MEDIA
•
POWER
•
POLITICS

MEDIA
·
POWER
·
POLITICS

David L. Paletz and Robert M. Entman

THE FREE PRESS
A Division of Macmillan Publishing Co., Inc.
NEW YORK

Collier Macmillan Publishers
LONDON

The Free Press
A Division of Macmillan Publishing Co., Inc.
866 Third Avenue, New York, N.Y. 10022

Collier Macmillan Canada, Inc.

First Free Press Paperback Edition 1982

Library of Congress Catalog Card Number: 80-1642

Printed in the United States of America

Paperback printing number

1 2 3 4 5 6 7 8 9 10

Hardcover printing number

2 3 4 5 6 7 8 9 10

Library of Congress Cataloging in Publication Data

Paletz, David L.
  Media power politics.

  Bibliography: p.
  Includes index.
  1. Journalism--Political aspects--United States.
2. Government and the press--United States. I. Entman,
Robert M., joint author. II. Title.
PN4888.P6P3 1981   071'.3   80-1642
ISBN 0-02-923650-9
ISBN 0-02-923660-6 pbk.

     Excerpts from the following publications have been reprinted here by permission of the authors and/or publishers: William Adams and Fay Schreibman, eds., *Television Network News: Issues in Content Research* (School of Public and International Affairs, George Washington University, 1978); Jeff Fishel, ed., *Parties and Elections in an Anti-Party Age* (Indiana University Press, 1978); David L. Paletz, Roberta E. Pearson, and Donald L. Willis, *Politics in Public Service Advertising on Television* (Praeger Special Studies, 1977); *Public Opinion Quarterly; Political Science Quarterly; The Nation.*

For Darcy and Francie

Contents

Preface

This book is the result of a genuine collaboration, a thoroughly cooperative process of creation. Our contributions have been equal. Our purpose is to explore the effects of television, news-papers, and newsmagazines on power in America; to show how media organizations and personnel, by following their own inter-ests and habits, unintentionally but often markedly influence the political thinking and behavior of the few Americans who possess power and the vast majority who do not. We reveal the sometimes successful, sometimes disastrous, media-manipulating activities of presidential candidates, presidents, members of Con-gress, Supreme Court justices, police, and leaders of powerful and fringe interest groups. We then show how media content (news and "entertainment" alike) socializes the majority of Americans into accepting the legitimacy of their country's political, economic, and social system; how public opinion on both domestic and foreign issues is strongly affected by the media and their powerful manip-ulators; and how the media often undermine the fitful attempts of ordinary citizens to participate in politics.

This book is personal, interpretive, openly speculative; but it is not ideological. We critically analyze the media, to be sure. We are not apologists. But we show how the media simultaneously disrupt and defend the status quo, how they can both assist the radicals and marshal the forces of reaction. Most important, we reveal how they inadvertently promote confusion, discontent, dis-cord. In other words, we try to portray the effects of the media on American politics in all their complexity and contradiction.

This book is not exhaustive. Although much of our analysis could be applied to movies, radio, and records, these three are excluded. Movies in particular demand another book—which we may write. Missing too are the methodological apparatuses that usually accompany content-analysis case studies. They are omitted for reasons of space and clutter but are available to interested scholars.

No book is without sin. Because our prime concern is with power and the media's political effects, we tend to blur the differences in process, form, and content of newspapers and television. Our use of the term "press" to include both may compound confusion. We are, however, quite aware of the differences, and of the distinctions between the "elite" and "popular" press, between national and local media, and between the networks and local television stations, even if that awareness is not always apparent.

We are also aware of the difficulties, the dangers, under which journalists often labor. Our argument about the effects of media content is in no way meant to be a criticism of the endeavors of individual reporters and editors. For journalism is a hard and exacting profession even if, as one eminent reporter and sometime columnist once remarked, "It beats heavy loading."

This book, then, is a risky venture. It proposes an ambitious, incipient framework to guide investigation and understanding of the scope and complexity of the impact of the media on politics and power. Against all our critics we invoke Erasmus: "We have wished to warn and not to bite; to be useful and not to wound; to benefit the morals of men, and not to be detrimental to them."

Finally, in case it too is obscured by our topic and focus, we want to make abundantly clear our dedication to the proposition that a free and untrammeled press is indispensable in a democratic society. Such a press need be neither objective, nor fair, nor unbiased, nor even responsible (this too will be the subject of a book); but it must be free.

Acknowledgments

The making of this book was abetted by individuals and institutions. Among the latter, the National Institute of Mental Health granted Entman a post-doctoral fellowship to the Graduate School of Public Policy at Berkeley. The funds supported him in the unassuming style to which he has now become accustomed while he learned policy analysis and worked on the book. The Rockefeller Foundation awarded Paletz a Humanities Fellowship, affording time for reflection and writing; our gratitude to Professor Joel Colton. The Duke University Research Council supplied modest but essential financial support. The Council for International Exchange of Scholars provided perspective by sending Paletz to Denmark as a Fulbright Scholar.

For their good hearts and Danish hospitality, Paletz extends thanks to his friends Karen and John Dinehart, Anita Jakobsen, Sven Åge and Tova and Jan Michaelson, Joyce and Johannes Pedersen, and Ebba and Mogens Pedersen.

Jil Hansen, Marianne Jensen, Lis Fischer Nielsen, Tom Pettitt, and the other members of the English Institute of the University of Odense made Paletz's stay in Denmark gratifying.

Birthe Fearing, Mary Jane Sweeny, Patsy McFarland, and, above all, the extraordinary Nancy Kiefer typed and retyped the manuscript with tolerance for the toil and compassion for us. Beryl Slome and Louise Walker showed compassion in their different ways. Linda Stafford of the University of Michigan delved deeply into the back files of the Institute for Social Research's *Newsletter* to retrieve an obscure quote. Dean Brenner did the index.

Some of our words and ideas have appeared elsewhere. We are grateful to the publishers of the books and journals listed on the copyright page for permission to use material first published under their auspices.

Bruce Andrews, Tom Bonnett, Rhonda Brown, Ernest Callenbach, Neal Cohen, Charles Ebel, Dan Hallin, Doug Huron, David Kirp, Jerry Mander, K. Robert Nilsson, Duane Silverstein, and especially Clay Steinman variously and voluntarily denounced, deplored, applauded, and heralded the manuscript. Their thoughtful responses elevated our work.

There are some people who contributed more than they will ever know. Paletz gives thanks to his mother, Hetty Rochlin, for being her unique self; to serendipitous Willem Langeveld and mordant Dan Lundberg; to Jeri Cabot for diligence and unfailing good humor; Max Cohen for his vitality; Ibby and Sydney Nathans for their friendship; Nan Rabinowitz for care and custody; Harry Rochlin for his kindness; Golda Sklar for her originality; Elizabeth and Amy Tornquist for succor and inspiration; Rose Weiner for being indomitable; and Dale Williams and Beth Bunce for industry and perseverance.

Entman was similarly blessed. Chuck Barone, Neal Cohen, Don Flaherty, Lynn Garrett, Dub Gulley, Wib Gulley, Lucy Haislip, John Laird, Kathi Lipcius, Susan McDaniel, Arnold Meltsner, Sharon O'Brien, Andy Parker, Gary Pruitt, Connie Renz, Clay Steinman, Ken Vickery, Gary Wein, and Hans Warner helped in ways they may not realize. And this book could not have been written without Bernard Entman, Rose Pachter, and Barbara Entman.

Paletz acknowledges three special contributors to his pleasure principle: Darcy Paletz, Gabriel Michael Paletz, and Susannah Batyah Felicity Paletz. Entman's profound gratitude to Francie Seymour is best expressed in another place and form.

We are both thankful for you all.

PART ONE

•

Roots

CHAPTER ONE

•

In the Beginning

"Intelligence is the perception of how other people get power."

Jules Feiffer

THE MEDIA ARE RIFE with political implications. Consider the concoction of headlines, editorials, photographs, stock market quotations, cartoons, comics, obituaries, and wedding announcements which, out of convention and habit and inertia, compose the press. The active verbs of headlines often give a fallacious impression of vitality and effectiveness to the actions (and inactions) of power holders. Editorials—grave, considered, often innocuous—encourage the illusion that all newspapers are divided into two parts: news (factual, fair, objective) and opinion; with the twain never meeting. Stock prices facilitate legalized gambling while symbolically endorsing capitalism. Editorial page cartoons, the most bitter and biting parts of the newspaper, attack the powerful with an unbridled license denied reporters and columnists. Comics unselfconsciously parade traditional American myths and values (with conspicuous exceptions). Photographs elevate or demean the powerful. Thus Richard Nixon was delighted when one of his aides managed to insert into the press a photograph of Senator Edward M. Kennedy leaving a Paris night-spot with a woman not his wife. Obituaries reflect the commitment of the press to the social order and established institutions; but not as well as wedding announcements. Social prominence and heritage are the criteria for inclusion of weddings in the imperfectly egalitarian *New York Times*. More democratic, the *Washington Post* lists alphabetically. Both news-papers picture the bride, an (unconscious?) promotion of the blessed state of matrimony for women. In Denmark, wedding pictures contain bride, groom, any and all offsprings they have begotten with each other or others prior to the marriage. Neither in the United States nor Denmark do newspapers contain a divorce section.

Scholars are gradually moving from denial, past uncertainty, into realization and acknowledgment of media influence. Media practitioners sense but disavow their impact on politics. Politicians fulminate ever more confusedly and publicly about it. And yet, neither scholars nor politicians in and out of office, nor even journalists, have written explicitly and at length about the influence of the media on the distribution and exercise of political power in America.

Our book is a beginning. In this chapter we discuss power, consider the relationships between power, politics, and the media, state our themes, and outline the organization of the book.

Power

A Supreme Court Justice once observed that although he could not define pornography, he knew it when he saw it. Power, less visible than pornography and more difficult to define, is as ubiquitous as it is vague. We do not intend to stifle this book with its definitions. For we agree with Arthur Bentley: "Who likes may snip verbal definitions in his old age, when his world has gone crackly and dry." [1]

Nonetheless, it is appropriate for us to explain briefly what we mean when we use the term. At its most obvious, power is the ability to determine the behavior of others, even against their will. Thus power can involve compulsion. But it need not be felt as such; for the power-holder's objectives may be shared (rightly or wrongly) by the people over whom the power is exercised. A more encompassing defining criterion of power, then, is the ability of a person or group or class to manipulate relations with other persons or groups or classes in its interests.

Power is particularly significant when transformed into authority. Occupying a formal public office as president, judge, legislator, or police officer endows the incumbent not just with power but also with the right to use that power. But the authority of a political system, its institutions, its offices and their incumbents—any or all of these—can be quite fragile. It depends on citizens' support or at least their acquiescence. The basis and extent of this acceptance is the legitimacy of authority.

Legitimacy is often related to the way authority is used. For authority brings responsibilities. In a democracy it is supposed to be exercised in the public interest, for the good of society.

In practice, groups and individuals representing different interests in American society contend to have their diverse and often opposed policy objectives facilitated or achieved through government action or inaction. Authority holders are far from neutral in this contest. A few groups are favored, others listened to attentively, some ignored, others spurned.

Why? Some segments of society are more aware of their interests than others; are better organized to bring them to the attention of policy-makers; can impose sanctions (even to the extent of facilitating the removal from office of uncooperative policy-makers); and have the resources to persist if their demands are not adequately and quickly met.[2] These segments often find their interests acknowledged even before they have expressed them aggressively. When they agree on something, the government usually does it; when they disagree, their wishes provide the options the government seriously considers.

As one consequence, there is far greater inequality of power and property in the United States than in many democratic and undemocratic states. One percent of the households in this country owns 31 percent of the wealth and 61 percent of all corporate stock. The top 20 percent possess 76 percent of all wealth and 96 percent of all stock.[3] Yet social and political instability resulting from such disparities is surprisingly mute: the underprivileged rarely rebel openly against the privileged. The powerless, rather, seem to acquiesce in their condition; to accept the fairness of legal and social arrangements which insulate private property (private property they do not themselves possess) and the continuation of a market system that perpetuates inequalities.

The Mass Media

Much of what most adults learn about government—its institutions and members, their activities, decisions, defects, strengths, capabilities—stems from the mass media. The self-same media have the power to decide which issues will be brought before the public, the terms in which they will be presented, and who will participate, under what conditions, in the presentation. By dint of the subjects they cover (and do not cover) and the ways they structure them, the mass media tell Americans what to think about, how to think about it, sometimes even what to think. This coverage can help or hurt both the public who rely on it, and the powerful who need the media to attain or retain office and enhance their power.

In practice the mass media have contradictory effects. They crusade against injustice; they condone inequality. They prop up capitalism; they vilify big business. They dismiss or distort dissent; they exhume irrelevant fringe groups. They educate the public; they pacify the people. They mythologized John F. Kennedy; they helped topple Richard M. Nixon. Fighters for truth, spreaders of murky illusions, the mass media seem to jumble the pieces of power in America.

Despite both the confusion and the contradictions, the puzzle can be assembled, even solved. The media have several interwoven, usually unintentional effects on power and politics. Hardly comprehended by elites, the public, even by journalists themselves, the themes of this book are:

- The media influence the decisions and actions of politicians and officials, change their priorities, can reduce their ability to control events.
- The media's openness to manipulation by the powerful contributes to insulating some power holders from accountability to the public.
- The media reallocate power among the already powerful.
- The media decrease to a marked extent both the ability of ordinary citizens to judge, and their power to respond quickly in their own self-interests to, political events and power holders.
- The media foment discontent among the public.
- The media help preserve the legitimacy of America's political, economic, and social system.

Outline

Our book is divided into three parts. This chapter discussed power in America, showing how it connects to the media. The next chapter exposes the roots of media content as they originate in the interests and processes of media organizations and practitioners. We follow the advice of President Nixon's former Chief of Staff. H. R. Haldeman wrote in a February 4, 1970 "confidential, high priority" memo to his aide Jeb S. Magruder, urging the mobilization of the "Silent Majority" to bring pressure on the media: "concentrate this on the few places that count, which would be NBC, *Time, Newsweek* and *Life,* the *New York Times,* and the *Washington Post.*" Add CBS, ABC, and the wire services, delete *Life,* and we concur. Certainly the *Times* and, to a lesser degree, the *Post* are the media's references for subjects to be covered, stories, perspectives on the news. Similarly, what policy-makers read in the *Times* and the *Post,* see and hear on the television networks' news programs, influence their perceptions, their arguments, their political options, their actions.

The second part of the book analyzes and illustrates the efforts of power wielders to influence media content to their advantage. For these men (and a few women) are far too shrewd about the mechanisms of capturing and preserving power, of controlling the direction of public policies, to leave the media to their own devices. Our focus is broad. Starting with two presidential elections, we illustrate and explain the successes and failures of media manipulation by presidents and legislators, the Supreme Court, the Federal Bureau of Investigation, and allied police departments. They extend from the heights to the depths of authority.

We conclude Part II by analyzing the interaction between the members of the mass media and Americans trying to influence the activities of public officials. At one extreme are powerful corporations; resource-poor groups and the unorganized are at the other. We look particularly at Common Cause, for several years a successful manipulator and beneficiary of the media.

In Part III we analyze the media's impact on the socialization, foreign and domestic policy opinions, voting and other political participation (or lack of participation) of the general public—powerless Americans unable and rarely inclined to tangle with the mass media but victims (and occasional beneficiaries) of their effects. This section includes a chapter devoted to the special influence of television entertainment shows and advertising.

The conclusion returns to the central question of power in American society, summarizes our argument and evaluates the prospects for change.

Our focus is unconventional; many of the traditional questions about the media, topics of protracted debate, are sl. hted or ignored. Some of our ideas, arguments, and analyses a.e frankly speculative. We write in broad strokes. Indeed, if too much American social science consists of "crawling along the frontiers of knowledge with a hand-lens,"[4] we may be guilty of venturing into the unknown with neither compass nor parachute nor even an umbrella. However, we do not disdain past research. Where relevant, it is incorporated; where tangential, it is reconstituted, shown from a fresh perspective. And it is joined to the latest discoveries by scholars and journalists.

Some of our more provocative data come from the press itself: stories in the *New York Times* or *Washington Post*. In part, these stories are exceptional, nuggets plucked from the seam of conventional, uncritical news. Further, like the revelations of CIA and FBI misconduct and malefaction, the stories sometimes surface years after the actual events have transpired, to be found first in fugitive publications rather than the mastodons of the mass media. Nonetheless, their appearance is a tribute to a free press, to the courage, ingenuity, and indefatigability of individual journalists. These qualities are not to be gainsaid.

CHAPTER TWO

•

The Sources of News

"A journalist is the lookout on the bridge of the ship of state. He notes the passing sail, the little things of interest that dot the horizon in fine weather. . . . He peers through fog and storm to give warning of dangers ahead. . . . He is there to watch over the safety and welfare of the people who trust him."

Joseph Pulitzer in *The North American Review* (1904)[1]

"They're liars by instinct. They're cowards by nature. They're yellow journalists. They're unbelievable. They're irresponsible. . . . They're reprehensible. They don't have a patriotic impulse in the hand that writes the garbage they bring. They stink like a mackerel."

Al Binder, campaign manager for Mississippi Gov. Cliff Finch's unsuccessful Senate campaign, quoted by the *Memphis Commercial-Appeal* in a fundraising speech on the subject of the press.[2]

MEDIA CONTENT IS CRUCIAL: different content, different effects on power. So we devote this chapter to exposing its roots. And we begin with an apparent paradox. The world is complicated, its myriad aspects difficult to grasp. And yet the competing mass media depict the world so similarly. Seventy percent of all weekday stories are duplicated on at least two of the three television networks.[3] The average percentage of network foreign news coverage is 21 percent for ABC, 23 percent for CBS, and 22 percent for NBC.[4] This similarity extends across media and subjects. Local newspapers in the United States are fungible. With exceptions, the press generally reports the same stories similarly, most obviously in its coverage of presidential elections.[5]

Journalists invoke a fourth-estate explanation for the content of their publications and programs. Their purposes are to inform the public about the important events of the day, to report the actions of the powerful, to scrutinize these actions critically, to hold public officials to public account. Thus they gather, publish, and purvey news that is factual, fair, impartial, objective, favoring no person, party, policy, or system.

As an assertion of ideals, this statement is unassailable. But it is an inadequate description of actual practice. It ignores the two fundamental determinants of media content. On one side are the media, with their goals, practices, customs; on the other are the politicians, interest groups, activists whom the media cover, who have their own goals and exert their own pressures. Out of this relationship, sometimes tempestuous, often symbiotic, emerges the media's overtly political content with its accompanying effects on power.

This chapter focuses on the first side, the media. We begin with profits, the media's bottom line; continue with prestige; consider the backgrounds, attitudes, and socialization of reporters. Then we examine the nature of news, describe how it is gathered, discuss the importance and influence of sources. A widely neglected yet vital topic follows: news presentation.

Profit and Prestige

Most of the men and women who run media corporations are animated by traditional American values: individualism, free enterprise, competitiveness, and materialism. They want their publications or stations to grow in circulation or ratings; to be seen by important people; to earn a reputation as influential in the larger society. They relish scooping the competition; detest being scooped. They want their organizations to prosper in a competitive world. In sum, they want profit and prestige, and profit and prestige are not always compatible. Profit usually comes first.

With the problematic and dubious exception of public television and radio stations, all of the important mass media are in business for profit. Profit is their bedrock. As Clay Steinman points out, their goal is "to use information communication (or its appearance) to hook in large audiences in order to sell those audiences to advertisers for profit."[6] The profit motive is most nakedly visible among local television and radio stations: "To the extent that there is competition among stations and between TV stations and other media, individual stations have little choice but to attempt to maximize long range profits."[7] Thus the main reason that many such outlets in smaller communities throughout America program local news is because of the dictates of the Federal Communications Commission. And because a majority of the Commission members have dedicated the Agency to "compromise, stability and a quiet life,"[8] the stations fill their news programs with time-consuming sports and weather segments, automobile accidents, crimes and fires culled from the police wire, and truncated excerpts of stories aired earlier by the network. With the exception of a "consumer affairs" reporter (an inaccurate description, we would maintain) whose name and voice are often attached to a story fed by the network, journalists specializing in social and political problems are not employed. Investigative stories are so infrequent outside the large cities (and even within them) as to be almost non-existent. The reason: investigative reporters must be paid and supported, their work takes time, and it may not produce usable results. Genuine exposés antagonize powerful community interests, provoke the (threat of) withdrawal of advertising, and inspire libel suits. They all cost money, reduce profits. No wonder one Boston television station cited as an investigative achievement its contribution to the first disclosure that Jacqueline Kennedy would wed Aristotle Onassis.[9]

The evidence certainly suggests that the quest for profits is successful. The pre-tax income of the television industry rose 12 percent in 1978, to $1.54 billion.[10] As percentages of revenue or tangible property, television earnings are around three times the average for all corporations.[11] And although there exists what Ben Bagdikian calls the "myth of newspaper poverty," the profits of most papers are also large and growing. Productivity is improving, but little of its dividend is invested in upgrading news coverage.[12]

The passion for maximum profits is sometimes voluntarily curbed in exchange for prestige. At the networks, a respected news department brings power and prestige to the parent organization and its affiliates. It may even sustain profits in the long run. One of the celebrities on *60 Minutes,* Mike Wallace, contends that the "Tiffany" reputation of the news division directly enhances profit: "I'm sure that the executives of CBS during these last two or three difficult years know full well that had it not been for the Cronkite news and *60 Minutes,* there would have been many more defections of affiliate stations from CBS to ABC."[13] Fewer affiliates, lower profits. Nurtured from the network's early days, CBS News adds luster to its parent corporation and inspires jealousy and emulation from its rivals. Its reputation for independent journalism helps protect all the networks when they are beset by accusations of scandalous sex shows, excessive violence, and mediocre entertainment. Prestigious news departments link the industry to the tradition of constitutionally protected free speech, thereby making the Bill of Rights into a shield for the virtually untrammeled pursuit of profit. And *60 Minutes* now achieves high audience ratings too.

Newspapers have an even headier tradition. Certainly news of public affairs appeals to educated, influential readers and viewers. Substantial advertising rates can be charged by organs which deliver this audience. Still, as long as income exceeds expenditures, a few newspaper owners with profitable properties sacrifice maximum profit in search of quality reporting; they value their fourth-estate tradition and the prestige and power that accompany it.

But it depends upon the owner. With the growth of multi-paper chains and conglomerates, *noblesse oblige* is succumbing to mercantilism.[14] Thus, David Halberstam describes the changes in the *Washington Post*'s operating priorities as it has grown from a family business into a major corporation listed on the American Stock Exchange. Publisher Katharine Graham has "committed herself more and more to profit, to winning Wall Street's approval."[15] The *New York Times* has apparently responded in part to the same pressures.[16]

The most influential newspapers and newsmagazines are now the centerpieces of publicly held media conglomerates. The *New York Times* publishes books and other newspapers and magazines; the *Washington Post* owns *Newsweek* and television stations; Time, Inc. owns publishers, Home Box Office, and land in the Southwest. Most other daily papers—over 60 percent of the total, having 71 percent of total circulation—are small or large links in newspaper chains.[17]

In some instances, a few of the more conspicuous organs are allowed, even encouraged, to garner prestige, while the bulk of the

conglomerate maximizes profits. After the *New York Times* helped
rid the country of incipient Nixonian tyranny, its book publishing
subsidiary issued H. R. Haldeman's memoirs. The book earned
him an income substantially larger than that of the average American family. It also profited the company. This potential conflict of
interest (the *Times* did not send teams of investigative reporters
digging into Haldeman's more extravagant newsworthy claims), is
not exceptional. While the *Times* prints innumerable articles decrying Johnny's inability to read, it simultaneously publishes *US*, a
vacuous magazine that caters to and encourages shrunken vocabularies. Other examples abound: CBS, Inc., answers critics of its
news division by pointing to *60 Minutes*, which does expose (small-
time) con artists, charlatans, frauds, and fakes. CBS, Inc., also
publishes *Astrology Today, Astrology: Your Daily Horoscope,
Your Prophecy,* and *Psychic World.*

In sum, profits and prestige set the boundaries of media news
content. When the passion for profit predominates, the television
station is devoted to trivia, skimps on its local news programs,
slights its public interest responsibilities. Its newspaper counter-
part hires as small a staff as possible, underpays it, relies for content on wire services and syndicates, and fills its space and time
with as much advertising as the audience will bear.

Owners of the prestige press are no foes of advertising. They
welcome it, as any of their readers must know. Yet they are willing
to sacrifice some profits on behalf of investigative reporting, in-
depth stories, foreign correspondents, and creative columnists.

So profits and prestige establish the framework. Within them,
other factors determine actual news content. They are personnel,
definitions of news, process, and presentation.

Personnel

Journalists appear to possess the potential to transcend profit
maximization, to exploit the desire for prestige in the interests of
their personal beliefs and causes. To some extent they choose
subjects, sources, their stories' leads and organization.[18] In inter-
viewing sources, they determine, in part, what questions to ask,
what answers to accept or reject, whether to probe further.
Through the information they include and exclude, the emphasis
given to the various sides, the allocation of evidence and colorful

quotes, they can impose their will upon a story. Reporters' backgrounds, experiences, attitudes, may direct them to stories which their newspapers are not organized to gather and would not otherwise publish.

But journalists infrequently plumb their potential opportunities. To explain why, we briefly examine their backgrounds, their attitudes, their socialization, and their susceptibility to sanctions.

BACKGROUND, ATTITUDES, SOCIALIZATION

Journalists are not innocent. They are disproportionately white, male, middle-class, and middle-aged. Avowedly non-partisan, American reporters, especially those employed by the major metropolitan dailies and television networks, tend to traditional values. They are sympathetic to the poor, object to the principle and practice of segregation, espouse a modified welfare statism at home and international cooperation abroad. They almost all unilaterally reject "extreme" ideological positions from the dismantling of the welfare state urged occasionally by Ronald Reagan to socialist solutions. The overt bellicosity of Barry Goldwater and the cynical racism of George Wallace were equally unappealing.

Idealistic, even romantic, about their country's history and the American political system, reporters tend to be suspicious of living government officials. And even before Watergate, the deeds of the Nixon administration stimulated a shift, in the words of Max Frankel, "from simple credulity to informed skepticism."[19] It approaches cynicism. But the cures that journalists advocate for the rampant political self-seeking they find have often been procedural, not radical or substantive. The solutions are those first pushed by the turn-of-the-century progressives:[20] clean politics, immaculate politicians beholden to no party, decisions in open meetings, not smoke-filled rooms.

There is little, then, in the backgrounds and attitudes of reporters to inspire them drastically and dramatically to violate the expectations of their employers and colleagues. Their on-the-job training teaches them to be objective compilers, accumulators of information presented for public judgment. The preferred stance is above the contending parties, beyond the conflict, injecting no provocative or partisan opinions of their own, taking no obvious position at all other than an unexceptional, putative, public interest.

Reporters are encouraged to conform by the wish to simplify their jobs (minimizing stress, ego-deflation, physical and mental exhaustion), desire for career security and success, and need for prestige and acceptance among other journalists.

Then there is the publisher. Says Otis Chandler of the *Los Angeles Times:* "I'm the chief executive. I set policy and I'm not going to surround myself with people who disagree with me. In general areas of conservatism vs. liberalism, I surround myself with people who generally see the way I do. . . . We don't have extremes here. I consider myself middle-of-the-road and I feel most of my editors are centrist."[21] Like many publishers, Chandler unites an ideological test of purity with an apparently genuine desire not to know his journalists' partisan affiliations. Asked whether his editors were Republicans or Democrats, he replied: "I don't know. I don't even ask them. I think it is an invasion of their privacy."[22]

We do not deny the existence of conflicts between reporters and their editors. These disputes are usually resolved by editors deleting what they believe to be opinions injected and interjected in news stories. Thus the eminent *New York Times* reporter Homer Bigart, soon to retire after forty-five years in his profession, of which seventeen on the *Times,* included the following in his story on the conviction of Lieutenant William Calley:

> Although he had just been found guilty of 22 murders, Calley was treated far more gently than was Army doctor Captain Howard B. Levy four years ago after receiving a sentence for refusing to give medical training to Green Berets on the grounds that the training would be used unlawfully in Vietnam.
>
> Unlike Levy, Calley was not handcuffed and left the court unfettered. An officer explained: "His conduct has been exemplary throughout and he'll continue to be treated as an officer."

After revisions by the editor at the *Times,* the passage read, "Lieutenant Calley was not handcuffed when driven to the stockade."[23]

Which brings us to sanctions. Owners, abetted by the managers who administer punishments, have a range of options. The most lenient is editing a story as Bigart's was. Or not running it. If incidents pile up, editors can reassign recalcitrants to the obituary "beat," cut their salaries, delay promotions. If these warnings do not suffice, the mavericks are fired.

These weapons are employed sparingly. They are rarely necessary; overuse would damage morale. But they are effective when used and serve as reminders to the less assertive to remain that way.[24] Sanctions are more likely to be invoked under some conditions than others. According to one study, the larger the circulation, the closer the geographic proximity of the news topic, the more it involves the publisher and his personal activity, the more revenue might be affected, the more likely publishers are to intervene.[25]

Definitions of News

Reporters do not wander in limbo: they are industriously searching for something loosely called "news." The problem for journalists is that although they usually have a reasonable sense of what is not news, they are less certain what exactly and invariably news is. The novel and unusual are obviously news, but much news is neither. What else, then? There are general guidelines, vague criteria; most are neither held nor applied consciously. They include drama; the activities of the powerful, especially when conflict results; and threats and reassurance.

Drama is a defining characteristic of news. An event is particularly newsworthy if it has some elements of a dramatic narrative —a central conflict or dilemma to draw the audience; protagonists whose actions affect or reflect the lives of the audience; and the possibility of catharsis at the reported outcome. American officials held hostage in their embassy in the far-off but journalistically accessible land of Iran provide a particularly strident example.

Not all news possesses high drama, but most stories that receive prominent and repeated attention do. Other stories have drama grafted on. Journalists have been known to highlight if not concoct conflict and to find characters to symbolize its different sides. One reason: to attract an audience that is thought to have little patience for the abstract, the technical, the ambiguous, the uncontroversial.

CONFLICTS AMONG THE POWERFUL

Prime news generally involves prominent, powerful people in action or, more desirable from the media's point of view, in conflict. Usually, these subjects of news are politicians, government officials whose activities can have threatening or beneficent impacts on the lives of ordinary Americans.

But only certain aspects of these actions are covered, obscuring their full impact on society. Power seems to be understood in a limited sense by the media: the process of seeking political office; the statements and deliberations of prominent officials, especially the president, who as chief symbol of nation and government is the subject of as much as 20 percent of domestic news;[26] and conflict between or within parties or branches of government as prominent members compete over power and policy. Stories emphasize the surface appearances, the furious sounds and fiery sights of battle, the well-known or colorful personalities involved—whatever is dramatic. Underlying causes and actual impacts are little noted nor long remembered. Administrative activity—technical, complex, undramatic, but often with significant effects—is ignored. Politics, not government or public policy, is a defining aspect of news worth.

THREATS AND REASSURANCE

"For the press, progress is not news—trouble is news,"[27] said Richard Nixon. A partial yet astute truth. Threat is a defining characteristic of news; but so is reassurance. Journalists believe it their duty to report on developments that may adversely affect audiences or people audiences identify with. They also search for aspects of the story that calm, assuage, uplift. In a memo to his staff, Av Westin of ABC News wrote:

> The Evening News, as you know, works on elimination. We can't include everything. As criteria for what we do include, I suggest the following for a satisfied viewer: (1) "Is my world, nation, and city safe?" (2) "Is my home and family safe?" (3) "If they are safe, then what has happened in the past 24 hours to help make that world better?" (4) "What has happened in the past 24 hours to help us cope better?"[28]

These guidelines are often followed. Much news alternates threats or potential threats to the security of audiences with reassurances, often resulting from the reactions and responses of public officials, who claim that help is on the way.

There are two particularly significant kinds of threats: physical and social. The first involves natural disasters, human catastrophes like oil spills and plane crashes, violent crimes. The second occurs when there is rejection or disregard of the legitimacy of the structure and constitutional processes of established authority; such violations threaten the social compact that is supposed to envelop citizens within an orderly and secure society. Challenges or disruptions of the normal values and procedures of government often come from below in the form of "extremist" demonstrations or violence. But attacks may also originate on high, with the corrupt, cupiditous, or incompetent behavior of officials.

After the physical or social threats are described, there are usually assurances of assistance. Rescue teams, presidential tours and declarations of disaster-area status, police and court actions, congressional hearings, governmental investigations—whatever authorities feel is an appropriate remedy, journalists usually find newsworthy. Not that the reassurance is necessarily effective. And there are some threats, like inflation, which defy or outlast any reassurances proffered by public officials.

The threat–reassurance dialectic also underlies news from foreign countries. Some of the stories originating outside America's borders concern disasters and their aftermath, generally including U.S. assistance. Most of the rest describe activities and events that could pose dangers to American sovereignty and interests, and the government's responses to these challenges. With some exceptions, foreign occurrences that do not affect America's diplomatic or economic goals are covered only briefly in a few newspapers.

Portents of things to come and innovative ideas frequently make news. If they promise to disrupt existing patterns, they are depicted as threats; if they seem to allow solutions that will preserve the American way of life, they are put on reassuring parade.

Human interest stories threaten and reassure. They involve personal suffering; evoke fear and pity in the unafflicted audience; then usually reassure. A boy goes blind, yet graduates from law school; a poor woman loses her home in a fire, but an outpouring of public contributions enables her to rebuild. The other kind of human interest theme is the quirk, cute eccentricity, outlandish habit. These stories reassure us: even in today's threateningly homogenized and depersonalized world there is room for individual initiative and idiosyncrasy.

Process

Defining the characteristics of news is necessary but not sufficient. Clearly some events are news from their inception, others become news by dint of careful cultivation, and others have newsness thrust upon them. Why does one threat or conflict or disaster make the news? Why not another? How to explain the varying prominence and emphasis of coverage of different public officials? Why do reporters spend so much time—the precious time they need to get the facts first, fast, and as accurately as possible— consumed by fairly routine coverage of predictably recurrent events?[29] How to explain the prevalence of news which meets no discernible definition of newsworthiness?

The answer essentially is that journalists work in bureaucratic organizations characterized by hierarchy, division of labor, and routinization of working operations through relatively standardized rules and procedures. The purpose is efficiency in the gathering, describing, and transmitting of news.[30] Efficiency ensures the lowest possible costs of production—a need of all profit-seeking firms, one especially difficult for media under pressure to produce a somewhat new and different product daily. The result: packs and reliance on official sources.

PACKS

"Pack journalism" is the frequent tendency of different reporters to write (and editors to assign) virtually identical political stories. In part this comes from the comfort of individual conformity; it makes reporters' and editors' jobs easier. Unimaginative, rigid, cautious, stereotyped writing reflects the kind of behavior we usually expect of bureaucrats. The news homogeneity that results may conflict with the organizations' interest in having exciting, different stories that stand out from the pack and boost ratings or circulation. But pack journalism also serves the organizations' interests by lowering the cost of gathering and interpreting news.

The most predictable events are arranged and conducted by government officials: meetings and hearings, press conferences and briefings, and formal speeches. They recur regularly, have foreseeable results, and provide authoritative information. With predictable results. Some 60 percent of a sample of front page stories in the *New York Times* and *Washington Post* originated from such official sources. Another 15 percent emanated from less formal governmental outlets.[31]

SOURCES

Reliance upon official sources is both necessary and ingrained. Ingrained from the first professional steps when reporters are instructed to cultivate their sources. Necessary because reporters soon discover that public officials make what are believed to be (by editors, other public officials, other reporters) the important political decisions and often offer easy access to information about their activities.

Sources among the elite range from the candid and willing to the reluctant and recalcitrant, who need to be induced by promises, threats, or simple charm to reveal some of the information they possess. But in virtually every instance, the source has reasons for talking, a premium on a particular version of events. As Walter Lippmann observed: "Every official is in some degree a censor . . . every leader is in some degree a propagandist."[32]

Sources are crucial because most stories recount what someone says occurred, not what actually occurred. But reliance on sources is accompanied by snares: "some reluctance to offend news sources in the stories they write, considerable willingness to print whatever their sources tell them, and little or no insistence that officials take responsibility for the information they pass along."[33]

Reporters find it expedient to see the world from the perspectives of their sources. Sources provide reporters with the frames and themes to structure the news. What attracts the source's attention attracts the reporter's attention. What repels the source, repels the reporter. Reporters "ask questions appropriate to their sources' world,"[34] thereby understanding the nuances of language, changes of attitude imperceptible to outside observers, the hints which signify policy shifts.

Reporters know that "familiarity breeds only deference"[35] and seek to avoid it. As soon as they become too beholden to a particular source, lose credibility, or exhaust their reservoir of goodwill, they may be given a different assignment, a new beat. They also pit sources against one another hoping (expecting) thereby to attain balance, approximate truth.

Consequently, when elite sources conflict, the press will contain a diversity of views about issues, problems, events. When sources agree, depictions will be one-sided. Elite conflict is a prime cause of the nature of the news reports of any event or problem: the more conflict, the more coverage, and the more varied the views stories contain. Since few elites disagree about the essential desirability and perfectibility of the system they control, news about challenges to the system will be particularly one-sided.

PERSPECTIVES

Media personnel deal constantly with space and time shortages. There is always more going on of potential interest to some members of the audience than can possibly be included. A major task each day is selective elimination. Because deadlines continuously loom, there is little time for careful reflection on the deeper meaning of stories. Traveling in packs, relying extensively on official sources, journalists pigeonhole the news, develop oversimplified shorthand explanations, construct superficial links of today's stories to yesterday's.

Journalists are fixated on the present. This syndrome is inevitable, given the audience-attracting purposes of the press, the need for daily grist, definitions of news, and news-gathering processes. It means journalists define events from a short-term, anti-historical perspective; see individual or group action, not structural or other impersonal long run forces, at the root of most occurrences; and simplify and reduce stories to conventional symbols for easy assimilation by audiences. News, then, is primarily "surface descriptions of events and activity."[36] Far more difficult to compose than it looks, requiring practice to perfect, elegantly traced, wondrous to behold in special cases—but surface-skimming nonetheless.

News practices are not entirely static. Monopoly, television, and youth all might produce changes. Monopoly newspapers could afford to cover more perspectives, in the sense of expanding coverage and defying objections and obstacles from local powers. Television covers more of the spot news, freeing print reporters for trend and background stories. Some young reporters espouse advocacy journalism, in-depth investigative reporting. Less beholden to routine or even special sources, they search through secondary documents, more often invoke the Freedom of Information Act, and interview a wide range of people involved in, concerned with, or informed about the events under investigation. They solicit leaks and whistle-blowing.

Such reporters remain uncommon. Ben Bagdikian has pointed out how few reporters in Washington, D.C., were assigned to cover Watergate full time.[37] The initiative for most news stories still reposes upon public officials. Journalists rely for most of their scoops on official governmental investigations and reports, as Watergate in many ways confirmed.

Presentation

News is not neutral. As Kenneth Burke has shown, it is almost impossible to identify social actors and name an action without also nominating an attitude toward them.[38] Beyond the trap of language (which we will consider in Chapter 13), the very process of selecting, editing, structuring, and presenting stories renders journalists' claimed adherence to objectivity chimerical. As Epstein puts it: "News is essentially protean in character. Any happening can be reported in a multitude of different forms."[39] In sum, to edit is to interpret, to speak is to define, to communicate is to structure reality.

A simple example will clarify this argument. Consider a television news story on massage parlors in which the theme was "illicit behavior: sexual exchanges, drug use, organized crime, and venereal disease. Masseuses were interviewed to obtain answers to these questions and the film was edited to focus on these concerns."[40] But the massage parlor story could have been discussed from such other perspectives as good health, sexual satisfaction, onerous governmental regulations, free enterprise, and career opportunities.

The massage tale reveals that reporters in fact do have a stock of frames for encapsulating events. However, the requirement of (an illusory) objectivity confines them, in most cases unconsciously, to a limited number of themes, a hopelessly narrow range of explanations—themes and explanations based on cultural assumptions, values, and beliefs so pervasive and accepted that they are not perceived by journalists or politicians or the public as interpretive frames at all, but as objective facts.[41]

Thus the magnitude, complexity, diversity, and continuity of social, economic, and political problems are reduced to the same banal, stereotypical themes. The locations may change, but the political explanations recur eternally: bureaucratic inefficiency, congressional corruption, the cynical desire by politicians for more power, prestige, votes. While there may be substantial validity in these explanations, there are other reasons for political behavior besides self-aggrandizement, ambition, venality, and incompetence.

But the news format obscures the existence of perspectives and values, perpetuates the illusion of objectivity. The mode of presentation is designed to persuade the audience of the credibility of the news stories and the legitimacy of the media which present them.[42]

Consider television news. The form of the news, both of the entire program and of individual stories or items, is structured, repetitive, and ritualistic. There is pacing and rhythm; filmed or taped reports edited for visual interest are followed by the anchorpersons, who abide for years. Set changes are infrequent; the manner, format, order, and mode of presentation similarly persist. News may be unpleasant, and often is; but the ritualistic format is familiar, comforting, reassuringly embracing events no matter how unexpected or untoward.

Television news contains "clusters"—related stories packaged into a segment.[43] A cluster consists of a general topic, subdivided into two or more stories, and suffused with one or more ongoing themes. Clusters are created in three ways: through narration by anchorperson and reporters; through graphics and other visual aids; or through the juxtaposition of filmed segments and the anchorperson's narrative—which takes such forms as a brief introduction of each story at the start of the cluster, a complete listing of all the segment's stories, or a specific explanation of why and how the stories are connected.

In the 1970s the most prevalent clusters concerned Watergate, the economy, energy, pollution, presidential politics, and the Middle East. Clusters help viewers remember general categories even if, or as, they fail to recall specific stories. But the connections within a cluster may be forced, even arbitrary; sometimes quite disparate stories were grouped under Watergate although they all usually had something to do with trials and criminality. Since filmed or taped stories originating from different parts of the world are clustered, viewers may be persuaded of the national or international pervasiveness of the events and themes irrespective of the accuracy of that view.

The reporting mode and functions of anchorpersons are consistent with ritualistic form and use of clusters. Correspondents are authoritative and factual, their demeanor unemotional, uninvolved, dispassionate. They authenticate their presentations by reporting from the scene of an event (in front of the White House, the Capitol, the Supreme Court building), or from a studio simulation. They are almost always shown at an appropriate distance from the camera—no penetrating close-ups for them.

Anchorpersons provide continuity and stability in the inferno of world and national affairs. They bring apparent qualities of common sense, rationality, and sanity to the manner in which news is presented. They are reasonable, undramatic, low-key. Like the correspondents, they present, clarify, summarize. They do not reveal strong opinions about the events they so religiously bring us and they are hardly ever emotional on camera. They appear knowledgeable, informed and impartial, summon forth images at will, control what we see. Added to their credibility are the formal way they are announced, their dress, their vocal inflection and resonance, the camera's respectful distance, and the concluding nightly benedictions they bestow.

The form of television news is designed to sustain the legitimacy of its anchorpersons, correspondents, and commentators—of its producing network. In so doing, it enhances the credibility of the information and opinions, the assertions and assumptions which compose the news. This form disguises the process of selecting, framing, structuring, contextualizing, and linking stories; it conceals the reconstitution and reconstruction of reality. Sources may be unreliable, their motives partisan, facts disputed and confused, meanings unclear, yet the news is presented with a straightforward clarity which denies, even belies, uncertainty.

Conclusion

In this chapter, we have attempted to explain some of the causes of media content. Seeking neither to praise nor deplore, we have shown that much of the news is determined less by external "reality" than by the internal logic of media organizations and personnel. Obviously this logic is not immutable. Different imperatives would produce different content. But the media are only one side. On the other are the power holders and wielders who pummel, grapple with, manipulate, or submit ungraciously to the mass media. In Part II we describe and explain the interactions.

PART TWO

•

The Media Manipulators

CHAPTER THREE

•

Presidential Candidates: 1976 and 1980

"They are in their wooing phase."

W. H. Auden

WITH RESPECT TO SEX, W. C. Fields once remarked: "There are some things better and some things worse, but there is nothing quite like it." Except presidential elections. Full of derring-do and timidity, intensity and indolence, integrity and hypocrisy, their results at once predictable and peculiarly uncertain, presidential elections are covered like a blanket by the mass media. There are other reasons: organizational imperatives, habit, a response to formal and informal governmental regulation; but most of all, presidential elections are extensively reported because they are stuffed with news. Elections overflow with real or contrived drama, contain conflict (usually with two principal sides), recur at specified times (thus facilitating the logistics of coverage over the years), and have measurable outcomes—votes and victors. Like such other national ritualistic contests, even obsessions, as the World Series, the Super Bowl, and the Miss America Pageant, presidential elections start with many contenders and climax, after toil and trouble, with the triumph of just one.

The mass media need presidential elections, certainly; but not as much as presidential candidates need the mass media. Without extensive and favorable coverage, a candidate is a nonperson, required to slog through the United States until, if ever, deemed worthy of media attention. Especially during the pre-convention stage, candidates' activities are often devised solely and simply to seduce favorable coverage from the national media. The candidate who, one way or another, attracts the most favorable or least unfavorable media coverage visibly enlarges his or her chances of victory. As one candidate's campaign manager put it: "The media is the campaign." [1]

It is appropriate, therefore, to begin this section of the book on power seekers and holders with a study of candidates in the 1976 and 1980 presidential elections. For these elections reveal graphically the way that media messages arise out of the sometimes clashing, sometimes compatible interests of the press and their subjects—here presidential hopefuls. As we shall document, the interaction between media and candidates involves both deliberate and unconscious manipulation of each side by the other as each seeks maximum advantage. Both desire the best possible stories, but "best" often means something quite different to candidates than to reporters.

Our analysis will reveal how candidates skillfully or ineptly exploit their differing resources in their relations with the press. We shall show how and why reporters emphasize certain aspects of the campaign to the detriment of one or other of the candidates. Our conclusion is a critique of the media, not for their putative power to decide the winner but for their baleful effects on the process by which that decision gets made. The interactions of candidates and journalists, each seeking maximum gain from the other, has an unfortunate by-product: each side reinforces traits in the other that make elections less an expression of popular will than they could be. [2]

The Context of the Campaign

First comes context. Context—the nature of the constituency, the kind of election (primary or general), the division and degree of voter partisanship, the candidates in other contests on the ballot, economic conditions, the public records of the contestants, these and other factors [3] often decide the election results before a campaign is even waged; they can ensure one candidate will win no matter how sophisticated and lavish his opponent's use of the media. [4]

The news media help set contexts. Well in advance of the election year, politicians and journalists begin speculating about the competitors in the next presidential contest. Years before the election, adroit politicians try to create a favorable ambience for the ultimate run. Take Senator Howard Baker (R., Tenn.). So skillfully did he play at righteous indignation before the television cameras at the 1973 Watergate hearings that he became an immediate object of presidential talk.[5] It took John Dean to reveal, some years later, that Baker was, even as the cameras rolled, taking calls from and meeting with Nixon advisors, plotting strategies to protect GOP interests against the fitfully inquisitive Democratic majority.[6] The positive attention Baker realized in 1973 probably helped him secure the post of Senate Minority Leader in 1975. From that niche he became one of the most widely quoted Republicans in the land, well poised for his ultimately abortive 1980 presidential bid.

Media impact on presidential elections is cumulative. By concentrating on media messages during the election year itself, journalists and researchers render a foreshortened portrait. Watergate coverage, interpretations of the 1974 elections, stories of Gerald Ford in office helped to create the context of the 1976 campaign, just as inflation, energy, Iran and Afghanistan, Israel and the Olympics, colored the 1980 race.

By the time the general election campaigns were underway, the context was set. The task of candidates, their advisers, and managers was to exploit favorable contextual factors and minimize the effects of unfavorable ones.

At the best of times, contextual factors are not easy to manipulate. In the 1976 and 1980 general elections the candidates encountered two complicating problems. First there was the relatively high number of people who identified themselves as independents or who remained undecided throughout most of the campaign. The independents made it more difficult for candidates to rely solely on party labels to provide a favorable context. And the decline in party loyalty reinforced voter indecision. According to the University of Michigan Center for Political Studies, voters decided later in the 1976 campaign than in most other elections. Thirty-five percent of Republicans, 45 percent of Democrats, and over half the independents decided whom to support after the party conventions.[7] The failure of people to develop a set voting intention early in the campaign increases the media's importance.

The less definitely minds are set, the more media impact; in 1980, voters seemed even more undecided.

A second complication involved the expectations voters have of presidential aspirants, which they apply less vigorously to candidates for other offices. They tend to seek reassurance, a sense of confidence that the leader is aware of problems, capable of meeting them, and possesses a high degree of integrity and wisdom.[8] One reason for voter uncertainty was the pervasive feeling that no candidate possessed many of these qualities. Part of the explanation for these doubts was the widespread political alienation in the country. Voter distrust of politicians was at an all-time high,[9] a contextual fact presidential aspirants had to try to bend to their advantage, lest they succumb to guilt by association.

Given the situation, the candidates' tasks were clear. Each needed to show that he possessed the personal qualities and traits —the character—fitting the public's psychic needs and expectations of a president. At the same time, they had to convince a majority of voters that their policy actions and proposals had been and would be beneficial—that they were competent and prudent. The interests of the candidates in advancing such impressions shaped their dealings with the media.

The Media

The media are the main link between the presidential candidates and the overwhelming majority of the public. Media content may even determine election outcomes if party or candidate allegiance is weak among many voters, and the election is so close that a small percentage of voters becomes crucial. Both these conditions existed in 1976 and 1980.

That the media link candidates and public does not mean that they are neutral conduits. Far from it. Media–candidate relations are an ambiguous mixture of conflict and cooperation, support and destruction. The reason: the needs of the media and the objectives of candidates differ. The candidates strive to flood television and the press with selective information conducive to their election. Reporters and editors want news—defined as conflict, controversy, duplicity, scandal. They probe for candidates' weaknesses, deceptions, closeted skeletons. Candidates and their aides try to impose their definitions of what is important in an election on the media. They assert the primacy of the issues which favor them. As campaign consultant Gene Wyckoff put it, candidates also enact for the media "that selective aspect of their total character that favorably corresponds with publicly held images of what characters should be in high places."[10] The media varyingly accept, ignore, or reject these attempts while seeking stories of their own devising.

Still, there are limits on how journalists gather campaign news and what they report. Reporters for the national media are obliged to trek about the country recounting what the major candidates say and do and to do so with as much impartiality as they can muster. This limits their time for investigative reporting. Nor can they report with impunity rumors, innuendo, or uncorroborated gossip. These are the dictates of objective journalism under which many reporters chafe as they secretly long (perhaps) for license.

For their part, candidates, faced with media scrutiny of their pronouncements and behavior, avoid blatant lies as a detriment to electoral success. In time, they usually refrain in public from making directly contradictory promises in contiguous parts of the country. And yet, knowing the press is watching does not inhibit candidates from fudging their statements just enough to avoid contradiction, or from changing their positions or emphases as a campaign progresses. Thus Jimmy Carter's pledge in the early 1976 primaries to abolish the income tax mortgage deduction was quickly condemned to oblivion when its political unpalatability became apparent. Throughout his term and into the 1980 campaign, his energy (and some other) programs and pronouncements were models of volatile and tortuous ambiguity. Nor are candidates deterred from claiming credit for widely applauded policies with which their personal connection is at best remote. In some of Ford's commercials he claimed credit for policies initiated and approved by the Democratic Congress. Similarly, in 1980 Reagan associated himself with programs enacted by the Democratic-dominated California legislature during his time as governor of that state.

The Primary Campaign

The would-be nominee must first induce the news media to take him seriously. This can be done in two ways: be president already or be a front runner in the polls, or do well in early primaries.

MAKING NEWS

When there is no heir apparent, the primary process involves a competitive struggle to penetrate the nation's consciousness through the media. The best manipulator of news coverage usually wins the nomination. To make the news work for him, a candidate need not be the richest, nor the most photogenic, widely known, or charismatic. (Carter was none of these in 1976.) He does need to know what excites media interest most, when to time his moves for maximum response, and how to sustain and build that response to a peak during the national convention. With luck and skill, a good media relationship established during the nomination quest will last into the autumn campaign.

Jimmy Carter, whose activities we focus on here, was a superb news strategist during the 1976 primaries, the best among presidential candidates since John F. Kennedy. His success began with his recognition of the locus of media power. As Hamilton Jordan wrote in a November 4, 1972 memo to his boss:

> Like it or not, there exists in fact an eastern liberal news establishment which has tremendous influence in this country all out of proportion to its actual audience. The views of this small group of opinion-makers in the papers they represent are noted and imitated by other columnists and newspapers throughout the country and the world. Their recognition and acceptance of your candidacy as a viable force with some chance of success could establish you as a serious contender worthy of financial support of major party contributors. They could have an equally adverse affect, dismissing your effort as being regional or an attempt to secure the second spot on the ticket.[11]

Carter and his aides understood which media organizations mattered—and far more. They knew how to exploit the determinants of the media's campaign news to counter the natural conflicts between candidates and the press. They were aware that:

- The themes sounded earliest are often the ones reported longest.
- Competition and news gathering procedures tend to draw

each medium into convergence with the others so that they focus on the same events and develop similar themes.
• Cultural assumptions, such as the notion that every race has but one winner, shape definitions of the news.

Carter's most important insight was that the early (primary success) bird captures the media coverage worm. In 1976, the competing media seemed particularly hungry to unearth early trends, perhaps fearing to miss a promising candidate, as they had in 1968 and 1972. They gave a lot of attention to the very first candidate competition: the January delegate selection caucuses in Iowa.

Jimmy Carter came in second to "Uncommitted," with enough caucus support to claim 13 Iowa delegates (out of 47). Media coverage was the real prize. The week after Iowa, Carter was blessed with 726 lines of coverage in *Time* and *Newsweek*. Morris Udall, Fred Harris, Birch Bayh, Henry Jackson, and Sargent Shriver averaged thirty lines each. Carter also enjoyed five times more television time than any of his rivals.[12]

By textbook journalism standards, few editors could justify such an imbalance. But the crafty Carter knew those standards are often buried in the stampede of the pack to define the news in terms of a "winner" with "momentum." According to *Broadcasting*, media "whiz" Gerald Rafshoon invested $8,000 for television commercials appealing to Iowans to attend the caucuses and vote for Carter.[13] This was the best-spent money of the campaign. The night after the caucuses, CBS's Roger Mudd said: ". . . no amount of bad-mouthing by the others can lessen the importance of Jimmy Carter's finish. He was the clear winner in this psychologically crucial test. . . . So the candidate with that highly prized political momentum tonight is Jimmy Carter. . . ."[14]

The media had fashioned a version of reality based on their own needs, practices and imaginings, and foisted it upon actual campaign events. The Iowa "test" was "psychologically crucial," and the "momentum" was "highly prized" largely because the media said so. In 1972, by contrast, the caucuses had barely been covered. We counted 4 lines—one sentence—in *Time* and 72 lines in *Newsweek* (February 7, 1972). Iowa's intrinsic importance to the nominations had not changed in 1976; apparently media interests had. However curious, coverage of Iowa enlarged the dimensions of the Carter candidacy, opening the door to the path of victory.

By 1980, Iowa had been elevated even further. The caucuses were worth about twice as much newsmagazine space as in 1976, about 800 lines in *Time* and 900 in *Newsweek*. And surprise winner George Bush obtained the bulk of the attention this time as Carter had four years earlier, but not with the same ultimate effect.

The New Hampshire primary is an even more crucial portal. The state is remote from American politics in many ways. But because it offers the first primary election of the year, it has provided a central focus for media coverage of the nomination story. As a genuine election (not a caucus), it gives each press organization a chance to display its remodeled panoply of polls and projections, pundits and prophets.

Despite the considerable criticism they received for overemphasizing New Hampshire in 1972, the networks devoted more time to it in 1976.[15] From our informal monitoring, New Hampshire received somewhat less attention in 1980; but it still enjoyed abundant coverage. Apparently the pressures of competition are too strong, the commitment to entrenched news definitions too deep, to allow much change in campaign coverage.

Were it not for the media, the Iowa caucus and New Hampshire primary results would be about as relevant to the presidential nomination as opening-day baseball scores are to a pennant race. The media make the outcomes relevant, even crucial, to presidential candidacies. The Iowa and New Hampshire stories can elevate the winner out of obscurity, while dumping losers into the netherworld of the futile or the forgotten.

How well the canny Carter knew this. For his 28 percent of the vote in 1976 he earned this nomination-boosting news headline from Walter Cronkite of CBS News: "Jimmy Carter took a long lead tonight in the race for the Democratic presidential nomination. He won the New Hampshire primary handily."[16] Only slightly less exuberant, NBC announced: "So Carter emerges from New Hampshire as the man to beat."[17] *Time* and *Newsweek* apparently agreed; they both put Carter on the cover, and gave him a total of 2,630 lines of coverage. All other candidates combined got 300 lines. Udall's second place finish (24 percent of the vote) was worth 96 lines. Though not quite so lopsided, television and newspapers also devoted predominant coverage to Carter.[18]

Quantity is not the same as quality. Not all of the Carter stories were flattering: non-Aryans and Aryans alike chastized him for defending the "ethnic purity" of neighborhoods, while some people rebuked him for being fuzzy on issues. Better to be fuzzy, Carter no doubt thought, than to enunciate original or unconventional policy positions which reporters would immediately dissect, if not mock—witness the dismal experiences of George McGovern in 1972 and Ronald Reagan in 1976. No wonder most of the coverage favored Carter's candidacy. Its theme: Carter, an unknown, was sweeping his party by storm, addressing the voters' new "conservative mood," ministering to their *angst* and alienation. Because this theme was so firmly established in the early primaries —and because so little attention was given the later contests— strong showings by Udall, Jackson, and Jerry Brown in large industrial states did much less for their hopes than Carter's early "victories" in bucolic Iowa and New Hampshire.

The convergence of supposedly competing media on a similar focus (New Hampshire) and theme (Carter as unstoppable outsider) can be traced to news-gathering practices, individual journalists' interests, and news definitions. To the influential media with their concentration in and on Washington, D.C., and New York City, Carter in 1976 presented a new face from the rural South, a face full of news value. Sparked by Carter's emergence during the early primaries (which they facilitated), the media burst forth with stories about his background, family, and rustic life in the so evocatively named Plains, Georgia.

It was far more onerous, time-consuming, and costly to gather information and write stories about Carter as practical politician and millionaire agribusinessman; to analyze how he made his fortune, how he funded his political campaigns, to untangle his associations with bankers and businessmen. These stories appeared much later, if they appeared at all.

Reporters' egos and career goals raise the personal stakes especially high in presidential campaigns and merge with news-gathering practices and news definitions to influence media content. Being with the apparent winner can put a reporter's stories on page one. Having covered the candidate who gets elected can yield a prestigious White House beat. Knowing a president makes one feel important. The frontrunner's press corps has some incentives, then, to keep the drum beating. These can sometimes overcome professional norms and even habitual goals like getting scoops on candidate flaws and *faux pas*. Note the impression of self-inflation, hyperbole, and candor in these remarks by writer Curtis Wilkie of the *Boston Globe* in the late summer of 1976: "I'm

going to be in a position to actually know a president and a vice
president and be able to say to my kids if . . .[Carter wins] that I
covered probably the most remarkable political story of this cen-
tury. . . . If he sees me he'll know who I am. No president ever
knew who Curtis Wilkie was." [19] Even if intended humorously,
these remarks help explain why some newspapers try to rotate
their reporters among the candidates.

FROM OBSCURITY TO NOMINATION: CARTER IN 1976

There are two reasons to believe—as the candidate planned
—that early primary publicity would give Carter a big push toward
the 1976 nomination. First, name recognition appears to be a major
factor in primary voting. Second, portrayal as the man to beat
creates a bandwagon effect that stimulates primary voters, campaign contributors, party officials, convention delegates, and contributors to hop on board before it's too late.

Dramatic evidence of Carter's astonishing rise in recognition
and the media's role in it comes from a survey taken in Los Angeles and Erie, Pennsylvania. Respondents were twice given a list of
candidates and asked to indicate which they knew, once just before
the New Hampshire primary (late February), once just after the
Pennsylvania primary (late April). The first time, only 20 percent
said "I know something about him" when shown Carter's name.
Two months later, 83 percent did. The comparable figures for Jackson were 26 and 42 percent, for Udall, 23 and 36 percent. The three
started about even; within two months, Carter was better known
than any other Democratic candidate. [20]

The University of Michigan Center for Political Studies con-
ducts the only well-funded national study of voting in each presidential election. The Michigan scholars found that Carter's
"simple name recognition, which came with the national publicity
that he received during the very early part of the primary season,
may have been more important to his victories than his antiestab-
lishment image." This advantage apparently held nationwide, and
it helped Carter with voters in later primaries. [21]

The other factor that aided Carter with late-spring voters was
his image as the likely winner. In the first Erie–L.A. survey, about
30 percent of the respondents said Carter, Jackson, Bayh, Udall,
and Shriver each had a "good chance" of being nominated. By the

April poll, 80 percent rated Carter's chances good, while less than 5 percent said that about the other four.[22] In reality, Carter's delegate lead was slight: he had 263, compared to 176 for Jackson and 128 for Udall.[23] But his springtime winning image was probably more important than the delegate count for creating the Carter mule train that ultimately triumphed at the summer convention.

FAME AND LOSS: EDWARD KENNEDY IN 1980

In the early fall of 1979, Democrats chose Senator Edward M. Kennedy (D., Mass.) over incumbent President Jimmy Carter by 59 to 27 percent. By late March of 1980, these figures were reversed: it was Carter 58, Kennedy 32 percent. The president who had appeared thoroughly vincible a year before won the nomination handily.

The nearly unrelenting critical media coverage of the Carter presidency during 1978 and 1979 (see Chapter 4) made a vaguely mythic figure like Kennedy look deceptively strong. The 1979 polls compared a man whose faults and incapacities (real and imagined) had been front page news for two years with a man whose blemishes and peccadillos had been obscured by romantic nostalgia for a return to Camelot. The polls and the myth created unrealistic expectations by and about the senator which he would find difficult to fulfill.

Media stories about the senator's popularity and the president's weaknesses may have helped induce Teddy Kennedy to seek his party's nomination. They may also have contributed to the apparent lack of preparation with which he entered the race. The senator seemed initially unaware of the kinds of coverage he would receive and of the importance of arranging his public appearances with the media in mind. Nor did he or his advisers seem to comprehend that media coverage would not necessarily be conducive to the kind of campaign he needed to wage to unseat an incumbent president. Thus from the start Kennedy found himself submerged in questions about his private life. The Chappaquiddick events haunted much of the coverage of his candidacy as they were featured in investigative stories in such publications as *Reader's Digest* and the *New York Times*. Roger Mudd interviewed Kennedy for a CBS profile around the time of the senator's announcement that he was entering the presidential race. Not only were there questions about Chappaquiddick, the show also contained a scene in which the camera looked out from the driver's seat of a car as it drove toward a bridge at night lit only by the automobile's headlights. The image suggested something tawdry and furtive, impressions magnified by Kennedy's hesitant and clumsy responses to Mudd's questions.

Worse, Kennedy at first undermined his myth by his appearances on the television news. Too often he was shown haranguing his audiences at rallies, a crude and common campaigner. The print media focused on his tactics and problems. Neither television nor newspapers afforded him the time and space to establish his credentials as a serious candidate (instead of a myth), articulate his policy views at length (once he discerned the need to do so), and set himself apart from Carter. Increasingly, Senator Kennedy was transmitted as a rather desperate man attacking the president because of mindless ambition for the office. He fell to a combination of media imperatives and his own initial overconfidence.

Meanwhile, Jimmy Carter was acting presidential. Ford had done the same in 1976, remaining in the Rose Garden for much of the campaign. Journalists reported Carter's ploy without appreciably undermining its effectiveness. As Kennedy campaigned, Carter's rating in the polls rose in apparent response to the seizure in Iran of American embassy personnel. Between October 1979, just before that event, and January 1980, public approval of Carter's handling of his job spurted from 25 to 54 percent.[24] The number of Americans rallying around Carter peaked just about the time of the Iowa caucuses in which Kennedy was badly beaten.

The President's decision to remain in the White House was orchestrated for the press. According to Martin Schram, a memo was written to the President outlining the consensus views of some of his closest aides that he debate his rivals in Iowa. On the memo Mr. Carter wrote:

> I can't disagree with any of this, but I cannot break from my duties here, which are extraordinary now and ones which only I can fulfill.
>
> We will just have to take the adverse political consequences and make the best of it. Right now both Iran and Afghanistan look bad, and will need my constant attention.[25]

The memo and presidential response were written to be leaked to the press.[26]

A peculiarity of media coverage accelerated the demise of

Kennedy's candidacy. The media shape the perceptual environment of the nomination struggle in a way that tends to disadvantage
candidates whose support is concentrated in the later primary
states. The earlier contests receive the most coverage. In most of
those states, Iowa, New Hampshire, Florida, and Illinois, Kennedy lost convincingly. Because of the characteristics of nomination campaign coverage, his victories in later primaries were less
closely covered, less widely heralded than Carter's early wins.
Consider the different impressions of the two candidates' chances
if the New York and Pennsylvania primaries (with their large numbers of delegates), which Kennedy won, had preceded the much
smaller delegate contests in Iowa and New Hampshire.

Carter and his staff were well aware of this peculiarity of
media coverage and of the penchant of the press for magnifying
any early defeats suffered by the president or his opponents. Occupying the White House, they were able to take appropriate measures. First, knowing they had the support of the governor of
Florida, they went all out to win that state's fall 1979 caucus and
straw vote. Cabinet members and White House officials, many
bearing federal largess (or at least promises) descended on Florida,
in Schram's words, "like crows on a cornfield."[27] Then the Carter
campaign leaders tried to change the dates of several primaries in
ways advantageous to the president. They enjoyed some success.
They had feared that Kennedy would carry Connecticut and Massachusetts on March 4, early in the primary season, thus boosting
the senator's campaign. The Connecticut primary was moved into
April. The Carter aides then succeeded in moving the Georgia and
Alabama primaries to March 11 where they joined that of Florida.
Carter enjoyed his predictable southern sweep on that day.[28]

FROM OBSCURANTISM TO OBSCURITY: JERRY BROWN IN 1980

California Governor Jerry Brown also suffered from the
media's emphasis on the early contests. He was not the kind of
man, his issues were not the type of issues, to excite many of the
voters in Iowa and New Hampshire. But Brown suffered from
other handicaps. He was no longer the new face of 1976. He had
been around for four more years of reportorial scrutiny. Some of
his more unconventional behavior, particularly a trip to Africa in
which he was accompanied by rock star Linda Ronstadt, had been

widely covered. Besides, his rhetoric was unconventional; whatever the specific content of his proposals, the language and concepts he used—his talk of colonizing space, of holistic health—were alien to most reporters who responded with barely concealed derision. His scant coverage consisted largely of snide swipes at his assertedly typical California weirdness. Finally, not unrelatedly, but perhaps most important, Brown remained very low in presidential trial heat polls. Indeed, Brown's announcement of candidacy was depicted on CBS News by photographs of Kennedy, Carter, and Brown each relative to their standing in the polls—the governor's was postage stamp size. Lacking the manifest recognition and support of the incumbent Carter and legendary Kennedy, failing to score well in Iowa or New Hampshire, Brown would probably have lost even if he had been from Plains or Boston.

IMITATION, INEVITABILITY, AND INDEPENDENCE: THE 1980 REPUBLICANS

In January 1980 Ronald Reagan appeared assured of obtaining the Republican nomination for the presidency. He was well-known and popular among Republicans. Many of his party's voters were familiar and comfortable with his style and views. His media appearances were practiced and reassuring. He had spent years journeying around the country attending Republican gatherings, giving pep talks at party dinners and rallies, campaigning in caucus and primary states. Only a striking campaign by one of his opponents could disturb his stately march to the Republican nomination.

If Reagan was to be challenged successfully, it would come from one of the three men who, it seemed to us, had adopted distinctive strategies to exploit the media. John Connally's strategy was simple; it had worked for past candidates: raise and spend vast amounts of money. But Connally was campaigning under a debilitating handicap, a result of his many years in politics, first as Democrat and then as Republican, and from his various posts and roles in the Nixon administration. Connally was widely viewed both by the press and members of the public as a wheeler-dealer—not the kind of man we elect president or even nominate for the presidency in these post-Watergate days. Nothing he spent could apparently erase that image.

George Bush too had a strategy: he modeled his 1980 nomination campaign on Carter's 1976 strategy. At first it worked. Publicity surrounding his Iowa success apparently tripled the percentage of Republicans who had a favorable impression of him; it went from 20 to 62 percent between January 9–13 and January 24, two days after the Iowa caucuses. The segment professing ignorance or no opinion about Bush dropped during that period from 66 to 32 percent.[29]

But in 1976 there had been no actively campaigning, famous, and attractive alternative candidate for anti-Carter Democrats to rally around in the primaries. In 1980 George Bush was facing a well-known and popular opponent in Ronald Reagan. In November 1979, polls showed Reagan the preference of 37 percent of Republicans followed by Connally at 15, Baker at 13, and Bush, Crane, and Dole each with 3 percent. Reagan thus possessed the largest contingent by far of pre-campaign adherents. More important, he had a wide base of second-choice support among Republicans who initially favored the ideologically similar Baker, Connally, Crane, and Dole. By April, when most of the others had dropped out, Reagan stood at 57 and Bush at 11 percent.[30] Still Bush's strategy worked in part: Reagan chose him as his running mate.

In 1976, reporters were frequently hostile toward and critical of Ronald Reagan. In turn, Reagan's campaign managers harmed their candidate by succumbing to pressure from reporters and predicting or speculating about victory in New Hampshire, Florida, and Michigan. Reagan obtained a large vote in each state without winning a majority. The media having transmitted and therefore established expectations of a Reagan victory, his showing was widely defined, mainly by the same media, as a loss. For too long, reporters denied or were unwilling to accept the possibility that Reagan might indeed take the nomination away from the incumbent Ford. According to Christopher Arterton, "the daily reporting of Ford as continually closing on the nomination constituted the major strategic problem for the Reagan campaign as it entered the convention."[31] Yet Ford won the nomination by only 117 delegate votes. Different reporting, different outcome?

In 1980, Reagan was virtually the incumbent Republican. All he had to do was avoid egregious blunders. Thus he made no risky predictions of glorious primary victories, no provocative policy proposals on which he could be impaled by the press; and he quickly realized the error of avoiding debates with the other candidates. As a result, Ronald Reagan moved relatively smoothly to the Republican nomination.

But one of Reagan's opponents had made a significant impression on many voters and, more importantly, on the press. Congressman John Anderson's (R., Ill.) strategy had been forthrightly to espouse some distinctive policy positions, thereby differentiating himself from the other more conventional Republican candidates. His positions were too liberal or idiosyncratic to attract a majority of Republican voters in any caucus or primary states, but he attracted predominantly favorable coverage from the media. There are several reasons. First, he was the newest of the new faces. Every campaign needs one whether it be Eugene McCarthy in 1968, George McGovern in 1972, Jimmy Carter in 1976. Second, non-neanderthal Republicans usually receive respectful coverage from the elite press as witness the cases of Senators Percy (R., Ill.), Hatfield (R., Ore.) and Javits (R., N.Y.). Third, Anderson fit the progressive, clean-government, seemingly frank, articulate, thoughtful kind of Common Cause type whose values are compatible with those of editors and reporters from the elite press. Fourth, Anderson combined fiscal conservatism, a willingness courageously to lead in some progressive directions, and a determination to propose solutions to some of the apparently intractable issues of the day. He was indeed different from the conventional Republican candidates, less platitudinous; and he was a distinct underdog. So stories about him appeared lauding his capacities, intelligence, and integrity and explaining why he could not, would not, gain the Republican nomination. Nor did he win it. But the media coverage achieved a quite different effect: it made Anderson temporarily a viable independent candidate for the general election.

The General Election

In the general election, media focus is on the major candidates. In analyzing the struggle for favorable media depiction we distinguish three kinds of content. We call them unmediated messages, partially mediated messages, and mostly mediated messages. The contest between candidates and media is somewhat different in each of these three arenas. In the first, unmediated case, media interests and those of candidates are most congruent; in the second, a bit more inherent conflict exists; and in the third, the mostly mediated arena, clashes of interest are substantial. We shall briefly define the three categories and evaluate the success of the strategies Carter and Ford adopted for each in 1976. Carter's successes here were balanced by failures, while Gerald Ford made the most of his superior media resources.

UNMEDIATED MESSAGES

Advertisements are unmediated messages because the mass media are mere conduits for their dissemination. The candidate pays a fee for the privilege of having his say undisturbed by disparagement or disagreement.[32] Media interests here are simply in the profit from the fee. But the benefits for candidates are mixed. Political commercials are expensive: candidates and their media advisors spend millions of dollars for production and distribution. The art of purchasing time and space is hard to practice wisely and well: wrestling and "Bowling for Dollars" for a low-income audience, Lawrence Welk for the elderly are easy to discern; but it takes inside expertise to know which of New York City's news anchormen appeals to critically undecided, female, Jewish, suburban voters—and to persuade the station to sell the candidate commercial time on that news program.

Worse, unmediated messages are vulnerable to the Gorgons of selective exposure, selective perception, and selective retention.[33] Some people realize that unmediated messages are self-serving and incline to turn them off or tune them out (selective exposure). The longer the message, the stronger the inclination. This explains why many campaign managers prefer commercials, even though it costs more for a sixty-second spot on a top-rated entertainment show than for a half-hour of network time to deliver a speech. But even brief spots are vulnerable to selective perception in which some members of the audience interpret the message to substantiate their views—for a Reagan supporter a Carter commercial may have confirmed that the Democrat was callow and insincere. And if selective exposure and perception are inoperative, selective retention, in which voters tend to remember information benefiting their preferred candidate, may take over.

To overcome these obstacles requires subtle techniques and shrewd deployment of the media. The objective was (and is) to exploit voters' existing concerns, attitudes, and beliefs, not to change them. Commercials are devised to establish a personal bond between candidates and individual voters,[34] to show candidates conversing with (certainly not at) the individual viewer at home. Consider some examples from 1976. Carter was pictured sitting facing us across a porch table, or strolling through cultivated land, or standing near (certainly not straddling) a fence. Some of the Ford commercials took viewers into the inner sanctum of the White House and, particularly through the use of stills, connected them with the burden, even the anguish, of being the president. (Carter took that tack in 1980.)

The main focus of Carter's 1976 commercials was on the candidate's character: his empathy, responsiveness, integrity, and honesty. Carter initially eschewed advertising on specific issues, perhaps because taking stands was seen as potentially divisive, a way of dismantling the unsteady coalition which supported him. This left him vulnerable to criticism from his opponent that he was indecisive and lacked clearly articulated stands. In response to these attacks, Carter appeared toward the end of the campaign in commercials on such social problems as unemployment, unfair taxes, inflation, and inefficient government. When he specified what he would do to alleviate the problems, his proposals were rarely provocative.

Carter did too little to dispel the charges that he was avoiding explicit stands. Nor were there advertisements overtly attacking President Ford.

"He wavers, he wanders, he wiggles, and he waffles . . ." proclaimed Gerald R. Ford about Jimmy Carter. Ford's charge was translated into commercials appealing to the public's uncertainty about Carter's ability and experience, suggesting he was more soiled than from the soil. These attacks "exposed" Carter as a man unqualified to be president. A series of "everyday representative" Americans, concluding with several from Atlanta, described Carter's performance as governor of Georgia in unflattering terms, saying they never knew he had occupied the office, he didn't do much while he was governor, and he increased the bureaucracy—thus undercutting Carter's claim to administrative efficiency and his promise to reorganize the bureaucracy in Washington as he had done in Georgia. Carter used a similar technique against Reagan in 1980.

The Ford campaign benefited from its anti-Carter advertisements, which perpetuated and accentuated doubts about the Georgian's record and capacities. Ford's spots also sought to alleviate public qualms about his own competence and intelligence. The best of these cleverly struck several themes simultaneously. It showed him in the top third of a famous Yale law school class while a football coach, telling viewers that President Ford was a man of physical prowess and accomplishments, from an impoverished background, had worked his way through college in the American tradition of self-reliance and independence, and was, above all, intelligent and well-educated.

Neither Ford nor Carter ran a particularly inspired ad campaign. Given Ford's unprecedented rise in the polls—from a 2–1 underdog in July to a nearly even contest on election day—we can conclude his commercials did not hurt him. Carter's precipitous decline, on the other hand, may indicate the opposite.

Partially Mediated Messages

In this category the candidate or his representative has considerable leeway to say what he or she wants but is constrained in some way because the format includes members of the media. Instances are: press conferences, television talk shows, and interview programs such as *Face the Nation.*

In 1976, the debates were the most important setting for partially mediated messages. Each candidate used them to assert his campaign refrains, making mini-speeches repeating words, phrases, sentences, complete paragraphs, with which he was most comfortable from the campaign trail. But they were supposed to be responding to questions; they lacked absolute freedom to say anything they wanted. Indeed, their attempts to do so led to complaints about their lack of responsiveness. The interlocutors' lengthy questions and the presence of the opposing candidate also provided constraints.

But all the questions asked by the panelists during the debates accepted without question the terms of discourse of the candidates and the campaign. The journalists neither possessed nor expressed any radical ideas. They observed the requirements of polite and rational debate. Tone was inevitably restrained, not harsh; inquiring, not accusatory—reflecting the belief in good manners. The journalists were apparently chary of appearing partisan before the candidates and the huge television audience. The candidates were therefore left off the ideological hook, never confronted with questions beyond the limits of their rehearsed rhetoric.

Carter benefited more from the debates than Ford. He received equal stature by appearing with the president, and he showed no significant inferiority in information and poise. He was able to demonstrate that he was qualified to occupy the presidency. Besides, Ford as the incumbent was often forced to defend his record. No wonder Carter resisted debates in 1980 as long as he could. No wonder Reagan's electoral triumph was cemented by his debate performance, in which he deflected or denied Carter's attacks.

MOSTLY MEDIATED

By "mostly mediated" we mean material conveyed by the mass media, such as news stories, over which candidates do not appear to exercise control. Because these stories appear to be controlled by journalists they are less liable to provoke viewers' defense mechanisms. The result: they can have the most influence upon the public.[35]

During the course of a day, a candidate may travel from state to state, greeting factory workers in the rosy-fingered dawn, breakfasting with the unemployed, making speeches at rallies, berating his staff, brow-beating his wife, reading, reflecting, telling his relatives to desist untoward activities for the duration of the campaign, and issuing a position paper on crime. From all this, only a few minutes (if that) will appear on the network evening news, and more, although scarcely an exhaustive account, in the newspapers.

In the general election Ford was hurt far less than Carter from mostly mediated coverage. Ford was shown acting presidential: signing bills, greeting or conferring with foreign leaders in the Rose Garden, attending a football game. This symbolically reassuring portrait arose from the media's habit of treating virtually anything a president does as newsworthy, plus the assumed obligation of "objective" journalism that the two major-party candidates should receive roughly equal time and space. Such habits can be exploited and Ford's advisers did so. Rather than involve the president in several events each day, letting the media decide which one to feature—one that might be undesirable from the president's point of view—they devoted him to one advantageous public appearance daily. The media, especially television, had little choice except to show it.

Ford gained, too, from being excerpted: the full-length Ford was monotonous, sleep-inducing; the highlights of the abbreviated Ford were quite tolerable. And it was these forceful moments that were shown—not because television reporters, editors, and directors favored Ford, but because their shows require maximum visual and aural stimulation, and this was provided by (and guided the selection of) the chosen excerpts. The coverage helped fuel his almost successful catch-up campaign.

In contrast, Carter was hurt because he lacked the intermittently forceful and vigorous manner of Ford so conducive to television excerpts. He was less fortunate in another respect. One aspect of his 1976 appeal was that of the sleeping king, the leader who will return to his people and restore a lost golden age. This appeal, waning during the last few primaries, had been bolstered somewhat by coverage of the Democratic convention in which the media served primarily as a conduit for Carter's coronation. But it was devastated by the close scrutiny he received during the campaign. As Carter traipsed around the country giving speeches, he was depicted as just another politician telling people what they wanted to hear. Kennedy suffered the same fate during the 1980 primaries, as Carter cleaved to the White House.

UNDERMINING CANDIDATES

In most elections, mostly mediated coverage is difficult for incumbent presidents, as well as their challengers, to control. It is the category of coverage in which the interests of media personnel sometimes clash most dramatically with the purposes of candidates. To the occasional dismay and detriment of the candidates, the media impose some of their own news emphases on campaign events, focus on and isolate particular statements or actions by the candidates, and originate their own stories. The emphasis on controversy, focus on strategy, "investigative" reporting, and use of polls for horse race stories, usually undermine one or other of the candidates.

Controversy is news. When it is absent from a presidential election, reporters will stimulate it; when inchoate, they try to tease it out. They do so by encouraging each camp to respond to the statements, behavior, and actions of the other, and then publicizing the responses. The sides are presented and represented. But the concomitant stories of charges and countercharges depict the confrontation without resolving it. Reporters, ostensibly disinterested and neutral links, pass few explicit judgments in their news stories on the vacuity, veracity, and validity of the charges. They suggest, thereby, that the truth lies somewhere in between, or that all sides (except the reporter) are guilty.

When reporters do offer explanations and interpretation, the candidates' statements and actions, often the product of complex motivations, are almost invariably defined in strategic terms. Typically, Carter's failure to respond harshly to charges by his primary opponents was explained not by his good manners or personal style or even arrogance and contempt, but as the tactical response of a front runner in 1976.

The media originate several kinds of stories. First, "investigative" reports. It is assumed that somewhere among all the candidates, entourages, and peripheral staff lie intriguing gossip and even occasional scandals. Some reporters are assigned the ferret function or take it upon themselves. Their revelations are usually low-grade; they tease and titillate more than they uncover. Thus the New York Post discovered that a maker of television advertisements for President Ford was simultaneously producing a hardcore sex film. The newspaper confronted the producer with his dual undertaking and published the stirring news. The producer advised Ford campaign officials of his action and was summarily fired.

Then there are those inevitable "gaffes." Given canons of objectivity and the need for news pegs, reporters are inhibited from bluntly asserting their judgments about the candidates. One expedient is to invoke "some informed observers" or "a widespread feeling." Less sneaky, more effective and legitimate, is the "slip-up" story. Present in every campaign, these concern blunders by the candidates which can be reported and repeated, harped on by the media to illustrate and exemplify reporters' hitherto unpublicized opinions of the nature of the men running for president.

There were two major instances in 1976. One was the passionate coverage devoted to Carter's reference to adultery in his Playboy interview. Ford's turn came in the debates: his puzzling statement about the lack of Russian domination of Eastern Europe. In 1980, one such incident was the Carter Administration's vote at the U.N. against Israeli settlements. Unremarkable in themselves, these slips received extensive coverage because they symbolized defects in the candidates which journalists find it difficult to expose and report in any other way. Indeed, Arterton is led to propose that political reporters define major campaign issues as those involving "a destructive relationship between a candidate's stand and his support at the polls."[36]

The mass media also contract for and report the results of independent polls which measure some of the electorate's views. Yet the media's use of polls illustrates the selective coverage which so disconcerts some candidates: the emphasis on the horse race aspect of the election. Surveys can and sometimes do tap respondents' feelings about the state of the nation, their desires for new government policies, their hopes and fears for the future; but the answers featured most prominently during the campaign deal with voting intentions and purport to reveal the candidates' prospects of victory.

The emphasis on the strategic and horse race characteristics of presidential elections at the expense of both the candidates' records and their policy pronouncements is rooted in the imperatives and constraints under which journalists labor. Circumspect, couched in rhetoric, often boringly detailed, candidates' policy pronouncements are rarely dramatically newsworthy. If reported once, they are seldom considered worth repeating by the media.

Nor does the press systematically probe the challengers' records. Carter's gubernatorial actions were not dissected in 1976, nor Reagan's in 1980. Carter denounced Reagan's past statements and behavior in 1980, characterizing the Republican, in effect, as promoting the forces of racism, sexism, and nuclear madness. But by depicting Carter's charges as mudslinging attacks on Reagan's personal integrity and character rather than on his proposed policies, the media accommodated Reagan's defense, thus turning the Republican's record into Carter's liability. Carter was even moved to announce a change in strategy in a network interview with the rebarbative Barbara Walters.

By contrast, the records of presidents are continuous daily news during their incumbencies. Presidents can be disadvantaged by the media's obsession with the man in the White House, especially when, as with Carter, they preside over rising inflation, unemployment, and international tensions (as we discuss further in Chapter Four).

Profit maximizing underlies all these practices. Fear of missing stories that competitive media cover, unwillingness to risk boring TV viewers by giving them words instead of pictures, insufficient space to go into sufficient detail: all exist in substantial measure because of profit considerations. There are, of course, some inevitable boundaries of time and space, and the need to attract an audience. But if the media felt no need to be competitive on a day-to-day basis, if increasing ratings were unimportant, if space devoted to advertising could be decreased to meet the needs of the news, then the seemingly immutable goals and limitations that make poor campaign coverage inevitable would change.

The specific forms trivial coverage takes—the reason dopey stories are believed to attract and sustain viewer interest—originate in the values shared by reporters and audiences. It is no accident that in America's highly competitive culture the horse race metaphor saturates news about elections. And when journalistic shortcuts reduce the campaign to a personal conflict between two men instead of a jostling for control of government among different elite coalitions, they reflect (among other things) the individualism of the culture, traditional myths about the democratic process, and the failure to seek out radical analysts of the electoral process from left or right.

Conclusions

This chapter illustrates several of our basic themes. It shows how the media influence the decisions and actions of candidates, change their priorities, sometimes reduce their ability to control events. Yet at the same time, the media's susceptibility to manipulation by certain types of candidates, especially incumbents, helps insulate some politicians from full public accountability. Often campaign coverage serves, moreover, largely to misinform or to direct the public's attention to trivia.

Less obvious is the way the media decrease the ability of ordinary citizens to judge and their power to respond in their own self-interest to political events and power holders. One way the media do so is by denigrating or ignoring minority parties, especially those who make unconventional policy proposals. Libertarian, Prohibition, Socialist Workers, Communist, and U.S. Labor candidates perennially remain obscure during American presidential elections. Yet they have proposed to cut the defense budget by thirty billion dollars, curtail automobile use, cut the work week, repeal laws against victimless crimes, abolish all federal police agencies, eliminate all government subsidies to private enterprise, abolish civil rights laws and social security and federal welfare payments, and turn the United States into a giant Switzerland.

Despite the fact that the media campaign depictions tend to constrict rather than enlarge the universe of policy possibilities, election coverage legitimizes the political system. Any subject receiving such attention, the coverage implies, must deserve our support—even if the individual candidates do not. Yet it is the surface conflicts of power and politics that are depicted, the myth that all viewpoints get heard and represented that is fostered. The system's more venal weaknesses—underlying power relationships, what to do about them, vital alternatives—remain unexpounded, unexplored.

CHAPTER FOUR

•

Presidents Ascendant and Descending

"I fear three newspapers more than a hundred thousand bayonets."

Napoleon

CASUALLY ASKED WHAT HAD CHANGED during his years in politics, former President Johnson replied vehemently: "All you guys in the media. All of politics changed because of you." [1]

Presidents complaining about the press are like ships' captains objecting to the sea. Inevitably, the pattern of cooperation and conflict between the candidate and the press that started during the election campaign continues into the White House. Executive officials persist in preferring to release (and read) stories conducive to their personal, policy, and political interests. All presidents want to communicate beliefs, aspirations, decisions, actions which will improve their public standing and professional reputation; to make it in the self-interest of legislators, bureaucrats, foreign leaders to facilitate or at least accommodate their objectives; in others words, to enhance their authority once they have acquired it. [2]

If unpleasant news must be issued—and they realize its appearance is inevitable—presidents want to structure and interpret it for the media and thus for the public. Reporters, meanwhile, have their own objectives and needs which sometimes harmonize, sometimes clash with the interests of the president and his staff.

In the first part of this chapter we consider the advantages

54

presidents enjoy over the media and the methods they use to exploit them and so maximize their power. We describe the way presidents benefit from prevailing news definitions and practices; the large staff of media manipulators they call on; the ways presidents and their staffs grant, limit, and deny access to reporters; their exploitation of secrecy; their control over the timing of information releases; and their ability to dominate press conferences. We conclude this segment by discussing the temptation to tame the press by intimidation, punishment, and assault—an allurement to which only the Nixon administration succumbed completely.

The second part of the chapter illustrates the limitations of these seemingly boundless presidential resources with case studies of Richard Nixon and Jimmy Carter. For the incentives of reporters and presidents frequently clash. Under circumstances quite common in the years since John Kennedy, the media may undermine the power of chief executives, who become paper giants.

Ascendant

PRESIDENTS BENEFIT FROM NEWS DEFINITIONS AND REPORTING PRACTICES

The president is news: who he is, what he thinks, what he says (which may have little connection with what he thinks), where he goes, what he does. The reasons: for reporters and the public the presidency is the ideological symbol of American democracy and nationhood; journalists define the center of government action as the executive branch; they can personalize the institution in one man. This man is the only nationally elected policy-maker in American government; he participates in traditional, picturesque rituals and ceremonies; he can bring havoc to his countrymen and women and the world.

About sixty reporters plus camera and sound technicians work daily at the White House.[3] According to Bill Moyers, former press secretary to President Johnson and now himself a journalist, this "White House press corps is more stenographic than entrepreneurial in its approach to news gathering. Too many of them are sheep. Sheep with short attention spans."[4] Observed a Ford official, "You can predict what the press is going to do with a story. It is almost by formula. Because of this they are usable."[5]

Many White House correspondents are trapped and turned into conduits by the panoply of press conferences, news releases, briefings and backgrounders provided by the president and his minions. But the reasons for accommodation also have to do with routine, news definitions, restricted sources, and profit maximizing.

White House reporters are under pressure from their employers to file a constant supply of "hard news" about the president. It is such news that executive officials are only too willing to provide. "Editors who pay dearly to keep a man at the White House feel wedded to showing off his by-line on that day's major story, even though they may have received similar accounts from various news services."[6]

This attitude is linked to the "might" mentality. The press secretary might make a significant announcement; an aide might resign with a blast; the president might say something important in conversation with the folks back home; he might be assassinated. Absent correspondents lose the story; their embarrassed editors have to use wire service accounts.

Ironically, while White House correspondents spend much of their time transmitting similar stories of presidential statements and activities to their newspapers and networks, their preferred self-image is of the last of the American individualists. They imagine their profession to be one in which free enterprise is supreme: financial and career success are defined by the scoop which puts rivals to shame. The news exists to be unearthed by derring-do and other manly virtues. This machismo, inadvertently reinforced by the heroic and quite atypical endeavors of Woodward and Bernstein, disinclines journalists to unite to demand an end to White House manipulation and domination, while exposing them to exploitation by public officials.

Consequently, because the president is so newsworthy, because the press is predictable, he can produce news of his own devising, knowing the media will cover him and it. Especially in foreign affairs, his agenda items become the media's priorities—be they China, human rights, or the Arab–Israeli conflict.

LARGE STAFF OF MEDIA MANAGERS

At least fifty White House staffers make more than $40,000 annually. Of these, the number estimated to be primarily involved in public relations ranges from a low of 30 percent to a more credible 100 percent.[7]

One of their tasks is to advise the president and his staff how the media are covering the administration's statements, policies, and personalities. So they prepare a more or less comprehensive and accurate daily summary of major news stories culled from some thirty-five daily newspapers, assorted magazines, and the three television networks.

President Nixon annotated his copy of the news summary. The copies sent to his top aides frequently determined their daily behavior. In response to the news summary report of a speech given by the head of the Office of Education critical of the administration's stance on busing, Nixon wrote to aide John Ehrlichman, "fire that man by 2 o'clock today."[8] As Kumar and Grossman observe, the deadline afforded sufficient time for the story to make that evening's television news.

But the main task of the president's public relations practitioners is to manage the media. Among their duties: servicing the White House press corps; nurturing non-Washington-based media; arranging fireside chats, phone-ins, town meetings; writing speeches. On trips, the press secretary's office ministers to reporters by making their hotel reservations, arranging their charter flights, establishing communication facilities, providing accommodations, room keys, laundry and room service, telephones and typewriters: everything the press needs, in fact, except the entire truth about negotiations, decisions, actions—unless it is in the president's interests to provide it.

ACCESS

Their large staffs help presidents control the way news of their actions is reported. They can transmit a substantial portion of the news unmediated, as through radio and television speeches, or only partially mediated, as in press conferences. "They have a huge built-in element of control over you. You're locked into this little press room with only a telephone connecting you to the rest of the White House, and they have the option of taking your calls or not. All you get is staged events—press conferences, briefings, photo opportunities." So laments *Washington Post* reporter Austin Scott.[9]

As Scott implies, presidents have the power to bestow or deny access to journalists. They use it. When access is granted, the information may be dispensed subject to ground rules which limit what can be reported. ("Deep background means the reporter can write the information without attributing it to anyone, background means he can write it and attribute a 'high administration source,' off-the-record means he can't write it at all."[10]) Reporters gain inside information at the cost of letting themselves be used for trial balloons, anonymous political attacks, and advantageous and untrue revelations for which the source is not held publicly responsible.[11]

Denial of access is used selectively to maintain control, preserve power, prevent untoward information from reaching the public. During the Johnson presidency, CBS White House correspondent Dan Rather requested permission for a CBS crew to film the White House staff at work (not play, one assumes). The request was transmitted by press secretary George Reedy to the president, who replied in writing: "This guy and CBS are out to get us any way Bill Paley can. Tell him we are workers, not actors on routine."[12] Rather met the same fate with the Nixon administration.[13]

CONTROLLED INFORMATION RELEASE

Secrecy is another way of withholding the news. It can be asserted on the grounds of national security, executive privilege, and through a complicated and extensive classification system; or just by not telling anyone, especially the administration's formal spokespersons, what is best kept secret.

Secrecy is a potent weapon. Exposed policy initiatives can be thwarted by opponents, undone by public scrutiny. *Faits accomplis*, by contrast, resound with finality and redound with political triumph—as President Nixon anticipated and realized in his 1972 move toward China.

Secrecy is difficult to maintain. Sooner or later much information finds its way to the press. The adage "anything you don't want to see on the front page of the *New York Times* tomorrow you should classify"[14] is not entirely in jest. For executive officials, the question is often not whether to release information, but when and to whom.

The decision applies also to classified material. There are

many reasons for revealing secrets to the press: to intimidate or warn an adversary, protect one reputation, harm another, advance policy proposals, stimulate support, woo the voters. As former *Washington Star* Pentagon reporter Richard Fryklund wrote about the 1964 presidential election: "I learned more about our nuclear weapons, legitimately, during the campaign than I had ever managed to learn illegitimately before. The administration went out of its way to answer the Goldwater charges by leaking information." [15]

Johnson continued to practice and perfect the art of releasing information. In 1967 Senator Robert F. Kennedy (D., N.Y.) decided to make a major Senate speech breaking with the Johnson Vietnam policy by proposing negotiations and the halting of the bombing of the North. Johnson quickly delivered a previously unscheduled speech and held a news conference, which began just before Kennedy took the Senate floor, in which he announced a headline-making agreement with the Soviet Union to discuss arms limitations. Secretary of State Dean Rusk held a press conference to rebut Kennedy's proposal point by point—the president having called his close friend Frank Stanton of CBS to ensure Rusk would get on national television. [16] General William Westmoreland issued a statement insisting on the military necessity of continuing to bomb North Vietnam. And Kennedy's opponents prolonged the Senate debate so that he was unable to appear before the television cameras in time for the evening news. [17] This was a galling experience for Kennedy—the man reputed to have said that three minutes on the television evening news is worth almost all the other publicity available. [18]

PRESS CONFERENCES: ARENA OF PRESIDENTIAL DOMINANCE

The televised press conference is one of a president's more notable opportunities to enhance his power. He can use reporters and their questions spontaneously to exhibit his erudition, mastery of issues, and charm; or not so spontaneously, as when questions are planted with an accommodating reporter, the answers prepared and rehearsed. At best, a president who dominates the press conference and other forms of public relations gives the impression of a similar mastery of his office and of the political scene.

Presidents control the number and timing of their press conferences. When they have something to hide, scrutiny and challenge in a press conference are avoided. In his first four years in office, Richard Nixon held only thirty press conferences, and called even fewer after his overwhelming re-election in 1972.

President Carter's press conferences were announced to reporters from one to three days before they occurred, even though they were actually scheduled well in advance. When asked to explain the discrepancy, a Carter administration official "replied that he didn't think reporters had to be told everything." [19] The shorter the advance notice, the less time reporters have to prepare nasty questions. The shorter the advance notice, the greater the ability to cancel the conference if adverse news or events the president prefers not be asked about occur.

Presidents assiduously prepare for their press conferences. Ford spent several hours communing with his aides and briefing books; Nixon much of two days. [20] Questions are easily anticipated though: Eisenhower's press secretary James Hagerty claimed an anticipation figure of 90 percent.

Presidents conduct their press conferences in suitably arranged settings. Nixon appeared before a large blue drapery in a relatively small White House room; no rostrum or stand blocked his contact with reporters. The purpose was to impress viewers with a sense of intimacy, of the president's willingness to face the roistering crowd physically unprotected. Ford's aides moved him to another part of the same room so that the television cameras could show him in front of a doorway to a long hall, thus associating the fresh president with freedom and openness. [21] Whatever the setting, the reporters are the guests. They deferentially rise when the president enters the room, they sit at his nod.

Presidents have several devices to prime their performance at press conferences. They can begin the conference with a prepared statement. This mini-speech formally and uninterruptedly presents a presidential initiative, accomplishment or concern; transforms a partially mediated into an unmediated forum; restructures the reporters' agenda; and reduces the time available for questions. When questions eventually ensue, presidents can respond with statistical recitations giving an illusion of factual mastery, lengthily restate policy statements, respond to a planted question, decline to answer for reasons of state, ignore hostile reporters, dismiss a tricky inquiry with a quip, or lie.

Reporters are constrained. They do not want to enter the dens of millions of American homes as troublemaking bastards. They do not want to enter into personal combat with the president—a fight in which his power vastly exceeds theirs and which tumbles them from the lofty heights of objectivity. So they temper the toughest of questions with deference and respect. Even Nixon's Ron Ziegler admitted of White House reporters, "I don't think they probe for stories as much as they should."[22]

When the conference ends, the president steps down from the podium and eager reporters crowd round him as, on television, he moves comfortably toward the door, pausing to chat with this reporter or that, a part of yet apart from the crowd. What could better symbolize the majesty and common touch of the president?

Yet presidents are more dutiful than enthusiastic about holding televised press conferences. Some are uneasy before the cameras, their style unappealingly cornpone or aloof. Others, with things to hide, want to avoid press scrutiny. For, despite all the advantages they afford a president, press conferences do enable journalists to ask the chief executive about the issues and events of the day, to raise provocative questions which he may not want to answer.

Nonetheless, when asked whether the conference benefits the president or the press, twenty leading Washington correspondents and columnists "overwhelmingly felt that it is the president's show."[23] The result: an adroit president can convey an impression of command.

INTIMIDATE, PUNISH, ASSAULT

Striking as their advantages are over the mass media, presidents are tempted to pass beyond manipulation to try for control. President Kennedy had no compunction about advising the publisher of the *New York Times* that David Halberstam, the paper's dubious correspondent, had been too long in Vietnam. The suggestion was wisely resisted, but it perhaps inspired Murray Kempton's aphorism that politicians "are generally exempt from that ordinary decency which inhibits so many other persons from complaining against a man to his boss."[24]

Suggestion can lead to intimidation. President Johnson badgered and bullied newsmen and -women without much subtlety. CBS White House correspondent Dan Rather was reminded of the president's friends at CBS and advised to be cooperative. After CBS News showed American Marines setting fire to huts in a Vietnamese village, CBS president Frank Stanton received an early morning telephone call from his close friend Lyndon Johnson: "Frank, are you trying to fuck me?" [25]

Only the Nixon administration undertook a concerted, extended effort to punish—to assault—the press. Nixon's initial communications strategy was perfectly feasible and legal: evade the Washington press corps, spring momentous actions on the media and public, build on the innovations of previous administrations. These rational calculations were undone by the president's paranoia and the political naiveté and criminality of his associates.

The Nixon administration's assault was scary and crass. To mention only the instances involving pressure from powerful agencies of government, it included: lie detector tests and phone taps for officials suspected of giving information to the press; FBI questioning of the neighbors and friends of probing CBS television reporter Daniel Schorr, ostensibly because he was under consideration for a federal job; an Internal Revenue Service audit of the tax records of *Newsday* and its editor after the newspaper ran a series of articles exposing the financial affairs of a Nixon friend and confidante; [26] an official monitoring system through the Federal Communications Commission as soon as Nixon appointee Dean Burch took up his post as chairman; and investigations of media corporations by the anti-trust division of the Justice Department.

Leading the thrust, Nixon aide Charles W. (Chuck) Colson sent an "EYES ONLY, PLEASE" memo to H. R. Haldeman summarizing his meeting with the three network chief executives. We obtained a copy. The only ornament on the NBC President's desk, he recounted, "was the Nixon Inaugural Medal." He quoted ABC executive James Hagerty (the former press secretary to President Eisenhower) as saying, in the presence of ABC President Leonard Goldenson, "that ABC is 'with us.' " And Colson concluded: "the networks badly want to have these kinds of discussions which they said they had had with other administrations but never with ours. They told me anytime we had a complaint about slanted coverage for me to call them directly. [CBS Board Chairman William S.] Paley said that he would like to come down to Washington and spend time with me anytime that I wanted. . . . He also went out of his way to say how much he supports the president, and how popular the president is."

No doubt Colson is preening, reaffirming his toughness. Perhaps he is naive about the placid, apparently accommodating response from the network presidents, who may be insulating their news staffs while they placate the big bad wolf from Washington. The evidence is not entirely reassuring.

Nor is the result: crude, hostile, and abusive of constitutional values as it was, the Nixon assault succeeded for five years, helping at least indirectly to bring the president an overwhelming reelection victory.

Descending

PRESIDENTS' PROBLEMS

With such an array of weapons at their command, presidents might be expected to reign from the heights of public enthusiasm, party acclaim, and legislative complaisance. Not so, save in their dreams. In reality, presidential power is undermined in four ways: by untoward events presidents can do little, or fail, to control; by institutional conflicts inherent in the American political system; by the personal incapacities and failures at media management of the president and his associates; and by some of the news-gathering, reporting norms, and new skepticism of the press.

No president is master of his fate. Every president faces problems difficult to control. There are events which he neither wittingly inspires nor initiates but to which he must react or respond (seizing of embassy employees in Iran, placing of Soviet missiles in Cuba, a damaging strike by coal miners). He may be beset by debilitating, intractable conditions, usually the Scylla of inflation and the Charybdis of unemployment. Also, presidents have a propensity for undertaking foolish or disastrous activities (Vietnam, Watergate, who knows what next?). And every president has his constant and intermittent critics and antagonists: prominent members of the opposition party, ambitious rivals in his own, interest-group leaders. The conditions of the time, the actions or inaction of the president, the statements of other powerful men and women against him, are often news and receive media attention.

Presidents can often do no more than react to, in Elmer E. Cornwell's words, "the enormous frictions in the American political system." [27] Hard put to demonstrate a capacity for dealing with some of these problems, a president may appear impotent, unable to cope. He has much to answer, and answer for.

Complicating his situation, a president may never acquire the knack of media manipulation. Or, displaying it as a candidate, he may lose it once in office. He may develop it in one office only to discover that another position requires quite different media skills. Journalists treat various political institutions (and their members) quite differently. One of President Johnson's problems was that he expected to be treated as president as he had as Senate majority leader—to have the same intimate, confidential, candid, protective, and protected relationship with reporters. He never completely negotiated the transition from cloister to public spectacle. President Nixon nursed into the presidency his wounds incurred as Republican point man (or fall guy) before, during, and after the Eisenhower administration of the 1950s. He believed most reporters to be ideologically biased against non-liberals and personally biased against him; they were implacable enemies to be hated and beaten.

The president has a special aura of authority that can lend weight to any policy he endorses. But much of this weight is reduced by the way journalists have taken to reporting presidential forays into opinion management. What their reports do is to strip the aura away by placing his actions firmly in a political context. He becomes another politician seeking to retain and enhance his power, not a special leader.

Deference does reign on certain occasions. Journalists serve up respectful stories when the president participates in a ceremony that involves his role as symbol of the nation's identity, when he welcomes a foreign dignitary or represents the United States at an international conference. The president's symbolic embodiment of the nation also comes to the fore in coverage of foreign emergencies that appear to threaten national security or sovereignty.[28]

Presidents also enjoy a positive press during internal crises of instability. The most notable case is the unexpected accession of a new chief executive after the death or resignation of the old. Journalists and citizens look to the new president for reassurance. At these times it is unseemly for news reports to remind audiences of the political purposes of the man who has just moved into the White House.

So a president faces the press with an ambiguous mixture of strengths and weaknesses. He employs secrecy but is beset by leaks. He controls the release of information, but not for too long. He can badger, berate, and bully the press, but at the risk of resentful reporting. He offers up good news; the bad is sure to follow. The press responds by being accommodating, serving at times as a conduit for the White House version of events. But it also oppresses with a constant scrutiny of presidential activities, by giving voice to his opponents, and by seeking out bad news for which he may be blamed. Even a president most able to dominate the media can be undone.

We illustrate this argument with two case studies: the first of instant analysis,[29] the second of President Carter in office.

The Case of Instant Analysis

Presidents can dominate the airwaves.[30] Despite occasional resistance all three major television networks accede to White House requests to televise presidential addresses and news conferences.[31] A Library of Congress report reveals that over a ten-year period, "Presidents Johnson, Nixon, and Ford sought to obtain television network time to address the Nation on 45 identifiable occasions and received it 44 of those times from all three networks."[32] Most of these appearances were during prime time and each reached audiences of between 40 and 80 million people.

Conducive to a president's advantage is the inability and unwillingness of the networks to provide a comparable opportunity for his opponents to reach the public. The opponents may be divided on the president's pronouncement or action and unable to agree on a spokesperson. Or although united, their requests for television time may be refused. Even when the networks consent to grant time, it is invariably at a less desirable hour than that granted the president. The opposition speaker lacks the prestige and drama accorded the president. His ratings are far lower, often because of the confining of his appearance to one network in contrast to the president's monopoly of the three.

What galled and aggravated President Nixon was not the granting of air time to his legitimate opponents but the brief summaries-cum-discussions, disparagingly dubbed "instant analysis" by Spiro Agnew, with which network correspondents often followed presidential speeches and press conferences. Nixon wanted these events broadcast without comment because he believed that reporters undercut his message, thus damaging his power. He was right, as the following experimental study of the effects of instant analysis reveals.

Beset by the Watergate investigation and energy crisis, President Nixon undertook to take his case to the people. This brought him on March 19, 1974 to the annual convention of the National Association of Broadcasters. Generally sympathetic to the president, the audience applauded him several times during the news conference, which was broadcast live by all three networks and lasted roughly fifty-seven minutes.

President Nixon began with encouraging announcements on the energy shortage, then used the conference primarily to reiterate his accomplishments, especially in foreign affairs, and to defend his policies.

Of the eighteen questions, six were about Watergate. They concerned the alleged payment of "hush money" to Watergate defendants, the confidentiality of presidential tapes and documents, cooperation between the president and congressional committees investigating Watergate, and whether Mr. Nixon would resign the presidency as demanded that very day by New York's Conservative Senator James Buckley. The president said it would not be an act of statesmanship to resign, even though he had fallen in the polls, because the charges against him were false.[33] And he linked his fate with the office of the presidency and the needs of future presidents: "I will not participate in the destruction of the office of the president of the United States while I am in this office."[34]

Immediately following the news conference, CBS broadcast live roughly three and a half minutes of instant analysis (and this was both instant and analysis) by correspondents Roger Mudd and Bruce Morton. It focused exclusively on Watergate and analyzed the president's appearance in strategic terms. Mudd began it with, "I cannot see an awful lot of news in tonight's broadcast. . . ."[35] He then explained Nixon's purpose as "to be seen as many places before as favorable an audience as he can arrange" and "to clothe the presidency with as much higher responsibility as he can bring to it." Bruce Morton agreed and elaborated on Nixon's conflict with Congress. Morton then assessed the call for the president to resign as "a blow to that sector of his support where he could least afford it." And Mudd concluded with backhanded favorable speculation: "I suppose the president should be very pleased with his audience this evening. He has in three nights enlarged his clientele, so to speak, and he has done well in these press conferences. And I think that we'll notice, as following every presidential appearance on television, an increase in his rating in the popularity polls.''

A group of students who had not seen the original program was shown the question-and-answer session. The group was divided into half with no statistically significant differences of age, sex, class, party affiliation, presidential preference, political philosophy, or family income separating them. The experimental group then watched the "instant analysis." The control group did not. Both groups completed before and after questionnaires. The data showed that on all the scaled questions there was a shift toward the anti-Nixon stance of the instant analysis in the experimental as compared to the control group. The analysis had statistically significant effects on opinions of both Nixon and McGovern supporters, of both Democrats and Republicans. Respondents were influenced negatively whether specific issues were mentioned in either or both the news conference and instant analysis. These effects occurred even though the news conference lasted approximately fifty-seven minutes, the analysis three and a half. Let us now briefly analyze the more striking results.

A series of questions was asked about statements not mentioned in the news conference but asserted critically of the president in the instant analysis. These included the amount of news in the conference, the conservativeness of the convention audience, and whether anything which damaged the president's national standing would be of permanent harm to the presidency. On all these items the experimental group responded more negatively than the people who did not see the instant analysis.

A large difference occurred on questions concerning issues invoked in his support by the president during the news conference but contested by the CBS correspondents. On such items as the specificity of the Judiciary Committee's requests for presidential files on Watergate, how cooperative Nixon would be with the committee, and how much Senator Buckley's statement would hurt the president's chances of avoiding impeachment, the experimental group was more critical of the president, closer to the sentiments of the instant analysts, than the control respondents.

One result was particularly striking: the difference between the groups when asked to categorize from "very specific" to "very general" the House Judiciary Committee's requests for presidential files relating to Watergate. The control group only observed the news conference in which President Nixon characterized the requests for presidential transcripts and tapes as "a hunting license, or fishing license" and said he was not going to say "come in and bring your U-Haul trailer and haul it out."[36] The experimental group heard, in addition, CBS commentator Bruce Morton say: "Mr. Nixon said again that he wants it [the House impeachment investigation] over with, and accused the [Judiciary] committee of wanting every file the White House has. The committee members say that that's not true, that their requests are quite specific, quite limited. They are asking for information about the Watergate cover-up and information that Special Prosecutor Leon Jaworski did not get."

In this one instance Morton invoked external authority, the committee. Clearly, the credibility and authority of the source of disagreement may be a major factor in determining the magnitude of the effect—at least the short-term effect—of instant analysis on viewers' opinions.

Nixon had vigorously and favorably described his performance on the economy, foreign affairs, and Western Europe. These topics were ignored in the CBS instant analysis. Yet again the instant analysis negatively affected support for the president —even on subjects it did not include. The same effect emerged when we asked our respondents how they reacted to the news conference, whether they thought President Nixon had been candid, and to rate his performance in office since his election in 1968. The experimental group was more critical on every item.

The results of this experiment must be treated with some caution. The subjects were college students, a breed apart. And being placed in a study condition may have affected both the experimental and control groups, heightening their attention and recall. Thus even if the difference between them was caused—as we believe— by instant analysis, similar distinctions might not appear among real-world audiences, with their low attentiveness and uncertain memories.

Nonetheless, the results are highly suggestive: with the noose of Watergate drawing tighter, Mr. Nixon was on the defensive, challenged from many sides, his credibility under attack, his authority tottering. The NAB conference was a desperate attempt to recoup stature, to gain public support. But the instant analysis followed immediately and undid the knots the president had so laboriously tied. Those who watched and listened to the analysis heard the president separated from his office, the tactics behind his appearance identified and specified, credible sources invoked to contradict his protestations and claims. No wonder the experimental group responded so much more negatively to the president, so much more in keeping with the content and tone of the instant analysis, than the control group. Instant analysis not only prevented President Nixon from getting his message to the public unmediated but also made his attempts to defend himself counterproductive.

TYPICAL

How typical was this particular instant analysis? Are network correspondents usually so assertive? Under what circumstances do they eschew reciting and summarizing the gist of a president's remarks in favor of factual contradiction, judgment, and speculation? The answer depends upon three factors: presidential status; solemnity and gravity of the occasion; and the extent of opposition.

The first factor we call presidential status. During the waning days of his presidency—but only then—with his prestige and power in dramatic decline, and his attempts at media manipulation more transparent than ever, Mr. Nixon's appearances received instant analysis rife with negative judgments and speculation. There were even more political interpretations of his actions than usual. They contributed to the further undermining of his authority. In conspicuous contrast, instant analyses of President Ford's initial press conferences and speeches consisted primarily of summaries, supportive amplification, and favorable judgments about how well he was doing.

The second factor involves the solemnity of the occasion and the gravity of the issue addressed. An inauguration speech or a State of the Union message personally delivered to Congress tends to be treated by the networks and their correspondents with due deference. Instant analysis consists primarily of a summary.

There is an incentive for presidents to magnify, then milk an event in order to limit opposition from other elites, the media, and the public. The graver the issue addressed appears, the more instant analysis is confined to summary and favorable explication. As we recall, neither President Kennedy's speech about the appearance of Soviet missiles in Cuba and our concomitant blockade nor President Johnson's Tonkin Gulf speech was followed by analysis questioning either president's data or definition of the situation.

But there are limits. Those were foreign policy issues. The public was asked to approve decisions made, actions already taken. Public approval of the president's action peaks following his television performance and subsequently declines. Presidents, moreover, who take too often to the airwaves to enunciate or defend their policies may inspire skepticism or, worse, cynicism.

The final factor affecting the content of instant analysis, and clearly related to the other two, is the extent of elite and public opposition to a president and the particular policies he defends or enunciates in his public appearance. Quite simply, the greater the opposition is believed to be, the more emboldened network correspondents are in their analysis.

Critical instant analysis undermines presidential authority by transforming him from presentor to protagonist. The president's performance, if not the president, is laid out like a cadaver for dissection. Credible, familiar, apparently disinterested newsmen and -women, experts too, usually agreeing with each other, comment on the self-interested performance of a politician. Usually the president's rhetoric is deflated, the mood he has striven to create dissipated. Cadavers are rarely improved by dissection.[37]

From Consummate to Comatose: Jimmy Carter in Office or "Why Not the Worst?"

In contrast to Richard Nixon's late days are Jimmy Carter's early ones. For happy is the newly-elected president. Happy are reporters with him. Following his victory, the new president offers the media generous access and enjoys favorable coverage. During this honeymoon period, the objectives of press and president coincide: they both want maximum publicity for the people and policies of the new administration. But the honeymoon passion withers, to be replaced by bickering and conflict. Press and president rediscover their incompatibilities. In the ensuing struggle an adroit, tough president, one willing to use all the weapons at his command to exploit the manipulability of the press, can preserve and even enhance his power. But if the president is beset by social and economic problems he gives no impression of solving, if his policies are problematic and encounter caustic opposition in Congress and from other elites, if he and his staff miscalculate the reactions of the Washington press corps, then the president is prey to the media and his power is undermined—his re-election chances jeopardized. Jimmy Carter's one term in office vividly illustrates our argument.

The honeymoon is the time for stories about the president, his family, closest associates, decision-making processes, and goals. The personality and family stories are almost invariably favorable, recounting, as they do, foibles, cute traits, the human interests of the new faces. The decision-making and policy stories are equally favorable, reporting the (good) intentions of the new administration to come to grips with old problems. The rhetoric is the news story; there is no performance with which it can be compared. Nor are other public figures yet prepared publicly to criticize the president.[38]

Because of a leaked memorandum from pollster Pat Caddell to the president-elect, we now know the Carter administration carefully planned to exploit the honeymoon, to maximize symbolically favorable, image-enhancing coverage of Carter's actions. Example: the new president's celebrated—but not impromptu—walk down Pennsylvania Avenue immediately following his inauguration. The picturesque symbolism of the open-air walk of a brand new, vigorous, precedent-breaking president and his family from the Capitol past the buildings of the executive branch to the White House was a natural for visually oriented television and news magazine reporters.

Also a natural was the president's decision, taken with daughter Amy, to build a tree house. The edifice constructed, the White House press corps, photographers and camerapeople trooped over to interview Amy and the president's 20-month-old grandson Jason, who were squatting in the house above them. Complained Ed Bradley of CBS News, "this is the sort of thing that eats up our time. Photo opportunities, briefings, releases, more photo opportunities. Most of it doesn't mean a damn thing. But the White House grinds it out and we eat it up. The network wants everything we can give them on the president."[39]

These two examples are typical of the new president's many public relations coups. Other innovations included his town meetings, which provided media appeal by using nostalgic (even atavistic) small town settings for sessions of ersatz democracy; his "talk to the president" sessions with Walter Cronkite and others; and the less noted tactic of delivering brief statements rather than long televised addresses. According to James Fallows, one of Carter's speechwriters, all "most people hear is about a minute or two on the news anyway . . . the same amount of coverage you get if you go out there and talk for one or two minutes." [40] Besides, brief statements are not susceptible to instant analysis.

Carter and his staff were aware of the benefits of secrecy, the controlled release of information, the necessity to reduce leaks and intimidate leakers, and the advantage of communicating their messages to the public without the mediation of the White House press corps. The president demonstrated a crafty understanding of our basic contention: if a political actor maximizes the match of his interests with those of the media, he will enjoy maximally favorable news coverage.

Inevitably, the honeymoon ended. Social and economic problems are difficult to resolve. In trying to resolve them, a president's proposals are often frustrated as he conflicts with members of his own and the opposition party, powerful figures in Congress, the leaders of business, labor and other "legitimate" interest groups. Because reporters thrive on two-sided conflicts, fanning them when they fade, they publicize the sources of elite opposition and then ask the president and his associates to justify and defend their proposals and actions.

Having helped raise great expectations of the president's performance, the mass media then helped contrive the chorus of dismay and disillusion when Carter's effectiveness was found wanting —wanting against standards of action and achievement propounded and promoted by presidents and the press. Carter was not aided in this evaluation by having to preside over the lowering of living standards, the raising of oil prices, and rampant inflation.

Fresh to Washington, Carter and his immediate staff inadvertently fueled this negative coverage. They made obvious early errors: inept congressional liaison, incompetent staff work, the pre-appointment financial juggling of Budget Director Bert Lance to whom the president clung too ardently too long, and the off-duty jiggling of aide Hamilton Jordan all received due notoriety in the media.

It was the president's promise of an open administration which, in time, caused him the most trouble. Openness is an image-enhancing commitment. In practice, it vitiates the weapons of secrecy, access control, and timed information release the president possesses. It permits, even encourages, White House aides and cabinet officers to argue for their policy positions in the press, to express their disagreements publicly. The result was an exaggerated impression of the chief executive as indecisive, stubborn, unable to control events or command obedience—a failure. Senator George McGovern (D., S.D.) had a similar experience during his 1972 campaign for the presidency: the disputes among his advisers were widely publicized; far more vicious conflicts within the committee to re-elect President Nixon were successfully concealed from the press. Consequently, the McGovern campaign seemed a shambles; Nixon's, immaculate.

It took only a few months for officials of the Carter administration to be embarrassed by press disclosures of their discussions, disputes, and policy decisions. As with previous administrations, moves were made to exercise greater control over the flow and release of information. At a Camp David retreat session, President Carter hectored cabinet members and senior aides about unity. Once enunciated, presidential policies were to be supported. Later, the more outspoken and independent cabinet members were dismissed and a White House chief of staff established.

This attempt to assert control contradicted the previous commitment to an open administration making open decisions openly arrived at. But Carter was in a double bind. Reporters had been appropriately exploiting the laissez-faire administration, depicting it in disarray. Now they wrote stories about an administration unwilling to countenance dissent, a president who retained only the obedient cabinet members, a White House peopled by a small band of loyal acolytes from Georgia.

Th continued decline in the president's standing in the public opinion polls had been perceived by the White House in part at least as a problem in public relations. The advertising specialist who had handled Carter's campaigns for governor of Georgia and the presidency thus joined the staff. Titled presidential communications director, Gerald Rafshoon announced: "We'll try to have more fireside chats on specific issues and presidential goals, more town meetings and call-in shows, more direct communications with the people, in other words." [41]

Following Rafshoon's employment at the White House, President Carter undertook a highly publicized tour of Civil War battlefields, journeyed to New York to sign legislation aiding the city, and traversed part of the Salmon River in Idaho by raft. The president hosted a series of intimate dinners for powerful executives of major news organizations, began granting requests for interviews, and started rehearsing his significant speeches and preparing more sedulously for his press conferences.[42]

Bringing back pomp to the Carter presidency, Rafshoon returned the president to his imposing, long, black limousine and resurrected the playing of "Hail to the Chief." The decisions are not trivial. Ritual is an important sustainer of authority. To the extent the media can be used as a conduit for ritual, they support the incumbent, the office, the political system as a whole.

What it took Carter and his aides, even Rafshoon, too long to appreciate was that they were dealing with a Washington press corps stung into suspicion by the official deceptions of Vietnam and Watergate. Inhibited by Ford's role as national healer and trustee (un-elected, he had waged no campaign, made no public promises to obtain the presidency), the media's wariness blossomed with the advent of Carter. After the honeymoon, Carter was increasingly treated as guilty unless he proved himself innocent. More than ever, White House reporters interpreted presidential actions as politically motivated. The media events undertaken by the president were described by reporters as attempts to manipulate press and public rather than taken at face value as efforts by a conscientious president to communicate with the American public.

The Rafshoon story reflects this attitude and illustrates the limitations of presidential media manipulation. The advertising man is hired to improve the president's communications strategy. Then the fact and purposes of the appointment become the substance of flamboyant press coverage throughout the country. "Advertising Man Hired By Carter To Sell Policies"[43] headlined one newspaper, while another entitled its front page story: "Adman Called In to Polish Carter's Tarnished Image."[44] The immediate impact of the stories was to expose Rafshoon, undermine his effectiveness, and highlight the deficiencies of the administration—why else would Carter need to hire the adman?

Pack journalism contributed to Carter's decline. Stories about the president's inadequacies (real and imagined), punctuated by regular, well-publicized surveys charting his falling in public approval (but not explaining why people lacked confidence in him) appeared frequently. Each defeat in Congress, each defensive speech was linked to the theme of incompetence and waning popularity, thereby contributing to the descent—or doing nothing to brake it.[45] Carter's extraordinary show during July 1979, when he retreated for ten days to reassess his presidency, coming down from the mountains of Maryland to dismiss several of his cabinet members, was treated by official Washington as the behavior of an insecure man trying to appear strong rather than of a decisive and determined president. In unison reporters transmitted this view across the country.

Then some Iranian "students" invaded the American compound and embassy in Teheran and took roughly fifty Americans hostage. Coverage by the American television networks was immediate and intense. Stories from and about Iran could have recounted the sins of the Shah, examined the nature and effects of American involvement in Iran before and during the revolution, explained the massive hostility expressed toward the United States by many Iranians, shown how much of Iran was functioning normally. News coverage could have tried to deal with the complicated post-revolutionary situation in Iran, the conflicts between and within the westernized middle class, economic and social radicals, and the various factions of the Islamic clergy. The hostages could have been put in the context of the struggles for power among the different groups in Iran and the attempt by the Ayatollah Khomeini and his followers to create an Islamic theocracy. But for reasons we outlined in Chapter 2 and will elaborate in Chapter 13 on foreign news coverage, the media inevitably emphasized not the complexities of the situation but the brute fact of the Americans' captivity and the reactions and responses of the Carter administration as it tried to effect the hostages' release. The coverage was unremitting. On CBS, the anchorman, the widely respected, avuncular Walter Cronkite, now concluded the evening news by giving the number of days the hostages had been held captive. ABC television introduced a new late night news program entitled "America Held Hostage." Such coverage riveted public attention on the plight of the hostages. It thereby transformed an unusual and disturbing event into a major crisis, a symbol of worldwide challenge to American power. Under these circumstances, President Carter would have had difficulty playing down the importance of the occurrence even if he had wished to do so. He could not turn his back on the hostages. Nor would he have been wise to try. For the events in Iran, followed by the Soviet invasion of Afghanistan, are the very kind of unifying foreign crises which a president can exploit to recoup esteem. This is what Carter sought to achieve. Iran became a centerpiece of his attention and the ostensible reason why, he claimed, he could not and would not leave the capital to campaign for renomination. For the president, the crisis transcended politics. This left rival Edward Kennedy out campaigning frenetically around the country while the president stayed statesmanlike in the White House. The strategy worked long enough for Carter to receive his party's renomination, but well before that time (although too late for Kennedy), as the hostages remained in Iran, the president's rating in the polls began to decline again.

When the stories he has emphasized reflect favorably upon a president, his personal standing, influence, and re-election chances are enhanced (Nixon and China). When the stories he has elevated reflect poorly (Carter and energy), the president's agenda-setting ability may haunt him. The president's panoply of media resources may allow him virtually to dictate the issue agenda of the press; it does not ensure that he can sway elite or public preferences on the specific actions he takes and policies he proposes.

Effects

The early phase of coverage generates expectations of quick results. During the post-inaugural honeymoon, the president is always pictured as about to embark on long-postponed reforms with the backing of an energetic new cabinet, a brilliant young staff. Then reality intervenes. Innovation is not easy in our system of limited government initiative, checks and balances. Because the media cannot deal effectively with such structural complexity but love a colorful fight between personalities, the stalemate is portrayed as a conflict between the political will, influence, and savvy of the president and his opponents. If the innovation fails (as most do), the media's framework allows but one explanation: a personal failure of the president.

This description applies well to coverage of Jimmy Carter's initiatives, which met with little success because of the opposition of powerful interests whose access to veto points is built into the system. Carter could have been as crafty and competent as Roosevelt or Lincoln, but he would still have had trouble taming Exxon and slaking Senate Finance Committee Chairman Russell B. Long (D., La.).

The media's obsession with the presidency can victimize the president, making him an easy target. It is less burdensome and more in keeping with journalistic routine to focus on presidential as opposed to legislative aspects of policy-making. For Jimmy Carter this meant that Congress's failure quickly to pass his programs was blamed on him. Although some prestige journals offered analyses of Congress itself, the sheer volume, the overwhelming concentration on the president as well as the actual content of reports made it appear that Carter's incapacity was at the root of congressional demurral and inaction. A more gregarious president and a more skillful staff could have expedited the legislation. Still, the greater difficulty of covering hundreds of legislators, of investigating the actual reasons for congressional decisions that are often made in private, excused Congress. And the reports of Carter's botching only decreased his influence in Congress, enhancing that body's independence. Through no fault or plan of their own, the media's routines and limitations, which lead them to converge on the presidency, contribute to the fragmentation of the policy process.

The implication of the media's personalized coverage of presidential policy-making is that all we need is a "good" president. Then problems would be solved. So new candidates appear, are elected, raise great expectations. The cycle repeats.

The presidency is the one office with some potential to push through domestic innovations against the claims of entrenched interests. By weakening the ability of the occupants of the office to innovate, media practice (again, these are not deliberate media intentions) props up the status quo. By taking the public through cycles of unrealistic hope and cruel disillusionment, the media may discourage voting. By attacking a president who pushes new ideas, they reward inactive presidents who do nothing to challenge the prevailing order—who can then take credit for "restoring normalcy" and "healing wounds." The media may deter presidential tyranny at the price of presidential—even governmental—paralysis. Underlying power relations are reinforced.

Conclusion

When events cooperate, a president who skillfully uses his considerable power assets to manipulate media coverage obtains a potent power resource. Journalists purvey images that enhance his control.

With less malleable circumstances and less skilled manipulation, different outcomes may ensue. Media needs and practices are likely to shape the actions and priorities of declining presidents struggling to regain esteem. Nixon in 1974 and Carter in 1978 are examples. Critical coverage of those very actions can further reduce a floundering president's ability to control events; the coverage portrays his behavior as a series of cynical and doomed ploys to recover the public's trust by manipulation. Only a unifying crisis can reverse the decline. Such a crisis may be real, contrived, or imagined. Its effect on the president's fortunes usually depends on the way it is covered and depicted by the media.

Without a redeeming crisis, media coverage which undermines a president has two effects. There is a reallocation of power among the powerful, a shift in the political momentum to a president's opponents within and outside his party. And there is a reinforcement of public discontent with political leaders whose failure to lead is partially traceable to media power. Neither media nor politicians propound solutions to the disaffection other than new presidential candidates: more of the same.

CHAPTER FIVE

•

Congress and Its Members

"The Press, Watson, is a most valuable institution, if you only know how to use it."

> Arthur Conan Doyle (Sherlock Holmes, *The Adventure of the Six Napoleons*)[1]

THERE ARE TWO KINDS OF COVERAGE of Congress. One undermines respect for its members as a whole. The other promotes the re-election of individual legislators. In this chapter we analyze the sources of the coverage: they stem from the news needs of the media and the news-making and -evading efforts of Congressmen and -women. Then we describe the dolorous implications of our analysis for representation of the ordinary citizen in Washington.

Disparity

The United States Congress is a cornucopia of news. Its members constantly make news. Most newsworthy events originating elsewhere have repercussions in Congress. And it is the most permeable of all the institutions of American government. Yet Congress clearly receives considerably less coverage than the presidency.[2] It may be argued that presidents enjoy a preponderance of coverage because they are more important, make more significant decisions than members of Congress. But in fact presidents often merely ratify decisions organized and structured by people far lower in the hierarchy. On most issues, the president proposes and the Congress disposes.

The disparity in coverage is based on several media needs and practices that work against extensive coverage of Congress. They are:

- Limits on space and time act to prevent running all the significant stories even if enough reporters are there to cover them.
- The legislative process does not comfortably fit journalistic needs for a smooth, uninterrupted flow: bills are considered intermittently; bursts of activity are followed by inaction, even elimination.
- News values clash with congressional norms: the former relish personalized conflict; the latter condemn public expressions of personal animosity.[3] Members can, however, berate people outside the legislature—the president, bureaucrats, lobbyists—and do so to obtain publicity.
- The ideological assumption is held by reporters no less than by other Americans that the nationally elected president is the most legitimate spokesman on public issues of general concern.

Further, there is one president, centrally located, who speaks (or appears to speak) for the executive branch. But who speaks for Congress? Searching for a single voice beggars the media. Covering all the conflicting subcommittees' and committees' markup sessions, overlapping hearings, the floor deliberations, is an expensive proposition. Enter profit maximizing. Some 99 percent of American radio stations, 96 percent of television stations, and 72 percent of daily newspapers have neither Washington correspondents of their own nor contact with stringers. Of the 1,400 domestic Washington correspondents, roughly 400 cover Congress, but work mainly for national news organizations.[4] Parenthetically, the condition is even worse in state legislatures. Most newspapers and broadcasting stations receive all the news about their state legislatures and legislators from the AP or UPI wire services.

The Media's News Incentives

Nonetheless, Congress does regularly make news, the content of which varies somewhat according to medium. As presently constituted, television coverage of Congress is yet another example of commercial considerations subjugating the public interest. We see little of Congress, learn less of the activities of its members, because the television corporations make more money showing "entertainment." Consider, though, what might happen if the technology used to transmit sporting events from throughout America were applied to Congress. Viewers could be swept from committee hearings to subcommittee votes, to floor debates, to conference committee decisions, all replete with slow motion, instant replay, and "color" commentary by former legislators. The technology would be abused, to be sure, but how it could illuminate the legislative process, how accountable and responsive it might make the members of Congress![5]

The more important congressional decisions, if covered at all, are read from wire service reports by anchorpersons. Rarely does television break original stories about the legislature. At best, viewers are offered corridor snippets in which legislators may be gently quizzed or witnesses belligerently badgered. Accompanying this news are occasional disparaging, even snide, comments from anchorpersons and commentators about congressional indecision, inaction, and incompetence. Only committee hearings attract much serious attention.

Newspaper editors devote a consistent amount of space to congressional stories, according to Susan Miller: "Despite enormous shifts in the number of hearings and other coverable events, the four newspapers [studied] maintained roughly the same total numbers of stories on topics and Congress month after month."[6] But what is this content?

The institution has its automatic newsmakers, most notably dynasty-laden, mystique-ridden Senator Edward M. Kennedy (D., Mass.). His pronouncements are news if he wishes. Other legislators occupy positions of power enabling them to attract occasional media attention. They include party leaders, especially of the majority or president's party, chairmen or chairwomen of significant committees, and actual or incipient presidential candidates. Other legislators flit across the national scene and are impaled by the media, rarely to reappear—a fate exemplified by Missouri Senator Thomas F. Eagleton once he briefly became the Democratic vice-presidential nominee in 1972.

Among the major categories of congressional stories are: fights for leadership positions; final passage or defeat of some kinds of prominent legislation; the progress, stalemate, or enactment of a few select bills, usually those proposed and promoted by or in the name of the president; and, particularly, dramatic hearings.

In covering this material, the Washington press corps tends to reduce issues to partisanship and personality. Policy proposals and the legislative process are reported as they expose conflicts between the parties and as they contribute to the legislators' personal power and political careers. Thus, health insurance legislation was presented primarily as a conflict between President Carter and his rival in the Democratic party, Senator Edward M. Kennedy. Far less in evidence are the strengths and weaknesses of these policies and proposed legislation, their potential effects on American society. They do not receive the extensive attention needed to penetrate public consciousness. The reasons for the disagreements over the substance of legislation are rarely laid to conflicting visions of the public interest. Even less are the details of such disagreements explained.

The Washington world perceived by many reporters is one of ambition and elections in which policy is often at best an expedient. But policy disagreements, serious and deeply held, are also a feature of congressional life. Their depreciation in most coverage results from the incentives and constraints of daily journalism. And it results in a more unflattering portrait than Congress deserves.

Policy differences are hard to explain and tedious to recount. Nor are reporters particularly equipped by training or inclination to discuss the merits and policy implications of proposed legislation. Indeed, such a discussion would be viewed as arrant speculation, violating the norms of factual journalism. In contrast, attributing politicians' policy positions to political motives is acceptable journalistic practice. Invoking personalities is the conventional device for attracting and retaining readers' attention.

In Congress these personalities are mainly male, white, middle-aged, wealthy, and egocentric. They possess the semblance and often the substance of power. Illicit funds are available to them through internal finagling and external favors; illicit sex through the aphrodisiacal attractions of power. Instances of graft, junkets, and love nesting are widely reported when participants are indiscreet and tattling serves somebody's interests. The reports can destroy individual careers, as witness those of Wilbur Mills, Wayne Hays, and Edward Brooke.

Scandal pricks the lives of only a few members of Congress each term. The actual number of scoundrels is larger. A lot of peculation and philandering probably is never reported. And the lack of investigative zeal that characterizes the press corps as a whole means that exposés often evaporate without producing significant institutional reforms or even punishment of errant solons.

Seeking and Avoiding National Coverage

Congressmen dislike stories about their soiled linen and laundered money. Indeed, many desire no coverage whatsoever in the prestige and national press. Coming from uncompetitive districts, in predominantly one-party states, some legislators are able to enjoy constituency approbation and re-election, rise through the seniority system to power if not eminence within Congress, all the while assiduously avoiding the prestige press. Anonymity suits them fine. As one multi-termed senator once remarked: "when you've got the votes, you don't have to talk"[7]—votes in committee, on the floor of Congress, and in the constituency.

But there are compelling reasons why many members of Congress seek favorable publicity in the national press for their policy preferences. Media mention of a topic can stimulate public interest and pressure on legislators. How an issue is defined and structured for public discussion by the media influences how legislators think about it. The way bills are reported in the press can impel representatives to vote in a particular way for fear of outraging their constituents.[8] Well-timed and appropriate publicity can force an issue onto the congressional agenda, remove obstacles to stalemated bills, and facilitate their final passage.

The two other uses of congressional news are more individualistic. At any one time, several members of the United States Senate are running for president, while the rest are thinking about it. All of them believe they could do a better job than the incumbent. Simultaneously, many members of the House of Representatives are considering challenging the senators of their states or hoping that the Senate seat will fall vacant as its occupant seeks the presidency. Without name-recognition, without favorable publicity, ambition for higher office is usually frustrating and frustrated. So members of Congress need the media to attain higher office and, under certain circumstances, to facilitate their policy goals.

There is a third, perhaps less respectable but equally compelling reason: status. Favorable media attention gives cachet, adds legitimacy to a legislator's activities by plucking him from the congressional morass: he has been deemed worthy of being brought to public attention. For constituents, the public, officials in the other branches of government, for colleagues who grumble as they envy, the legislator is marked as a person distinguished from his or her fellows. Being favorably presented on the television news, even in the papers, confers status. External recognition of a legislator's supposed worth is no detriment to power.[9]

Unfortunately for the legislators, the national press needs any single member of Congress less than members desire the press. The opportunity to broadcast unmediated speeches and invitations to participate in television panel discussions rarely accrue to ordinary members of Congress. In practice, Congressmen and -women court the press as the press courts the president. Their problem is the relative uninterest of the mass media in most of their activities and the reporters' belief that the information released by legislators is even more self-interested than that emanating from the White House.

Susan Miller's investigation suggests some general rules for congressional committees and their members desirous of making news. They include accepting reporters' definitions of what is newsworthy, ready accommodation of journalists' inquiries, and riding on topics already in the news.[10] These rules give the press substantial influence over certain aspects of congressional activity. Matthews exaggerates only slightly (and covers both houses) when he writes that "much senatorial behavior is shaped by the senators' perceptions of the reporters' notion of news. . . . The types of bills a senator introduces, the committee assignments he cherishes, how he votes on roll calls, and what he defines as an 'issue' are influenced by anticipated press reactions."[11]

The prime path to a national press is holding a newsworthy hearing. The best way for Congress to get covered "is to become the best and most complete source of information about a topic already being covered or to pick a topic that is more 'newsworthy' (negative, unexpected, elite, unambiguous) than the topic the President is pushing."[12] Hearings generate such information; they can be highly attractive to the press. They take place at predetermined times, in convenient locations equipped for coverage, and they respectably relieve journalists of some of the burden and expense of investigative reporting.

Many hearings are held, but few are extensively reported. Widespread coverage occurs when media interest unites with public disquiet, genuine congressional concern, and potential partisan advantage. Such hearings usually contain flamboyant ingredients: peccadillos, scandals, corruption, crime, exploitation of the public by greedy corporate executives and once smug now scared officials, reassessments of a presidential policy, probes of the causes of man-made disasters.

Many legislators crave media coverage of their hearings but are limited by the jurisdiction of their committees and subcommittees to topics that lack glamor and are difficult to transform into media fare. Even diligent efforts may fail to induce coverage. Daniel Schorr recounts the pleas of the staff director of the Senate poverty subcommittee that CBS cameras cover a scheduled hearing. Witnesses "would include a black, a poor white and an Indian in full headdress." When Schorr demurred because of conflicting assignments, the staff director indicated the date of the hearing could be changed, pleading that without the presence of television cameras most subcommittee members would not attend.[13]

Many committees are engaged in parceling out goodies—tax breaks, subsidies, or other preferential treatment. Publicity is the last thing they want or usually receive from the typical reporter. Servicing special interests requires mastery of the technical minutiae that editors habitually equate with the unnewsworthy (I. F. Stone was the proverbial rule-proving exception).

MOLDING COVERAGE OF HEARINGS

Here is how the general counsel of a congressional committee advised members to conduct a hearing for maximum media effectiveness:

> Decide what you want the newspapers to hit hardest and then shape each hearing so that the main point becomes the vortex of the testimony. Once the vortex is reached, adjourn. . . .
>
> Do not permit distractions to occur . . . which might provide news that would bury the testimony which you want featured.
>
> Do not space hearings more than twenty-four or forty-eight hours apart when on a controversial subject. This gives the opposition too much opportunity to make all kinds of countercharges and replies by issuing statements to the newspapers.
>
> Don't ever be afraid to recess a hearing, even for five minutes, so that you keep the proceedings completely in control so far as creating news is concerned.[14]

Other tactics include eliciting testimony from witnesses who make news because of their prominence or notoriety; scheduling witnesses who support the legislator's position during the first few days of hearings, when press interest is high; and having these supportive witnesses testify early in the day to facilitate newspaper and television coverage. Opponents–defendants are relegated to waning days when press interest has probably declined, unless they can be discredited, in which case they are encouraged to testify on the first day. Information is presented in its most head-line-grabbing form. Making the case against the predatory prescription drug companies, Senator Estes Kefauver (D., Tenn.) gave the drug markup from production to selling not in dollars and cents but in percentages, 1,118 percent to be precise.[15]

The incentives of the news media combine with the responses of members of Congress and the increasing sophistication of witnesses to produce a species of congressional hearings featuring confrontation, muck-raking, and moral outrage.[16] Here the interests of media and member most closely correspond. These are the hearings most frequently shown on television and in excerpts on the evening news. They sometimes dramatize rather than investigate policy issues. A network cameraman called television news coverage of congressional hearings "the biggest hoax in American theatrics."[17] But often the publicity does start a process of education and arousal of the public and even its servants in Washington. The mutually satisfying media show put on by Senator Abraham Ribicoff's (D., Ct.) Government Operations Subcommittee and Ralph Nader in 1966 elevated automobile safety onto the congressional agenda and into the statute books.

Unfulfilled Expectations

The national news organizations focus on what they believe are the big issues and leaders. Following their news incentives, they highlight conflict, controversy, inaction, and venality. Legislators' actions are predominantly ascribed to self-interest and political and electoral expediency. The accomplishments and failures of Congress are implicitly compared by reporters against a mythical standard of efficacy, diligence, and probity hard to attain and sustain.

In promoting themselves and their policies nationally, in pub-

licizing their hearing room indignation, members of Congress inadvertently reinforce in part this negative impression. Hearings are
newsworthy; they expose problems. Discord and debate are newsworthy; they sketchily air solutions. Expectations are raised, then
dashed. For the outcome of many congressional hearings is no
positive action at all: bills repose in committee, are waylaid in the
legislative shuffle; tabled, defeated, or vitiated. Others are passed
as tepid and timid compromises unlikely to resolve what the president and coverage of Congress—and people's own experiences—
have identified as serious dilemmas. And, with rare exceptions,
even when major legislation is enacted, it fails to change most
citizens' lives significantly. Thus legislators' action and inaction,
their necessary and inevitable pandering to the national press, usually combine with media news needs to yield an impression of
congressional ineptitude and irresponsibility.

But there is another kind of coverage of Congress with a quite
different result. Beneath the waves of the networks, prestige newspapers and newsmagazines is the undertow of local television,
radio, and newspapers' treatment of their hometown legislators.
Local coverage is predominantly composed of neglect and puffery,
insulating individual members from accountability to their constituents.

Seeking and Avoiding Local Coverage

Some members of Congress want to stay there indefinitely.
Others stay only as long as they need to in order to advertise law
practices or lay the basis for higher office. Others retire voluntarily, in disgust, relief, or remorse, clutching their ample pensions.
Whatever their goals and plans, as long as they want to remain in
Congress, members must face the voters. They know that, irrespective of their skill and reputation within Congress, their power
rests on the whims and proclivities of their constituents. Personal
image-building and -polishing is the solution; the local media are
the means.

Individual congressmen and -women make news, are made by
the news, and may be destroyed by the news. Many are ignored as
non-news. Three-quarters of America's daily newspapers rely on
the wire services for accounts of events in the nation's capital. But
wire service reporters are preoccupied with the major news stories,
not the minor members. Even when newspapers have bureaus in

Washington, the reporters are likely to spread their attention over several members of Congress from their state, as well as covering the departments.

Most American newspapers therefore originate few stories about their local members of Congress. Often they publish little more than an obscure summary of their legislators' votes on final passage of major legislation. Votes in subcommittees and committees, on motions to table or return bills to committee, are rarely published, although they are usually far closer and far more vital than votes on final passage. Nor is there much investigative reporting of the local legislator's decisions, statements, and actions or his or her business and political cronies at home. A typical press secretary, who insisted on remaining unidentified, told us that his job was to get news about his congressman into the local paper. "They don't care what we do," he said, "they don't think their readers are interested." And "what we do doesn't sell papers unless it's sexy or about sex."

Because most media owners do not want to incur the expense, and because editors and news directors think the routine behavior of legislators is of no interest to their audiences, the average legislator goes unscrutinized by the press. But, like lovers refusing to accept rejection, members of Congress embrace the spurning media. As so often happens in life, their fervor, their persistence, are rewarded; they penetrate the languorous press.

INSERTING AND WITHHOLDING NEWS

The members usually employ one or more aides to handle media relations. These press secretaries perform the usual activities: press releases, advance notification and texts of speeches and other formal statements, leaks, off-the-record interviews, exclusives, and social interaction with and cultivation of relevant reporters. They know about deadlines and slow news days. They write the releases claiming credit for government largess received (whether or not through the legislator's efforts) by the district. Construction of defense installations, highways, dams, libraries, government buildings; contracts received by district firms; alfalfa allowances; and fellowships for faculty members at local universities—the list of subjects for releases is endless.[18]

Newspapers succumb to this wooing by printing at least some

of the press releases as news stories. In fact, when Paletz worked on Capitol Hill, he was astonished to see a reporter (somewhat besotted to be sure) pick up a press release, cut off the congressman's logo and substitute his name. The release appeared verbatim, as the reporter's independent work, the following day in the home-town newspaper for which the reporter had been long employed as chief Washington correspondent. This practice is supposedly uncommon, although (public) besottedness by reporters may not be.

Attention is not limited to the printed media. Most congressmen and -women use at public expense the expensive facilities in Congress to make television and radio tapes, featuring themselves alone or with a prominent guest, for distribution to stations in their districts. Often, these stations have low news budgets and are willing to include a spliced excerpt on the local news, or fill a sleepy half-hour on Sunday morning with an unmediated "report" from the legislator.[19]

The numerous small radio stations in America are unable to obtain live reporting from Washington unless they subscribe to a network, which most of them do not. Adroit congressmen and -women have been known to try to exploit this deficiency by providing the stations with "live" feeds. In North Carolina, the staff of former broadcast executive and editorialist-turned-senator Jesse Helms (R., N.C.) sent radio stations the senator's recorded answers to questions. The local broadcasters were instructed to read the questions and then play Helms's responses. The illusion is of a thoughtful interlocutor posing spontaneous questions to a "live" senator who, accessible as ever to the people, replies with his customary spontaneous candor and facility. Imagine what a roguish reporter could do by posing scrofulous questions then playing the senator's pre-recorded responses.

Another technique is the local hearing. Legislators hold hearings in their own constituencies over which they preside, usually alone. This enables them to reap local media coverage and publicity as they are shown caring about, but not necessarily taking a position on, an issue of local concern. (Migrant workers is a good one, as is the cost of health.)

Then there is indirection. The press secretary of one Maryland senator leaked stories to a Washington reporter for the *Los Angeles Times,* knowing that the item would be unsuspectingly picked up by the *Washington Post* from the *Times* and appear in the capital and Maryland. More circuitously, Representative Frank Horton (R., N.Y.) called the attention of congressional liaison staffer Henry Hall Wilson to an editorial in the *Rochester Democrat and Chronicle* in which the congressman was attacked for voting with the Johnson administration. Wilson sent the clipping to White House aide Marvin Watson with a note describing Horton as a very helpful Republican. Horton's purpose, Wilson explained, was for the White House to talk to one or more of the newspaper's editors—individuals who apparently frequently visited the White House.[20]

All of these stories socialize constituents to a certain set of expectations about what their representatives should be and do, a set of criteria for judgment. The announcements of pork barrel projects, the publicized poses of concern on major issues, tell the citizens that members of Congress are supposed to procure projects and voice concern. The skillful media-managing legislator not only plays the re-election game but also shapes the rules. He or she may also benefit from the way national coverage diminishes esteem for congressmen and -women as a class. National reporting sets low general expectations of members of congress, which individual incumbents can easily surpass by the impressions they convey via the local press. They can blame the failings of the membership at large for their lack of substantial accomplishments and the persistence of myriad social problems, while simultaneously taking credit for the benefits they have brought to their districts in spite of congressional incapacity.

Keeping news out of the media is equally, perhaps more, important. In many cases a legislator can actively pursue policies firmly opposed in his or her district—but only by the grace of the press. Should a reporter decide that such pursuits are newsworthy, the solon's career may be put in jeopardy. Since the most effective policy-making is done in private and involves technical details, however, misrepresentation of the voters' views most often goes unreported.

For an electoral challenger to overcome the incumbent's advantages, to bring his or her name and views before the electorate, requires money and media. But challengers are often barely visible in skimpy campaign news coverage. A substantial per capita expenditure on broadcasting is therefore necessary to disrupt established voting patterns, increase supporters' turnout, and challenge the incumbent's hold on the electorate. Indeed, broadcast expenditures have an evident impact on winning vote margins, particularly in Senate contests.[21]

The local media can originate the kind of information about an incumbent's effectiveness and competence, his or her policy stands in the nitty gritty of subcommittee and committee, which might lead to an informed voting decision by the electorate and enhance the challenger's chances of victory. They rarely do.[22] At best, the media transmit the challenger's charges; but these are self-evidently self-interested, lacking credibility with the incumbent's supporters and most independent voters. Yet occasionally local coverage can have an effect, and intense scrutiny can be lethal. The 1972 defeat of Iowa Republican Senator Jack Miller is attributed in part to stories in the *Des Moines Register* about a special-interest amendment he promoted on behalf of a Bermuda insurance company. (Would it have mattered had the company been Iowan? One wonders.)

Below the waves of national coverage received by Congress and its more prominent leaders and characters, then, is the undertow of the local press. Abetted by their aides, members of Congress expend vast quantities of time and effort and taxpayers' money to tell their constituents about their decisions, statements, and activities, in ways designed to insure re-election or elevation to higher office. This objective is promoted through the selective withholding, release, and structuring of information. But these efforts would be fruitless were it not for two factors: the reluctance of most American newspaper proprietors to pay for scrutinizing members of Congress; and the willingness of many American newspapers to transmit at least some of the self-serving stories these legislators provide.

Anticipating Reactions

Members of Congress and most public officials are well aware of the media's impact on their political successes or failures, achievement of their policy objectives, their careers, their fates. They devote considerable time and attention to their media relations. Blarney, cajolery, manipulation, deception, threats, and destruction are but a few of the tactics in which they and their aides indulge, as is chronicled throughout this book. More difficult to document are the effects of potential media coverage on the behavior and decisions of power holders and seekers, their calculations and conniptions as they try to anticipate the reactions of reporters.

Fortunately, we have documentary evidence. It comes from a confidential transcript from the House of Representatives' Select Committee on Assassinations. Culling our copy, from which all quotes in this section are taken, we show why and how the committee members behaved in anticipation of media coverage.

Behind closed doors, members of the House of Representatives' Select Committee on Assassinations gather. A feud between the Committee's Chief Counsel and Staff Director Richard A. Sprague and its former chairman, conducted in part by press release, has been exuberantly ventilated in the press. The new chairman, Louis D. Stokes (D., Ohio) is meeting in executive session with committee members and staff to try to rectify the situation. The aim: to continue the committee's existence against charges that it has wasted the taxpayers' money while accomplishing nothing. At stake is the survival of the committee. In jeopardy are the potential benefits to be enjoyed by its members. The committee's demise will tarnish their reputations for competence and efficiency, associate them with ineptitude. Its perpetuation offers the opportunity for national publicity accompanied by burnished prestige with congressional colleagues, constituents and the public.

To achieve their objective, the committee members need to create the impression—the illusion—of competence, of knowing what needs to be done and of doing it: "The public and the Congress have to be reinforced that the committee is in control and that the committee is pursuing the investigation in an orderly fashion." It is the way to gain support from the House leadership, elicit approval from the Rules Committee to continue this committee's charter, and convince a majority of the House to vote for its budget. The media are the means. But before they can exploit the media, the committee members have to stop the media from exploiting them.

The chairman reads to his colleagues from his home town newspaper, the *Cleveland Plain Dealer:*

> James Delaney, Democrat of New York, the Chairman of the House Rules Committee, said the panel will have to produce something more substantial than witnesses refusing to testify to justify the House spending more money on the investigation . . . Delbert L. Latta, a key Republican on the committee, agreed. The committee has to come up with something that gets to the point that the investigations are more than just a wild-goose chase, he said.

The self-same media which brought the asserted views of Delaney and Latta to the committee can be used to save it. Members therefore discuss how to act in anticipation of media reaction. They plot strategy on the assumption that the media are crucial intermediaries between and among elites and the mass public. To the extent that they sacrifice the committee's legitimate objectives for media favor, the members are reprehensible; but their assumption is right.

With the exception of Committee Counsel Sprague and Chairman Stokes, the speakers of the quotes which follow are not identified. This is not to protect the innocent. Rather, it means that the comments represent all segments of the committee: Democrats, Republicans, liberals, conservatives, males and females, old and young. They are a composite of the members' attitudes toward the press. Perhaps some members objected to or disagreed with the substance or tenor of the discussion; if so, they did not speak up for the record.

The first task is to divert reporters away from the conflict between Committee Counsel Sprague and the former chairman which had stimulated so much harmful publicity. Members begin by discussing what information should be made available to the media, when, how, and why. It is agreed that the transcripts of the executive sessions should not be released. They contain material on the feud which, the members fear, would make the headlines. For this reason they will also exclude them from the *Congressional Record*, where they would be available to the press.

The committee members' familiarity with press coverage of their activities is extensive, their analysis astute. They read the stories and judge the journalists. George Lardner of the *Washington Post* is described as having reported the committee's activities "pretty badly." And that is significant, because the *Post* is the local newspaper, common reading for most of literate and not-so-literate Washington. The committee members are shrewd too in the media ways of their fellow legislators in the House: "I think the only thing basically that is read is the headline, not the story." This being so, both reporters and headline writers are causes for concern as the members choreograph the next public session:

> If we know what we are going to do and the microphones are all working and move into a meeting and we look over and we look like we are moving . . . and we have our two top investigators share a very carefully-drawn comment on the King and Kennedy Assassinations, that I think will set the stage, followed up immediately by a

"dear Colleague" letter that would go to every congressman indicating what our resolution and budget request will be and urging their support. Wednesday night's public media would announce our information . . .

The favorable publicity could induce support from the leadership of Congress, Rules Committee members, and House colleagues. It might even encourage the public to contact their representatives on the Assassinations Committee's behalf. When the committee's problem is the widespread impression among members of Congress of its inactivity, just holding public sessions which are reported by the press may erode negative feelings. In this sense, any news is good news, no matter how badly reported.

There are additional ways of exploiting the media to communicate an illusion of committee activity. One technique is to put a provocatively recalcitrant witness on the stand. "We had Mr. Traficantee there and he was pleading the 5th Amendment. I think we did more yesterday, even without getting factual information, simply because it focused again on the fact that we are looking into the issue." Even though such displays sacrifice the committee's investigative purposes, they are necessary. "This, of course, is not the way to conduct an investigation . . . But what we are talking about today is survival."

Holding public hearings is intimately connected with decisions about the nature and amount of information possessed by the committee which should be released to the press. Members cannot be too wary. The Kennedy and King assassinations are controversial subjects rousing intense passions, suspicion, and widespread interest among some segments of the public. The news media are quick to leap at the hint of any new disclosure. As the committee chairman complains:

> I posed a question, would the briefing be in the nature of matter that should be undertaken in executive session and he [Mr. Sprague] in response to that, said, yes, Mr. Chairman, we will present testimony regarding others who may have been involved, and so on. The newsmedia went wild with that. Calls came in from Canada about the fact, didn't Sprague say this, that he has some others—evidence of conspiracy. This and that. They ran wild with it.

After this experience, careful thought is given to how the press will treat statements and actions coming from the committee: "I have been sitting here, wracking my brain, trying to figure out what would be in the public presentation, and I cannot visualize it, because every time I think of something that immediately the press is going to do what you are talking about here"—that is, exploit the statement for its own needs and purposes. Says Committee Counsel Sprague: "It is very difficult to think of what is being presented publicly that is meaningful, that does not get into that which ought to not be presented. . . ." If only commonplace informantion is released, the committee is vulnerable to a "ho hum" media response. If the information is revealing, unrealistic expectations can be generated, hampering confidential investigations in process. Worse, the committee might upstage itself. The dilemma is never really resolved, but when the committee errs, it does so on the side of self-preservation. For if the committee is not continued, there will be no further investigation—at least not by these members.

They cannot always totally control the release of information to the media, especially when other sources exist with reasons for talking. Thus James Earl Ray is to be interviewed in jail by committee staff, with his attorney present. It is the attorney who has told the press of the forthcoming interview and who, to the dismay of some committee members, proposes to hold a press conference to announce that the meeting had occurred and even recount what had transpired. Still, he could perhaps be persuaded to delay his press conference until the chairman had reported on the interview to the committee.

Meanwhile, a decision is required about the next public session. The committee must revise its budget, but the chairman is still worried about the media. He proposes a solution: "I do not think that we ought to let the media to just focus in on budget . . . but would rather see it sandwiched in with something else so that, among other matters taken up that day is not just the budget. If we give them just the budget, they will go wild on that." But what other information might divert press attention away from the budget? A four-part session is proposed: "skeleton review of where we are on the Kennedy and King assassinations, response to that, the resolution for reconstitution, connected with the discussion of the budget, and finally some specific focus on some specific piece of evidence . . ."

Finally, the immediate problem: what to tell reporters at the end of this executive session? The members of the press are waiting outside the hearing room. Some have been there for several hours. Their presence is hard to ignore. They have to be told something. Now the attitude of the committee members toward the press is most graphically revealed: a mixture of hostility and fear.

"Are you prepared to meet these wolves outside the door?" the chairman asks. He is unsure and seeks advice from his colleagues. One suggests telling about the budget, another the report. A third says, "I think you should keep them right where you have them now, champing at the bit, and not tell them anything." And, when he is told the afternoon meeting will be in a different room: "Have the people think we keep moving around just to keep them off balance."

Conclusion

The two flows of media coverage, national and local, result in a thoroughly misleading impression of both Congress and its members. Congress is a deliberative body: its members devote much of their time in subcommittees, committees, on the floor, and in conference committees, to discussing the purpose and substance of legislation. After argument, through negotiation and compromise, its members seek the most favorable outcome for the diverse groups and interests with which they are allied—not all of whom are located in their individual constituencies.[23] At the same time, many members of Congress are part of the cozy triangles of congressional subcommittees, executive agency bureaus, and interest groups which govern by accommodation.[24]

Congress can also be a protector of minority rights. Its rules and procedures are designed to permit minorities to express their views. Its organization encourages the frustration, the blocking of enactment of majority sentiment. Time-consuming delay is a built-in feature of the legislative process so that many laws pass, if they do pass, *en masse* at the end of a session. Most of the work of Congress is the undramatic and tedious manipulation of language: adding a word or phrase here, deleting a comma there. The business is painstaking and complicated; the results can significantly affect people's lives.

It is the legislative process—the heart of congressional policy making—that is conspicuously absent from media coverage. The powerless public is told what major laws are passed by what majority and, if it is lucky, given a summary of the main provisions. This is like reporting box scores without describing the games— save that box scores are more revealing than press accounts of Congress. What changes occurred during subcommittee, committee, and floor passage and why; what the legislation actually means in substantive benefits to individual and organized Americans; whose interests are advanced or impeded by individual members of Congress—these topics receive scant attention. Well-organized groups, powerful key decision-makers, operate in Congress with minimal scrutiny by the mass media and, therefore, without public knowledge and understanding of their activities. Autonomously, often quite efficiently, too many of the people's representatives in Washington service the powerful few.

We conclude with a paradox. Recent polls put the public approval of Congress about even with that of public approval of used-car salesmen; yet, in the 1978 election, 95 percent of the incumbents in the House running for re-election were successful. There are many reasons—gerrymandered districts, one-party dominance, and limited choice for voters; but the media are one of the most important.

In 1980 the Republicans were in a potent position to change this situation. The United States was in the midst of substantial inflation and burgeoning unemployment. These ills could be blamed on the Democrats who had controlled the presidency for four years and Congress for twenty-six. The presidential contest would receive ample media coverage. But, given the obstacles to adequate coverage of individual members of Congress we have described, how might the Republicans indict the Democratic congressional majority for the woes of the country in a way that would rouse potentially disaffected Democratic voters to turn to Republican congressional challengers? The answer: unmediated advertisements shown during popular television shows. Well-financed and widely used, this strategy spurred the defeat of some of the more marginal and even a few of the hitherto impregnable Democratic incumbents.

Despite the success or failure of the Republicans' unmediated attacks on Congress, our basic argument stands. Journalists for the national media paint the grand picture of congressional mal- and non-feasance. They probably overstate it in their cynical explanations for all politicians' actions. But at the same time, by their openness to incumbent manipulation, the local media help to insulate the members of Congress from electoral accountability. By failing independently to investigate legislators' activities and decisions in Washington, by failing to probe into the 435 individual stories in the House, or the 100 in the Senate, the mass media let more than one sleeping dog lie. The result: the press contributes to the public's deepening despair about Congress while helping to insure the re-election—the power—of the kind of people who make that body what it is.[25] Representative democracy decays and with it the citizenry's ability to use the electoral process to enforce accountability. An ignorant, impatient public is left discontented with Congress but bereft of the knowledge to replace its membership.

CHAPTER SIX

•

The Supreme Court

"It is better to know the Judge than to know the law."

Richelieu

OF ALL THE AUTHORITY WIELDERS in American politics, judges seem to need the mass media least. Federal judges are appointed to office, remain during good behavior and, with few exceptions, voluntarily retire, or die in office at an advanced age. At the apex of the judicial system, the Supreme Court is an elite institution dealing through specialized publications (professional and law journals) with other strategically placed elites in American society, on whom it relies to implement its decisions.

Legitimacy

And yet, the judicial system and the individual courts and judges within it need the mass media more than they acknowledge. For they labor under a limitation not shared in so extreme a form by the other branches of government: the implementation of judicial decisions relies upon voluntary compliance by the affected parties. When that fails, the courts depend upon enforcement and the application of sanctions by other governmental agencies. As Johnson observes: "Broad-scale compliance . . . necessitates implementing activities well beyond the normal confines of the legal process with its court orders, law reports, and formal opinions." [1] President Jackson's perhaps apocryphal words remain an apposite warning: "[Chief Justice] Marshall has made his decision, let him enforce it."[2]

At the head of the judicial system is the Supreme Court, its decisions affecting the exercise of politics and the distribution of power in America. We shall analyze the advantages the Justices can employ to protect and enhance their media image, consider how reporters cover the Court, describe the resultant coverage, and speculate about the consequences.

Justices must strive to maintain the legitimacy of the Court as an institution. In a putative democracy based on periodic elections, the specter of nine unelected men making policies to deal with many of the society's most disharmonious dilemmas could be disquieting. Yet popular and elite acceptance of the Court persist through all the dissension that surrounds its controversial rulings. That they do is attributable to the public relations skills of the justices and to the beliefs of journalists.

Justices' Strategies

Members of the Supreme Court seem to be aware of the potential flimsiness of their authority. They have a number of ways of coping. Perhaps most important is the prudent restraint of their decisions. The Constitution gives the Court a formidable weapon for asserting individual rights and liberties in the face of social and political antagonism. Yet a majority of justices avoid the temptation and opportunities for provocative decisions. They are reluctant to provoke, to clash with the more powerful institutions of government, notably Congress and the presidency. Usually not until the other branches of government have convincingly demonstrated their refusal to tackle the problems or have temporized eternally does the Supreme Court enter the thickets of controversy. Examples are its decisions on reapportionment, civil rights, racial equality, and busing.

When Supreme Court decisions do not reallocate power among parties, groups, or institutions, they may still require social adaptation and adjustment, antagonizing one or both of the contending sides. Consequently, because judges are conscious of the opposition they may provoke, the most forthright-seeming decisions may include clauses permitting delay or outright avoidance of their requirements. Other decisions acknowledge social forces with discreet language and verbal formulas designed to placate the contending sides.

But the justices, like politicians, know that the reality of their behavior is often less important than its image. Enter the media. There are two main strategies: accentuate the majesty of the Court, and minimize access to its inner workings.

The justices take extraordinary pains to emphasize that the judicial process is magisterial and depersonalized; to convey the impression that the function they perform is to interpret the law with fairness, neutrality, and objectivity. They cite precedents; support their constitutional and statutory rulings with persuasive arguments; emphasize the logic, the reasonableness—the inevitability—of their decisions. These techniques contribute to the widespread belief that judicial decision-making is unsullied by politics and should remain so.

What reporters see inside the Courtroom—all they see—is designed more to elevate than to display the judicial process. The ornate setting, the ritual, the ceremony: the way the justices preside in their robes and high-backed chairs, physically and metaphorically raised up, occasionally deigning to pose and press questions while the lawyers plead their cases below; all sanctify the authority of the Court and its members.

Meanwhile, the crucial decisions are reached in private, out of sight and earshot of reporters. For, of all the institutions of American government, the Supreme Court is the least permeable to the press. As Congress is relatively open to the mass media, as its members court publicity, the justices shun it. How decisions are reached; the kinds of informal contact among the justices; the appeals and persuasion; the sometimes pragmatic compromises, negotiation and bargaining; all are kept confidential. Only a few eminent law school graduates, privileged to be serving as law clerks to the justices who selected them, are privy in any part to the deliberations. They have few incentives to leak, substantial reasons to keep silent. Secrecy is the norm, revelations are infrequent.

Access denied is reinforced by information controlled. Supreme Court justices—all judges—preside, commune alone or deliberate one with another, and reach their decisions. They speak to the mass media, when they speak at all, through official spokespersons, not in person. The representative, in turn, is mainly a conduit for transmitting the decision and servicing reporters; he or she neither expounds on the decision nor describes the process by which it was reached.

Despite their tight control over access and information, Supreme Court justices have not always avoided damaging coverage from the mass media. For many years, no summaries of decisions were released. Important rulings were handed down simultaneously at the term's end. Reporters found themselves scurrying around, hastily reading entire decisions, trying to analyze scope and meaning without much guidance from the court. Inevitably, some decisions were subject to misinterpretation. Headline writers wedded to the short and snappy, relying upon wire service characterizations of decisions, were prone to make the Supreme Court decisions seem more drastic and dramatic than they in fact were.[3] There was no communication from the court with editors and editorial writers.

It took some bad experiences in which their decisions were misconstrued to jolt the justices into understanding the full significance of the mass media for their legitimacy. Changes ensued. A press office has been established at the court, summaries of decisions are prepared for reporters, and the limits of decisions are usually clearly specified to avoid misinterpretations—for example, accusations that the court is abolishing the right to religious practice. Some decisions contain a little bow in the direction of public relations. As Johnson puts it: "It is helpful for the Court to take special pains to grant symbolic rewards to widely respected interests, especially in instances where substantive rewards are being withheld."[4]

Media Practices

Largely by denying access, justices minimize the production of behind-the-scenes stories that might reveal politics and contention and undermine the Court's magisterial image. Part of this is conscious strategy, part an inevitable by-product of the confidential nature of the judicial process. Yet the media themselves contribute to deferential coverage, most importantly by their adherence to the myth of the judicial exception. Most reporters seem to think that the Supreme Court is above and beyond politics, unsullied—in contrast to the executive and legislative branches. Legal scholar C. Herman Pritchett called that notion the most po-

tent myth in American life.[5] All courts are political. Judges enjoy
considerable discretion in interpreting and shaping the law. Their
personalities and ideologies bear strongly upon their conduct and
decisions, as scholarly research has repeatedly shown.[6] Prosecutors show they understand this fact when they maneuver to select
the judges before whom to prosecute certain cases. Civil rights
workers painfully learned the fact as they pled and bled in the
South before racist federal court judges.

Yet the myth persists. Its workings are best illustrated by
contrasting media treatment and popular mythology of legislators
and judges. Legislators are elected on the basis of popular appeal;
judges are elevated (the word resonates) to the bench. Legislators
are expected to be responsive to public needs; they are blamed
when conditions go wrong. Judges are expected to follow the law
—the law which many people wrongly suppose has little to do with
causing social and economic conditions. Many legislators conspicuously need the media, and there is a certain contempt for the
needy. Judges appear not to need reporters at all. Legislators lack
much of the protective panoply of judges; they are ordinary folks
or try to appear so when they are not. No real sense of expertise
accrues to legislators. Judges are special people who supposedly
have demonstrated appropriate legal ability, temperament, and
skill. The legislative process—bargaining, manipulation, compromise—is petty if not sordid and lacks the majesty of the law. Reporters have intimate familiarity with legislators, little personal
contact with judges. Legislators are properly seen as politicians;
judges improperly are not perceived as politicians.

Reporters sometimes lack legal background and training. Gen-
eralists are relatively circumspect around professions and institutions without a history of journalistic scrutiny. This does not mean
reporters are ill-equipped to understand and comment on courts'
decisions, merely that they think they are. Believed to be the solution, legal education is no real avenue to critical *political* reporting of the Supreme Court. Law courses generally stick to the facts
and doctrines of decisions, not their political sources and consequences.

Journalists who cover the judicial system accept and respect
the majesty of the law as it issues from the Supreme and lower
federal courts—and most state courts too. They sense, if they do
not fully comprehend, the vulnerability of the courts' legitimacy.
To dissect the courts, expose the fallibility and frailties of judges,

could undermine the legal system by encouraging disrespect for court decisions by the public officials who should execute, and the public who should obey them.

Court Depictions

What news issues from the combination of Court actions and reportorial custom? Press coverage is predominantly confined to reporting Supreme Court decisions. Nonetheless, there are substantial differences in content across media. According to an exhaustive study by David Leslie, Associated Press stories emphasize who is involved in a case, what happened to them, the legal history, and the Court's holding. The wire service reports very little about impact on policy, whether compliance or resistance is likely, reactions of different groups. No doubt this sketchiness is traceable to the AP's need for speed. Television normally covers the ruling, skimps on the details, and concentrates on reactions and possible policy impact. A group of major newspapers which tend to go beyond wire copy had a more evenly balanced mixture of information on the decision and on its political ramifications.[7]

But, as is true of many congressional actions, a number of Court decisions are not reported. A study of the *New York Times*'s coverage of the Court's October 1974 term found that 33 of the 145 written opinions received no mention at all. Of the 112 covered, David Ericson rated 32 "complete." Stories about 31 decisions had "essentials" only and 49 were "incomplete." By comparison, the less prestigious *Detroit News* reported only 44 decisions.[8] In Leslie's study an important predictor of coverage was the degree of conflict on the Court. Unanimous decisions received less attention than those over which the Court was split.[9]

The limitations imposed by definitions of news and by reporters' lack of access to the interstices of the Court circumscribe coverage. In addition, space limitations severely constrain journalists' ability to convey the full flavor of decisions that are often difficult for legal scholars, let alone harried reporters and barely attentive audiences, to decipher.

Court actions that do make news are labeled in an intriguing way. They are called "decisions." But often they are also public policies: they allocate scarce economic resources, redistribute political power, alter social relations as surely as the actions of the president and Congress. By not calling Court decisions "policies" the media acquiesce in the belief that the Court merely insures that laws enacted through a democratic process are carried out properly and constitutionally. Journalistic language makes it less apparent to the public that nine unelected justices make policies as significant as those of the elected president and Congress.

Though it may be elitist, the Court is not unconstrained. It cannot be the purely inward-looking body, mulling morality and debating legal philosophy, that media depictions convey. It must consider the lineup of political forces that will contend with or over its ruling. The reason is quite practical: the stronger an offended group and its feelings, the more likely are the Court's decisions to be challenged successfully or disobeyed. Too much disputation and flouting of the Court would threaten its legitimacy. This means that the Court must take account of the structure of power and the dominant consensus as it decides. The Court cannot be as insulated from politics as it is portrayed and still retain its authority among elites. The portrait as neutral arbiter of democracy does help protect its legitimacy among ordinary Americans, however.

The final omission is of coverage of the justices as human beings. Whereas coverage of the president and Congress is often personalized, Supreme Court reporting is quite the reverse. We rarely learn much about sitting justices as people or even as lawyers and legal philosophers. Unlike other politicians, their peccadillos and predilections are not dissected; personal or ideological conflicts are not seized upon and played up. Indeed, except in their written opinions, justices are quoted only rarely. They are shadowy (though not shady), mysterious figures. This distance evokes authority.

One of the few times judges or potential judges are personally inspected by the news media comes when they have been nominated by the president and are before the Senate for confirmation. Even then, the scrutiny consists mostly of covering the hearings into the nominees' backgrounds and credentials. Senate examination can be severe, revealing an appointee's dubious past behavior, judicial inexperience or errors, and partisan passions. But Senate hearings are usually cursory for many appointments below the Supreme Court. Nor are they intense for all nominees to that court —witness the speedy Senate confirmation of Nixon's man, conser-

vative ideologue William J. Rehnquist. And once appointed, no
matter how sullied, how highly political and partisan their previous
lives, the new justices are invested with judgment and sagacity as
they are divested of political preferences.

Effects

THE GENERAL PUBLIC

The first comprehensive national survey of attitudes toward
the courts reveals that the public's main sources of information are
"formal education and the media." [10] Most people, 37 percent,
gave the media, divided among newspapers, magazines, and
books, and television news programs (14 percent). When respondents were permitted to list more than one source, the figures were
44 percent for schools, 61 percent for newspapers, magazines and
books, and 60 percent for television news. [11]

To the surprise of the surveyors, who failed to anticipate it as
a variable, 6 percent of the respondents, increasing to 34 percent
when more than one source could be listed, cited television entertainment shows as a source of information about courts. [12] What a
source! Television entertainment shows portray American courts
as immaculate, the judges as efficient, compassionate, and immaculate too.

What then are the effects of the mass media's sporadic, mani-
festly incomplete and benign coverage of the judicial system? Predictably, the survey revealed a low level of public knowledge. But
"those having knowledge and experience with courts voice greater
dissatisfaction and criticism." [13] In other words, the more people
know about the courts from their own encounters, the greater their
discontent. In contrast, the mass media's contribution to public
enlightenment about the courts is ignorance and bliss. [14] Ignorance,
because they fail to report the manifest defects of the legal system
or expose the courts as political instruments. Bliss, because the
way the judicial decisions are reported perpetuates the myth that
judges apply pre-existing legal rules after adversary proceedings in
which justice triumphs. The result is what we can only call the
"oracle effect." People may not like what the courts decide, but
they accept that judges are qualified and reach decisions by de-
tached application of esoteric rules of law. It is no surprise that 70

percent of a panel agreed with the statement: "the Constitution is a mighty complicated thing, so it's fortunate that we have a body of well-trained judges to tell us what it means." [15]

ACTIVISTS AND POLITICIANS

Besides diffuse support of the institution among elites and masses, Supreme Court justices seek specific acceptance, preferably not grudging, of their policy pronouncements. They are less successful here than in maintaining the Court's overall legitimacy. In a conflictful society where the executive and legislative branches are as prone to tergiversate as to tackle complex problems, the judiciary cannot avoid controversy entirely. Some justices even relish it. Intermittently, the Supreme Court's decisions as reported in the media are excoriated by indignant members of Congress, political leaders in the states, and ordinary Americans. The reaction is exacerbated when the justices themselves are split and condemn each other's stands with uncharacteristic vigor. Acquiescence to decisions may then be replaced by resistance, even rejection among some Americans.

Inadvertently by news emphases or deliberately in editorials, the press may fan controversy and spread opposition. The media naturally, compulsively attend to organized opposition on emotional issues involving religion, race, or sex. Court coverage may activate people deeply interested in such issues, helping existing groups to recruit new members, encouraging the formation of new organizations. The activists then use the media and other resources to pressure legislators to pass new laws or amendments and administrators to ignore rulings. While they may fail to overturn a decision completely, the pressure groups may successfully induce Congress to narrow the effect of Court rulings. Indirectly, the media's effect may be to discourage the Court from further pursuit of a line of policy decisions. In the 1970s, school integration and abortion exemplified this process. Congress passed laws that discouraged effective desegregation and vastly reduced the number of legal abortions received by poor women. The Court then reduced its innovative thrusts on these policies—not merely because of the growing conservatism of its membership but because of the sensitivity of its majority to the dangers of dwindling authority and congressional usurpation.

Court–Press Conflict

There is one area in which press attempts to cultivate opposition to specific rulings are overt: cases involving the press's own autonomy. During the 1970s, a Court majority began to curtail journalists' freedom, to reduce the First Amendment-based rights the press had enjoyed.[16]

Press cases pose genuine, difficult conflicts between rights of the press and of defendants in trials, free speech, and libel. But many of the Court's rulings in these and less complicated cases suggest that several of the justices have little sympathy for the argument that the press warrants special protection under the First Amendment.

The media covered and commented on these decisions with a loud chorus of outrage and dismay. One study of ten newspapers from 1970 to 1977 showed that they gave far more news coverage to cases involving freedom of the press than to ones about free speech of individuals. And their editorials defended the free expression position and criticized the Court's decisions in 81 percent of the press cases, 56 percent of the individual cases.[17]

Because the media vigilantly remind their audience of the importance of a free press to democracy, such coverage tends to undermine the legitimacy of the decisions criticized. After all, the Court is supposed to protect democracy by upholding the Constitution and the Bill of Rights. On the other hand, because of the nature of news practices, coverage of even the press-threatening cases is sketchy, evanescent. And the limited inclination that most media owners and managers show toward investigative, disruptive reporting means that editorial indignation is rarely feverish or long-lasting. There is probably only limited awareness of these decisions and their import among the public, or even among non-journalistic elites.

Conclusion

Media coverage of the Supreme Court illustrates several of this book's basic themes, revealing that press reports have political sources and consequences even for what is often thought of as the least political aspect of the policy-making process. For example, how particular decisions are reported stimulates opposition to some of the Court's actions, thereby quite possibly affecting the justices' behavior and promoting shifts in the direction of public policy. When other decisions are left uncovered or reported only cursorily, the ability of ordinary citizens to judge and their power to respond in their self-interests to political events and power holders is decreased.

Persistent legitimization of the Supreme Court is the most important function of the media's coverage, more significant than it may seem to most of us, conditioned as we are by news practices. The Court's members are not elected and may be highly unrepresentative of the public; they sit for life and make laws on some of the most conflictive and vital issues of each generation. In so doing, they reallocate power for years to come. We do not mean to imply that the legitimacy of the Court is undesirable. The founders designed a third branch to resolve conflicts and impasses that the other two could not or would not resolve; in fulfilling its mission the Court has often advanced laudable goals, sometimes not.[18] But the legitimacy of such a body might easily be tenuous in a country where obeisance or commitment to representative democracy is so deeply entrenched. That the Court's legitimacy is nonetheless secure is in considerable measure a testament to the portrait provided by the mass media.[19]

CHAPTER SEVEN

•

Law Enforcers

"Men can only be highly civilized while other men, inevitably less civilized, are there to guard them."

George Orwell

SOME 671,000 PEOPLE ARE EMPLOYED in police work in the United States, one for every 331 Americans. Most of them come from working-class backgrounds; they are usually high school graduates who do not immediately go on to college. They value, to the point of preoccupation, cleanliness, thrift, punctuality and, above all, order. Police departments promote from within. Senior officials have taken evening courses emphasizing textbook memorization. As a consequence of these promotion and training practices, police management is hidebound and inflexible. Despite or because of these facts, the police have managed to put almost 300,000 Americans in prison. Each year there are approximately 412,000 arrests for violent crimes.

Police work is not without risks. In 1977, 123 officers were killed while on duty (30 in accidents, the rest by homicides). This is a ratio of 18 per 100,000. But miners, lumberjacks, and construction workers have higher rates.[1]

Police functions have only partly to do with crime and violence. Indeed, the average officer labors for more than a year without making a single felony arrest. Rather, the police are an all-purpose social agency performing the dirty work of society. They reluctantly handle as a court of first—and sometimes last—resort, all the problems, the human dregs and debris, other governmental institutions prefer to avoid or reject. In the process, the police enforce the law, maintain order, reduce threats of violence, and exercise force. These activities are undertaken selectively, sporadically, capriciously, because the police lack the resources, the inclination, and the public support to do all the jobs asked of them simultaneously, consistently, and continuously.

Beyond their overt and obvious functions, the police are the most visible representatives of authority—the most powerful figures with whom powerless Americans have everyday contact. In this capacity, they symbolize and serve as scapegoats for more powerful but less visible figures and institutions. They serve, too, as a palpable reminder of the power and sanctions the state can impose on its lawbreakers, rebels, and revolutionaries. And by protecting property and the propertied class, they insure that the redistribution of wealth in American society is confined to legal and conventional, not unlawful and revolutionary, processes.

Police Protection

Clashes between press and police should be inevitable as ideal reporters—inquisitive and probing—conflict with the secretive hierarchy and centralized structure of police departments. But this potential for conflict is buried under a blanket of cooperation. Crime news sells newspapers, and the police have a virtual monopoly on crime stories. Reporters learn of crimes from police scanners and "hotlines" to police patrol dispatchers. Police departments are reporters' prime sources of the details of criminal activity and of police responses. Since most perpetrators are not caught, they are unavailable for questioning by journalists. The accused lack credibility; the convicted have less. Witnesses and victims may be asked for their reactions to the crime, but they are not usually asked to evaluate the performance of the police handling the case. The only competition to the police control of information comes from convicted felons who have turned to prose.

Predictably, most of the stories about the police concern crimes; and most of the stories about crimes are taken by police beat reporters from official investigation reports and police department press releases. Thus a study of several years' press coverage of the Durham, North Carolina, police found only two stories that originated from non-police sources. Both contained charges of police misconduct. But in both stories the paragraphs with the charges were immediately followed by the Police Chief's denials. The reporters' respectful and uncritical approach, lack of substantial information supporting the charges, and police denials, tended to minimize possible negative effects from the stories.[2]

If reporters lack the requisite respectful attitude, the police may deny access. The Los Angeles Police Department consistently refused the slightly subterranean *Los Angeles Free Press* a "press pass" for its reporters, thereby preventing them from observing the police in action. The decision was upheld by the United States Supreme Court when it voted six to three not to hear the newspaper's argument that press passes are part of the Constitution's guarantee of freedom of the press. Four votes are necessary to grant a hearing. Meanwhile, the Police Department issues the passes to its own undercover officers for the purpose of observing meetings and demonstrations.[3]

To increase protection from undesirable media coverage, police departments emulate other government bureaucracies by establishing or expanding public information offices to formalize and control relations with the press. Press officers arrange for reporters to accompany police officers in their grubby, depressing, sometimes dangerous work. They establish personal contact between ranking police officers and reporters, editors and publishers. Within this framework of access, the release of information is controlled as much as possible. Police passes are not issued to all reporters; special folders marked "not publishable" are devised; in some departments only written questions will be answered; and in many towns beat officers are not usually permitted to respond to newsmen and -women unless a superior or public information officer is present.

This explains in part why individual police officers are often absent from police stories. In the Durham study, "no patrolmen or other beat officers, the group comprising over 85 percent of the department's personnel, were directly quoted in any article."[4] In many cities, the Police Chief or Commissioner, sometimes not a career policeman or -woman at all, symbolizes the department in the media. This enhances the mystique and thereby the power of the police.

A few editors and reporters, dissatisfied with crime stories and cozy contacts with police information officers, want to probe police practices. Departments are protected against these malcontents by the adroit invocation of legal restrictions, buttressed by departmental regulations. A North Carolina law designed to preserve the privacy of municipal employees' personnel records effectively prohibits the compiling of data about the backgrounds of members of the police force. Then Rule 1-20 of the department requires that "before an officer makes public statements adversely criticizing any departmental policy, order, or operating procedure, the officer shall make known the substance of his criticism to his superior officer and shall avoid any public criticism until a reasonable time for departmental action has elapsed."[5] Officers who break the rule can be subjected to formal punishment up to dismissal plus such informal sanctions as ostracism and violence.

One result of all this is bland reporting. A report on the reorganization of the detective division of the Durham police for reasons of "greater efficiency" told readers nothing about "the problems the move was trying to correct, the role of a detective, or the effects of such a reorganization on service to the community."[6] But it did preserve the power of the top officers over their subordinates and the department's power over the citizens.

Without much overstatement we may conclude that the mass media's stories about the police emphasize crimes, recounting information the police have uncovered (or stumbled across). They do not examine the police, their organizational practices, or how they obtained the information they release.[7] Recruitment, training, working conditions, career patterns, are all neglected. There is little mention of procedures, search and seizure policies, incentives to issue traffic citations, or other aspects of police administration. Rarely defined as news, the information is not made available by police departments or assiduously sought out by reporters. Pressing for it disrupts harmonious relations between reporters and departments. Collecting it would consume the time police reporters have available for covering crimes. For similar reasons, few attempts are made to assess the efficiency of police departments in combating crime. Yet a recounting of crimes committed compared to the arrests made and the paucity of convictions obtained would discredit most police departments and raise questions about their use of power.[8]

Behind the scenes, meanwhile, a pattern of cooperation insidiously undermines journalists' independence while furthering police-press unity in the fight against evil-doing (actual, alleged, and imaginary). It begins innocently enough when, at the request of police departments, the mass media relay appeals for information about particular crimes and advertise most-wanted miscreants. But then reporters informally share with the police information they have gathered from the unwary in pursuit of their stories. Television outtakes (visual material not used on the air) have been secretly given to the police. Despite pockets of resistance, and some changes, much police-press cooperation persists.

The breakdown of social cohesion and comity might be expected to strain this pattern of cooperation. Instead it strengthens it, as the following case study reveals.

Press Coverage of Civil Disorders

During 1967, many of the black citizens of Winston-Salem, North Carolina, rioted.[9] At the height of the disturbances, people broke windows, looted, started fires, and threw rocks at policemen, firemen, and passing cars. The riot continued over three nights. In the four-day period, almost 200 individuals were arrested (150 with previous arrest records—not necessarily convictions). The charges were store-breaking, larceny, violating the curfew, carrying a concealed weapon, public drunkenness, and disorderly conduct. More than 100 were injured. No one was reported killed.

The proximate cause of the riot was the death of a Winston-Salem black following his arrest for drunkenness. Some rioters used the disorder as a means of trying to accumulate otherwise unobtainable worldly possessions; for many more it was an attempt to strike back for years of indignity and deprivation inflicted upon them and their forebears. Their targets were the police, stores, and other symbols of white power. Thus, when faced by what must have been overwhelming force, the rioters did not immediately desist, but continued the disturbance. While some looted, others were bent on destruction alone. In addition, those who rioted were regarded with favor, or at least not with disfavor, by many other blacks who themselves played no active part in events. In other words, the causes and conduct of the Winston-Salem riot differed little from that of its Los Angeles and other predecessors in the 1960s in being a form of social protest, although absolute property damage and loss of life were substantially less.

The Winston-Salem riot usefully illustrates the cooperation we have outlined between police and press. We will show how and explain why the town's leading newspaper covered events from the police perspective and in the interests of local power-holders.

THE WINSTON-SALEM JOURNAL

The *Winston-Salem Journal* is a respected and responsible newspaper with a progressive attitude on race relations. It subscribes to and uses the *New York Times* news service. It editorialized in support of federal legislation for the cities. For its help in obtaining a federally supported legal service program in North Carolina, it received an award from the National Legal Aid and Defender Association.

The *Journal*'s riot coverage was of uncommon importance. It seems that on the first night of rioting, all radio and television stations reported nothing. Their initial involvement came when they requested National Guardsmen to report for duty. This reticence apparently was the result of a previous agreement; its purpose, to avoid inflaming the situation. This meant that the *Journal* was virtually the public's sole source of information from the media.

The *Journal* had provided a precursor of its coverage by publishing a story on a joint news conference given by Winston-Salem's mayor and police chief. Mayor M. C. Benton was quoted as saying that "racial violence is not expected in Winston-Salem this summer." But, he added, "if trouble does develop, the city is ready to take vigorous action. Live ammunition would be used; the National Guard would be called in if needed."[10] The *Journal* quoted Police Chief Justus M. Tucker as saying "trouble is less likely to come from Negroes staging a racial protest than from 'thugs and hoodlums' who see a chance to profit from looting."[11]

The inferences are plain; if a riot occurred it would be the work of the criminal few, and it would be vigorously suppressed. When disturbances did arrive, some three months later, this was the image conveyed by the *Journal*. The *Journal*'s motivation in so depicting the riot seems to have been to help curb violence and reduce racial tensions. These two somewhat overlapping objectives were sought not by a calculated suppression of facts, but by selection and placement. The guidance for this approach came from written instructions issued by editor-publisher John W. Carroll.

As formally updated after the disturbance, these can be summarized as follows: making information as precise and specific as possible; fixing the limits of the affected area and indicating surrounding tranquillity; avoiding words that convey an exaggerated idea of the turmoil; not recapitulating in any more detail than necessary the grievance that set off the rioting; omitting late-breaking news of violence that might subsequently prove to be exaggerated or might have been suppressed before the reader received his paper. "When in doubt, leave out," was the admonition. This meant avoiding rumors, predictions of future trouble, and threats of further violence; using photographs that would discourage rather than inflame lawlessness.

The *Journal*'s coverage conformed to these instructions. The riot news was presented in such a way as to calm racial tensions, at least in the short run, and curb violence.

But there was a further slant to the *Journal*'s coverage which explains why the paper concentrated so heavily on suppression of the riot and displayed no understanding or empathy for those engaged in civil disorder: the *Journal* presented the riot almost exclusively from the perspective of law enforcement and city officials.

A few examples must suffice. On the first night of the riot the mayor was quoted as saying that the trouble came from "unorganized roving gangs and hoodlums." [12] The same news story continued: "At 12:55 A.M. the mayor said: 'It looks like things have quieted down considerably. This is what I expected at this late hour. Most of the young hoodlums are young people, and I imagine they are worn out.' " A feature article described what it was like to be a National Guardsman when a sniper shoots. [13] Apparently the only UPI article printed dealt with a Guardsman who was almost shot by a sniper; the bullet, while penetrating his coat, missed his body. [14]

The zenith of this coverage was reached with a feature article devoted to the control center at City Hall, including a photograph. [15] Riot coverage ended in the same place. A front page article on November 7, began: "In the police command post in the basement of City Hall, the telephone rang seldom yesterday."

The *Journal*'s white authority orientation resulted in part from the way the paper's staff was organized to report the riot. The *Journal* editors had no preplanned method for reporting such racial disturbances; they merely attempted to cover the events as if they were normal criminal activity writ large. Approximately nine reporters were sent to gather material. Several of these were located at City Hall, while some traveled with police. A few traversed the city tracking down rumors. During the curfew nights these reporters were given passes and allowed to travel freely. They were dispatched to the scene, however, by their editors at the newspaper office. The editors used a police-broadcast radio to become informed of incidents and as a guide to the nature and extent of the riot.

Little or no attempt was made to cover the stories from the perspective of those engaged in the violence. Because of the heavy reliance on the City Hall control room, where the mayor, police chief, and other enforcement officials were accessible and as accommodating as possible, and because reporters traveled with police, the story was seen almost exclusively as a successful encounter of law and order and legitimate authority against blatant lawlessness. This was not the whole truth.

By neglecting the underlying social problems that led to the riot, reporters prevented the participants from communicating political grievances to potentially sympathetic whites. Far from evoking support, the paper probably prompted opposition to black demands by handling the events as a police-crime story, not a political one. The coverage probably reduced the political power of already inefficacious poor people. Simultaneously, it may have enhanced the prestige of the police department—at least among whites.

The FBI

The Winson-Salem police and their "accomplices" on the *Journal* pale in comparison to the Federal Bureau of Investigation. Under the leadership of media-conscious J. Edgar Hoover, the FBI enjoyed more authority-boosting coverage in books, movies, television, and newspapers than any other American institution. A brief discussion is instructive.

The FBI rivaled even the courts in its ability to keep unfavorable news out of the hands of the mass media. Its members spoke with a monolithic voice. Significant information was narrowly circulated among a few top officials. Official spokesmen monopolized communication with journalists. Ostensibly part of the Justice Department, the FBI had its own public relations office that was quite separate and independent. "Don't Embarrass the Bureau," was the motto. Certain illegal activities were condoned; all bad publicity was condemned. Agents observed a norm of secrecy. Violators were severely punished. Leaders had no shortage of sanctions at their disposal. The FBI's opponents might have wanted to harm the agency and diminish its authority. They were discouraged by lack of access to negative information, deterred by fear of revenge.

Formidable at keeping unfavorable news out, the FBI was even more successful at filling the mass media with stories of its accomplishments. Often investigative activities were undertaken with the mass media in mind. Hoover and his men often directed their might at bank robberies and kidnappings, which are visible, highly publicized and relatively easy to solve. And the agency's public relations staff indulged in statistical gyrations which reporters published at face value for more years than they should care to remember. Two brief examples: First, a suspect was convicted of writing ten worthless checks totaling $887. The FBI reported ten convictions to add to its luster. Second, before the FBI could report the results of its investigation of the backgrounds of two plaintiffs suing the government for $1 million in a land transaction, the claim was dismissed by the court. FBI statistics recorded the case as a $1 million saving by the Bureau.[16]

"Traditionally, the FBI has cooperated only with those it has had reason to believe would tell its story in its own image."[17] In this it hardly differed from other police agencies. But the FBI went much further. The Bureau kept files on newspapers from the large to the small and obscure. FBI field offices supplied headquarters with lists of cooperative and reliable reporters. (The office in New Haven, Connecticut, provided a list of 28.) Wrote the head of the San Francisco office to FBI headquarters about the *San Francisco Examiner:* "The cooperation of this newspaper in the past has been pledged to representatives of this Bureau."[18] Other outlets included the *Jackson* (Mississippi) *Daily News,* the *Chicago Tribune,* the *New York Daily News,* and television's *Mike Douglas Show.* They were variously referred to as "reliable," "cooperative," "established," "friendly," and "exceptionally friendly."[19]

Some publishers, editors, and reporters cooperated, connived, and conspired with the FBI because of ideological agreement, a shared belief that America faced dire, imminent danger from the perils of internal subversion. A foolish but understandable fear in the years following the Second World War, it was a delusion by the time John Kennedy became president, and idiocy thereafter. Other journalists acted on the principle that exchange is no robbery. They provided the Bureau with tips, information, details of situations, and received stories in return. Whatever the reasons, the FBI and its cronies in journalism exhibited an impoverished understanding of the purposes of the press in a democratic society.

What came of this relationship between the Bureau and the mass media? Damaging information, whether true or false, about individuals and organizations the FBI intended to discredit was supplied to reporters and, apparently in most instances, dutifully published. Stories were planted, editorials written for pliant newspapers. The victims were radicals, black militants, and critics of the FBI. The purposes: to dissipate their energies, disrupt their activities, stir dissension between and among them. As one typical example, stories would be leaked to the press before anti-Vietnam war marches or rallies. Agents would write press releases grounded in fantasy warning that violence was expected on the day of the rally, communists were involved in organizing the march, and so on. The Internal Security Division at FBI headquarters would transmit the information to conservative newspapers for publication. The general public was misled, potential marchers deterred, dissension stirred among the organizers, and the rally subverted.[20]

Meanwhile, at production costs of approximately a quarter of a million dollars per episode, millions of Americans were regaled every Sunday for many years by the television show *The FBI*, which is still seen in immortal re-runs. Featuring angelic agents (portrayed by actors), it showed the FBI in peace and war busting gangs, tracking down communists, and in its spare time (overtime) disposing of run-of-the-mill kidnappers and bank robbers. Every proposed show was cleared in order through QM (the producing company headed by Quinn Martin), the FBI, the ABC network, and the sponsoring Ford Motor Company. Any one of the four could veto any show for any reason which it did not have to disclose. A resident FBI agent was assigned as a technical adviser to the series. And only actors, writers, and directors "politically acceptable" to the Bureau (read J. Edgar Hoover) were hired to work on the show after being screened.[21]

Producer Quinn Martin is perfectly clear: "I am a patriot. In the police stories that I do, I show the police in an idealized way. Without respect for the police, I think we'd have a breakdown in our society."[22] Thus, when a writer asked to do a show about police brutality, he was told certainly, "as long as the charge was trumped up, the policeman vindicated, and the man who brought the specious charge prosecuted."[23] Similarly, on the program no FBI agent ever bugged a house or tapped a phone or hired a paid informant. No writer was allowed to suggest that these stratagems were ever employed or existed.[24]

So convincing was this fictional FBI to its viewers that 85 percent of the respondents to a University of Michigan Institute for Social Research poll who had watched the program described it as "showing life as it really is."[25]

The FBI's use of the news and entertainment media was so effective that it took an act of larceny to breach its image. Documents incriminating FBI agents in illegal activities were stolen from the Bureau's office in Media, Pennsylvania. Exploiting the roots of media coverage, the thieves intermittently released the more newsworthy documents to competing prestige publications. Hoover was no doubt infuriated by the theft of the documents, their release, and the failure of his agents immediately to catch the perpetrators.

The release of the Media documents began a trickle of revelations about the FBI. Hoover's death broke the dam. Eventually, a special task force of the Department of Justice, in a report made public in 1977, revealed that under Hoover's prolonged reign, the Bureau operated as an independent fiefdom, keeping files confidential from its nominal bosses, the Attorneys General of the United States.[26] Operating autonomously under Hoover's virtual whim, the FBI fueled Senator Joseph McCarthy's (R., Wis.) attacks on democratic institutions by trading information with him. From 1963 until he was assassinated in 1968, the FBI waged a campaign of vilification, wiretapping and illegal break-ins to discredit the Rev. Martin Luther King, Jr., leader and symbol of the civil rights movement. The FBI inserted agents provocateurs into the anti-war movement: men and women who informed on the legal actions of their friends and associates and instigated illegal activities. No matter how legal their activities, black nationalists, socialist sects, and the Ku Klux Klan were objects of the FBI's campaign of disruption and destruction.

Hope springs eternal in the editorial breast. The revelations of FBI misconduct were greeted with suitable "deplore and denounce" editorials, then followed by credulously optimistic praise for the Bureau's avowals that its past misdeeds were no more, that its future behavior would be impeccable. The *Washington Post* described the agency "as undergoing profound change," and praised the call of then Director Clarence Kelley for "quality over quantity."[27]

Problems

The emergence of the truth about the FBI, partial, incomplete, belated, and ill-digested though it may be, is a testament to the Freedom of Information Act, Hoover's mortality, and the vitality of the free press. It suggests, too, that there are problems, some inherent in the practice of law enforcement, which render the police susceptible to adverse media coverage.

Certainly the police do not believe they are indulged by the mass media. Suggestive albeit primitive evidence comes from a study of police reactions to press coverage of a Chicago rock concert riot in which many police and youths were injured. A group of police cadets almost unanimously accused the two newspapers (one liberal, the other conservative) of anti-police bias, even though the stories clearly stated that the rioters had attacked and injured the police. Asked the causes of the bias, the cadets responded with every conceivable explanation: the profit motive, giving the people what they want to read, ideological (liberal) values, the press as partisan, past mistreatment of reporters by the police, reporters' resentment of restrictions imposed on them for security reasons by the police, the police as scapegoat, and failure to understand the role of the police in American society.[28]

All institutions, programs, and people are vulnerable to media exposure, to having their deficiencies dramatized in the cause of news. An organization is likely to suffer media coverage adverse to its authority under the following conditions and circumstances: first, when it willingly or unwillingly expands its scope of activities, thus subjecting its members to unusual demands and strains; second, when it undertakes unpopular or controversial activities; third, when dissent breaks out among its members and attracts or is brought to the attention of the media; fourth, when its members, who have been insulated from the press, are placed in the position of jousting publicly with reporters.

The police are vulnerable on at least the first two counts.

During recent years their responsibilities have increased manifold, even extending onto formerly tranquil campuses. They are required to quell college student disturbances, to supervise school busing in pursuit of racial integration, to prevent the consumption of relatively harmless weeds.

The police are beset by additional problems peculiar to their profession. Their power is conspicuously inadequate to accomplish the vast responsibilities with which they are saddled. They are charged with upholding morality even as morality changes. Constitutional boundaries fence them in. Lacking prestige, they are tempted to break the law to uphold it. They are organizationally inert, purblind, clinging to outmoded procedures and techniques. Opportunities for petty corruption surround them.

The police are out in the streets and highways of America. Their misbehavior cannot be concealed permanently. Besides, the police are the inflictors and the lightning rods of violence. They are therefore subject to periodic investigations by higher public officials intent on rooting out corruption (for a while), finding scapegoats, and enhancing their own authority. Howsoever exposed, venality is news. That is why, in addition to coverage of violent crimes, the mass media periodically feature revelations about police graft and corruption, laziness, inefficiency, and permissive attitudes toward lawbreaking.

As the police struggle with their jobs, they encounter a public only too willing to judge their performance and find it wanting. Where do Americans obtain these standards? In television entertainment programs. The most popular television police heroes are invincible, indomitable, ingenious, and inspired. They concentrate on one case at a time, make arrests without sufficient evidence to convict in real life, are not inhibited by constitutional niceties, benefit from confessions which real criminals are unlikely to make, and rarely suffer from the stifling bureaucracy and understaffing affecting real police. Their business is murder, rape, and kidnapping; no petty larcenies for them. And they always get their man or woman.

How can we claim that television's cop shows bolster the authority of the FBI, yet contribute to undermining the authority of local police forces? The answer is visibility. The local police occupy the front line of authority. The FBI, the courts, other governmental agencies, may deviate outrageously from their public images, be less efficient, more corrupt than the police; but most

Americans lack sufficient personal day-to-day contact with their members to contradict the images. The police, however, are at once the country's most visible, most exposed, and, because they do the dirty work of society, most maligned manifestations of authority. Fictional portrayals establish expectations which real policemen and -women cannot attain and probably shatter.

Conclusion

Stories about corruption and the invidious comparison with fictional cops undermine respect for police officers and cast doubt on their competence and trustworthiness. Respect for, even the legitimacy of, individual policemen and -women may be lessened. At the same time, the media's failure consistently to report overall police policies and effectiveness (the ever increasing amount of crime, the paucity of arrests and convictions), combine with public relations manipulations by law enforcement agencies to sustain the deeper legitimacy of the police as an institution and of the legal system behind them.[29] Individual officers, even an agency or two, may be rotten; but the barrel is both appropriate and necessary. Thus the police go about their business subject to occasional caviling and, less often, exposure by the media, but they are rarely subject to the kind of critical scrutiny which might question their underlying functions as an institution. In particular, the most important law enforcement function is implicit and thus essentially ignored by the mass media: protectors of property, the police are the basic arm of the social order and of existing power relations in the United States.

CHAPTER EIGHT

•

Interested Groups: Uncommon and Common Causes

"Newspapers make associations and associations make newspapers."

Alexis de Tocqueville

WHAT IS TRUE OF AUTHORITY HOLDERS also goes for manipulators outside the government: the effectiveness of their attempts to shape media messages depends on their capacity and ability to exploit the mass media's interests and practices. Media depictions matter because they provide almost all the information the public possesses about most interest groups. Even decision-makers acquire much of their knowledge about and attitudes toward interest groups from the media. Favorable coverage can generate public sympathy, activate reference groups, encourage existing members to stay and new ones to join, and stimulate financial support and foundation grants. Such coverage makes a group's policy agenda politically salient, legitimizes the group's demands and actions, and strengthens its ability to influence policy-makers in its favor.

Yet media coverage of various groups is drastically and dramatically different. Certain groups are scorned as pariahs, some ignored, others indulged. For a favored few, the media serve as a conduit, transmitting whatever news and views the groups' leaders care to provide.

In this chapter, we shall analyze and explain these different kinds of coverage. We begin with marginal groups. Such groups have few advantages: their values clash with elites'; they lack the capacity to generate the trustworthy data reporters desire; their goals are often unpopular with press and public; their members are few and poor.

In contrast, high-status organizations can bank on information and membership resources, trade on American values, and assume public support or at least acquiescence for many of their policy objectives. We therefore follow our discussion of marginal groups by considering the ways in which business groups are able to overcome the adverse coverage generated by their more public malefactions.

We conclude with a case study of Common Cause—the most successful group of media manipulators of them all. Our analysis will show that, in the main, media coverage of the nation's contending factions defends the powerful and defangs the threatening.

Marginal Groups

Unofficial strikers, urban rioters, welfare mothers, student militants, radicals, and impoverished reactionaries compose the more marginal interest groupings in American politics. These relatively powerless, often *ad hoc* groups have problems. They lack the ample resources of money, leadership skills, and a staff with status and expertise, possessed by established organizations. Their policy objectives are not widely shared, at least initially, by politicians and the public. Their credibility is low, their prestige lower.

OBTAINING COVERAGE

On the margin of American politics, of interest to few people, with little obvious impact on society, marginal groups do not make conventional news. They are off reporters' beats and lack the resources to package any news they do make in a usable form for journalists. Their leaders have few if any "exclusives" to offer the press and are often naive about the constraints and imperatives under which reporters operate.

Nonetheless, marginal groups do not go entirely uncovered by the mass media. There may even be regular contact, akin to the kind with which reporters routinely service elected public officials. As Goldenberg explains them, these instances "involved a reporter or columnist who specialized in precisely the area of reporting that was of concern to the group, who agreed with the . . . group's goals, and who accepted the desirability of advocacy reporting as necessary to correct what was perceived as a pervasive imbalance against the poor in most metropolitan newspapers today."[1] When regular interaction is achieved, future coverage for the group is eased and reporters are able to deflect any accusations from their editors of overtly engaging in advocacy reporting by claiming that they have been covering the group all along.[2] Reporters may even acquire a vested interest in perpetuating coverage of the marginal groups they report on. One *New York Times* reporter explained the continued coverage of a Harlem rent strike by saying "We had an interest in keeping it going."[3] No apparent progress, no more stories.

Regular interaction is rare. All of Goldenberg's examples come from the *Boston Globe,* the only one of the three newspapers in Boston "in which editors tolerated advocacy reporting on stories with a community perspective."[4]

In practice, fringe social movements and groups fall outside or through what Gaye Tuchman calls "the news net."[5] To achieve coverage from the press, they must impinge on institutions regularly covered by reporters, either by becoming a subject of concern or by forcibly intruding themselves. Alternatively, they can appeal to media interests by doing something—anything—newsworthy. Dramatic gestures, marches, sit-ins, demonstrations, confrontations, strikes, and riots are newsworthy and visual. As long as there is no surfeit of such activities and they remain novel, the media will tend to cover them. The prospects of coverage are improved if the activities expose injustice and exploitation and if they can be tied to a prevailing news peg.

The most dramatic and flamboyant and violent activities are the most newsworthy. Indeed, many of the incendiary theatrics in which terrorist groups indulge can be explained in part as attempts to catch and hold the public through the media. Thus did the Symbionese Liberation Army capture the headlines by kidnapping Patty Hearst and then apparently transforming her from captive to convert.

Less maniacal groups have no newspaper heiress with whom

to seduce the media. They can hardly aspire to manage the news. But they are increasingly aware of media needs. For example, spontaneous confrontations between, say, welfare mothers and embarrassed bureaucrats do not appear on television news for the simple reason that they end before the cameras arrive. So they must be arranged and sustained within the logistics of television coverage. Knowledgeable organizers therefore call the assignment editor at the local station in advance giving him or her the time, place, purpose and the reasons why an assemblage of reportorial and technical personnel should be dispatched. A promise or the possibility of violence is often a persuasive inducement.

Greater sophistication in handling the mass media does not necessarily lead to more favorable treatment. When an ABC television producer began a documentary on the Black Panthers, he was asked to sign an agreement to contest any subpoena for out-takes up to the Supreme Court, if necessary. He agreed, but network executives refused, reasoning that they could not withhold any information about plans for a crime. "We are citizens," the spokesman declared.[6]

TREATMENT

Dramatic, disruptive, controversial events are news. The mass media, moreover, are attracted to movements and groups which are ahead (but not too far ahead) of their times. Thus dissident or unconventional voices are sometimes heard. But they are usually treated in a way that deprives them of their eloquence and force; their threat to the larger distribution of power is muted. This occurs in three ways: through the reporting of "events," the use of balance, and the reporters' posture of conflict resolvers. We elaborate briefly.

The policy objectives underlying a group or individual's media-attracting behavior can be explicitly stated: for example, women demanding jobs invade a U.S. Employment Service Office. Or they may be implicit: for instance, the crude, obstructive antics of a defendant in a courtroom. But in both cases it is the behavior —the demonstration, the confrontation, the violence—which takes precedence in the media coverage. Even when the reasons for the behavior are clear, they are relegated to the background. When they are merely implicit, they are not reported at all: stories recount the necessity for gagging the prisoner, not his or her rejection of the judicial system as unjust.

When the leaders or members of marginal groups are afforded access to the mass media to assert their policy objectives, they are almost invariably subject to rebuttal, often on the same program or in the same story. Otherwise the coverage is immediately condemned as lacking balance or, worse, as advocacy journalism. The balance is provided by a representative of the opposite point of view. If one does not exist, it will often be created by or for the press. When the Vietnam Veterans Against the War were attracting media attention by such dramatic and newsworthy gestures as throwing the medals they had won for gallantry in Vietnam over the White House fence, Nixon aide Charles Colson organized a competing group of veterans in support of the administration's policies. Capitalizing upon the press norm of reporting all sides, this artificial creation received its share of media attention and coverage.

The reporter, narrator, or host usually poses as a disinterested, above-the-battle compiler, siding with neither extreme. In so doing, he or she frames the issue from a conventional perspective, thereby defining the views and objectives of the contending groups as extremist. This balance tends to equate both sides and certify their ineffectiveness, reassuring readers and viewers that the middle way—the government's way—is still preferable, no matter how inefficient and inept it may be.

THE CIVIL RIGHTS EXCEPTION

The success of Southern civil rights groups in the 1960s seems at first to belie our argument. By their coverage of the movement, the media contributed mightily to the surge toward black equality and thus to a marginal reallocation of power in America. But the circumstances were special, if not unique. Segregation is morally wrong, violates the democratic creed, and undermines national values. It can be squared with the Constitution only by the most tortuous and devious reading of that document. In the South, segregation was overt, blatant, and legally sanctioned. It was opposed in principle by all right-thinking Americans. It was opposed in practice by blacks and whites from inside and outside the South, men and women who risked their lives to confront it non-violently.

Their leader was charismatic; his very name resounded symbolically. His opponents were bull-headed; their responses only clarified the moral conflict between good and evil. Segregation was a
regional scar, and the journalists who courageously covered the
efforts to remove it mainly represented national media—newspapers and networks less vulnerable to economic, social, and political pressures than Southern-based newspapers and television
stations.

David J. Garrow argues provocatively that the Rev. Martin
Luther King, Jr., and his associates consciously devised an unspo-
ken strategy of deliberately provoking attacks from violence-prone
white Southern officials in order to attract widespread and by definition sympathetic media coverage of their activities.[7] Whether
they deliberately concocted the plan or not, they received the kind
of coverage they needed.

Southern politicians could assert that their Negroes were
peaceable, perfectly satisfied with the segregated status quo. But
the stories in the press, the television films of mostly home grown
demonstrations, of vicious whites screaming at little black children
trying to attend formerly all-white schools, of racist and brutal
policemen—none of these could be denied. Because of this media
coverage of the gallant actions of civil rights activists, segregation
was shown to be clear and present and dangerous.

As one of the black children Gov. Orval Faubus (D., Ark.)
tried to keep out of Little Rock's Central High School subsequently recalled (perhaps romanticizing what was a harrowing experience): "We spent most of the time gettin' interviewed. . . . We
felt like celebrities. Some of the kids who had been selected to go
to Central with us had got cold feet and dropped out. But they
wanted to come back in when they saw all the publicity we were
getting."[8]

This mass media coverage translated exposure into public and
governmental support, facilitating passage of a series of significant
civil rights laws, culminating in the 1965 Voting Rights Act. The
legal bulwarks of segregation were shattered.

Since that time, the civil rights movement has been
superseded by opposition to the war in Vietnam, concern for the
environment, and the campaign against nuclear energy. Yet the
economic and social conditions of most blacks are little changed.
What have changed are the conditions provoking favorable and
extensive media coverage of black grievances. With the legal im-

pediments wiped away, many elites agree that enough has been done; thus there is no chorus of white elected officials who articulately espouse the black cause for the press. Black groups' economic goals do not have the legitimacy their demands for constitutional treatment had. There is a dearth of colorful personalities and a lack of headline-making violent clashes.

REPERCUSSIONS

Mass media coverage can heighten the visibility of a marginal interest group and its demands. Reference groups may be alerted to come to the group's assistance. Sympathetic public officials can capitalize on the coverage to resurrect and promote their own (dormant) proposals to improve the conditions publicized. The group's members may be inspired by the publicity to greater effort and increased loyalty. New members may be recruited.

But negative repercussions are more probable. The very tactics of protest and disruption attracting news coverage offend many Americans who do not yet share a group's quarrel with established institutions and practices. Moreover, marginal groups have a multiplicity of targets. Media-publicized activities which increase the morale of a group's members and spur recruitment are simultaneously likely to conflict with internal group maintenance, dismay reference groups, and discourage foundation support. The price of publicity is further exclusion from the bargaining process. As Lipsky puts it: "People in power do not like to sit down with rogues."[9] Provoked administrators may feel compelled to show strength against rather than accommodate the demonstrators and their demands. Scrupulous or unscrupulous politicians can use well-paid, highly skilled public relations experts to exploit the events, turning them (and the group) into issues of law and order.

Media priorities can begin to dominate the planning of protest movements, thereby harming their effectiveness. By forcing groups into confrontational tactics to gain publicity (since other forms of political action by marginal groups are not deemed newsworthy), the media isolate the groups from the rest of the public, making them look like violence-prone threats to social stability. Radical groups are undermined by being indiscriminately equated with terrorists. Recognizing this, group leaders may then tone down their demands, easing pressure on established authorities, leading to co-optation.

This may have been the fate of the women's liberation movement. One of its first major media events was a confrontation at the Miss America Pageant in 1968. There, two bras were burned as cameras rolled. The ensuing publicity roused many people to the oppression of women. But it was soon apparent that "by choosing to work through the medium of public spectacle, demonstrators open themselves to the possibility that they will be appropriated as spectacular entertainment." [10] For ever since, the epithet used by strident opponents of liberationist women is "bra-burners." Then tactics were moderated. Now it's more the "women's movement" than "women's liberation." Equal pay and opportunity to advance to elite power positions are much easier demands for power-wielders to cope with than "liberation."

In the course of covering the newsworthy, then, media organizations can often be induced to convey messages critical of power holders. By clever exploitation of media interest in audience appeal, of media susceptibility to fad and conflict, to the unusual or unexpected, opposition groups can attract media attention to their causes. But under current media practices, this coverage may not advance the deeper goals of the marginal groups, especially when their aims are not easily accommodated without fundamental redistributions of power.

Business Interests

COZY

We live in a semi-capitalist economy. In contrast to marginal interest groups, businessmen and -women make vital decisions affecting the economic, social, cultural, and political lives of Americans. They determine the organization of the work force, decide the location of plants, facilitate technological innovation (consider the effects of the automobile and the contraceptive pill on modern life), and contribute to the income or lack of income of millions of Americans. They have power.

Government needs business. A flourishing, low-inflation economy generates jobs, tax revenues, and re-election for incumbent politicians. Business is supported by tariffs, tax rebates, cost-plus contracts, sponsored research, and regulatory agencies which often regulate in its behalf. But government also needs labor, and during the past fifty years it has increasingly intervened to curb the worst excesses of untrammeled free enterprise. Although business groups are far from monolithic, most of them usually oppose increased bargaining rights for unions, federally imposed safety standards at the work place, increases in the minimum wage, windfall profits taxes and other curbs on their autonomy.

To keep what they have, to resist further encroachments from governmental agencies on their private preserves, businessmen and -women intervene directly in politics. They expend vast sums of money, far exceeding any other sources including labor unions, to support the right political candidates, and to lobby for their interests at the national, state, and local levels. Much of what they spend is tax-deductible.

Beneath the overt political activity, many segments of business have quiet, comfortable, mutually beneficial relationships with congressional sub-committees and executive agency bureaus. The legislators and bureaucrats placate or please the interest groups and gain their useful support by responding to or even pre-empting their needs and demands. Embodied in public policy by governmental agencies, the wishes and demands of business and other private-interest groups are endowed with legitimacy and backed by social control. The result is political gain without appreciable cost for politicians and the groups involved. Public ignorance is public acquiescence, but only if these cozy arrangements are conducted out of the public's sight and mind.[11]

The mass media can disturb these cozy accommodations, give them salience and visibility, bring them to the public's attention. But scrutiny and exposure are infrequent. Part of the explanation rests in the inadequate coverage of Congress and its members analyzed in Chapter 5. But neither do the mass media scrutinize the more avowedly non-political activities of American business, the day-to-day affairs of industries and corporations.

Business activities are infrequently deemed newsworthy because they are usually devoid of glamor, sex, conflict, or suspense, and are difficult to personalize. Even the coarse details of financial speculation and misappropriation lack the simplicity and appeal of violent crimes and political skulduggery. The press thrives on people robbing banks, not banks robbing people. Yet the latter activity is probably both more thriving and more profitable. To expose business practices requires expertise with balance sheets and accounting practices, time, and access—usually denied—to corporate boardrooms.

More important than the superficial drabness of business activity, reporters' lack of expertise, and the access denied reporters to significant decision-making by corporate executives, is the public–private distinction. Increasingly obsolete, this distinction leads journalists to concentrate their attention predominantly on the public business transacted by government. Private institutions, whether profit or non-profit, involved in business, industry, education, medicine, and philanthropy, many of which are not easy to distinguish (try medicine and business), receive far less coverage. When covered, it is because of a scandal or disaster; some outrage it is no longer possible to conceal; or through the exposure efforts of congressional committees or regulatory agencies.

Why is the public-private distinction still maintained? Inertia, conventionality, the outmoded concepts to which some journalists cling. The distinction has logical although not analytical validity: public officials are held to be accountable to the American people, private executives less so, if at all. Public officials are expected to meet with the people's surrogate—the press—to justify, explain and if necessary defend their actions. Not so their private counterparts, who can and do refuse access with impunity. The effect is to perpetuate concealment, thereby adding to the corporations' behind-the-scenes political power.

Consequently, the business sections of newspapers, with the exception of the *Wall Street Journal,* usually consist of columnists expounding their soon outmoded economic analyses and forecasts, puff pieces about the latest marketing tactics, and a retreat into stories of epiphenomena: a flamboyant corporate executive's philosophy and life-style. This type of material, found at its worst in real estate sections of even the most prestigious papers, diverts attention from the more fundamental powers of business.

BAD PRESS

In nine years the number of people expressing a great deal of confidence in the heads of large corporations has fallen from 55 to 15 percent; between 1968 and 1977 there was a drop from 70 to 15 percent in the number of people agreeing that business strikes a fair balance between profits and the public interest; and a Gallup poll measuring levels of confidence in American institutions placed business at the bottom, below even organized labor.[12]

This decline is a product of people's disillusioning experiences with free enterprise economics in their personal lives. But it also stems from media coverage. Corporate executives are right to claim that their activities are sometimes critically and negatively reported in the press. But in part they have only their abundant, malodorous actions to blame. Corruption, bribery, illegal campaign contributions; feeding violence to children; promoting unnecessary, defective, dangerous products; automobile and airplane recalls; power failures, chemical dumping, price increases, and excessive profits—often the behavior of business—these are newsworthy when exposed.

For most of this bad publicity business should blame government, not media. Corporate sins are usually brought to, rather than uncovered by, reporters. Congressional hearings, regulatory agencies' investigations, even presidential attacks, are reporters' sources of information. Members of Congress can garner publicity by exposing callous and greedy industries and thereby enhance the chances of remedial legislation. Even the most decrepit and inert of regulatory agencies is sometimes invigorated to investigate an abuse or two in the industries under its jurisdiction. And presidents, from populist and political instincts, have been known to lambast an unpopular industry, as President Carter attacked the greed of big oil. Whether the attacks lead to legislation, to law, to effective elimination of the corporate abuses identified, is questionable, but they do receive coverage from the mass media.

The sins of business have an additional attraction for the press: they fit nicely into the consumer–business dichotomy. Perpetuated by Ralph Nader, the dichotomy provides reporters with a simple way of fitting business depradations into their news columns. Meanwhile, the accomplishments of business—jobs created, products invented, managerial innovations—have gone relatively unreported in the news columns of the press; they are not news.

PUBLIC RELATIONS

David Truman noted in 1951: "It is not astonishing . . . that trade associations and various institutionalized business groups have engaged in propaganda largely aimed at protecting established attitudes and positions."[13] With the abundant resources at their command, they still do. Their purposes: to combat whatever adverse news reaches the press about business transgressions, and to sustain elite and public support for their activities. These campaigns are a contemporary version of the "What Helps Business Helps You" slogan promulgated by the U.S. Chamber of Commerce and other organizations during the 1930s.[14] Publicity is sought to bolster an image of public service, to guide and control public opinion by imposing a business frame of reference on policy issues, and to capitalize on pre-existing, widely held public attitudes.

There are several techniques. Because advertisements are so transparently self-interested, groups try to give the impression that their unmediated advertisements are mostly mediated. Thus the cigarette industry placed articles favorable to its position and critical of the Surgeon General's Report into *True Magazine* and the *National Enquirer*. It was the same article, written by an advertising man, but issued under different names. After publication, reprints of the article were sent by the industry lobbying organization to doctors, medical researchers, educators and, of course, members of Congress.[15]

Or sponsorship may be concealed. The "Calorie Control Council" sponsoring newspaper advertisements that attacked the Food and Drug Administration's proposed ban on saccharin actually consisted of manufacturers and processors of dietary products. Similarly, business sources often originate editorials which appear in daily and weekly newspapers as journalists' own work. The National Association of Manufacturers is allegedly a prime practitioner.[16]

The most successful campaign, its effects still visible today, was that staged by the American Medical Association in the late 1940s against President Truman's proposal for national health insurance. It included advertisements, press conferences, and supposedly neutral experts who appeared on radio shows and wrote newspaper articles decrying "socialized" medicine. The campaign actually coined and popularized the loaded term as a substitute for "national health insurance"—on the correct assumption that anything smacking of socialism exudes negative vibrations in the United States.

Nowadays, television is available. Corporations vitally interested in creating and preserving a climate of opinion permitting their undisturbed operations and profit-making have found the ideal solution. They advertise their beliefs in free enterprise and promote their policy preferences to the extent the network executives allow. They support public television, "an act of advertising which happens to enjoy the legal and moral benefits of philanthropy."[17] The audience is elite, consisting disproportionately of wealthy, college-educated, opinion leaders. The advertisements are discreet: no jingles, no sex; just a cultured voice, usually male and English accented, telling Americans that the program was made possible by Exxon, Mobil, Xerox, and the rest. The corporations broadcast the news of their sponsorship in newspapers and on the commercial television networks, inviting Americans to watch the programs. They thereby advertise their good deeds on behalf of culture and enlightenment whether the public watches the actual programs or not and no doubt evoke feelings of gratitude for making a modicum of quality television available. Gratitude may yet be translated into the illusion that these oil companies and other quasi-monopolies behave in the public interest, that their power should be left untouched, for these corporations care about America.

NO CHANGE

Media coverage of corporate derelictions damages the images of particular firms, even entire industries. Business lobbyists may be hindered from obtaining their objectives without compromise. Some of the corporate power that would otherwise be unchallenged is redistributed. But despite the lack of confidence, the downright hostility toward corporations expressed in public opinion polls, business is surprisingly immune. Individual companies are faulted and falter, but the capitalist system within which they function remains unquestioned. According to pollster Daniel Yankelovich, whereas public confidence in business leaders has plummeted, "some nine out of ten Americans were still so attached to the free enterprise system in the mid-70s that they were willing to make personal sacrifices in order to preserve it."[18] Clearly the public relations campaigns we have just described contribute to the system's preservation; but there are two other reasons: the way the media actually report business activities, and what they omit.

The media do not contextualize. Thus each separate report of corporate malfeasance leaves an impression of companies being caught and punished. For example, the small fine of a huge oil company for knowing about safety law violations that led directly to the deaths of three workers in Oklahoma is reported. Undiscussed in the story is the question of the relations in corporate behavior among legality, morality, and profits. Similarly, many of the largest corporations have been found guilty over the past few years of bribery, of price fixing, of deliberate violations of safety or pollution laws. Many of these offenses, convictions, and sentences are (briefly) reported. Not reported is that many similar crimes have occurred without sanction. Not raised is the question whether there might be something inherent in corporate goals that induces immorality or illegality by even the most prestigious firms.

Since journalists are not philosophers, they report the facts rather than the implications of corporate misbehavior. Journalists are not conscious promoters of societal change; they do not go around looking for different ways of structuring the economy. But the result of avoiding analysis, of ignoring alternative ways of organizing work, is to reinforce the existing economic system in the United States. There is no pressure for internal reforms in the fundamental operation of the business economy. Worker participation, worker control, even social responsibility infrequently raise their insidious heads. The media can curb corporate political and economic power in specific instances, but rarely if ever can they basically alter it. Usually they protect and advance it. The essential character of capitalism persists.

A Common Cause

Putting the civil rights movement to shame (to flight also?), more effective even than business groups, Common Cause is the classic modern example of successful, sophisticated manipulation of the mass media. A case study of *New York Times* coverage of this interest group synthesizes the analysis and argument not just of this chapter, but of the entire book up to this point. We begin with a brief summary of our data, explain the reasons for the amount and kinds of coverage, and conclude by discussing possible effects.

Formed in 1970 primarily at the initiative of John W. Gardner, Common Cause is prominent among the so-called "public interest'' groups. Gardner described it as a citizens' lobby designed ''to revitalize politics and government''[19] and said its purpose was to ''protect the public interest against all comers.''[20] He used his initial funding from foundations to send out over a million and a half direct-mail solicitations and to purchase full-page advertisements in four major American newspapers. Partly because of this extensive publicity and widespread news coverage, Common Cause soon had over 200,000 members, adding approximately 5,000 more each week. During the first year, over three million dollars was raised, almost two and a half million of it in dues.[21] In 1976, the organization had a membership of roughly 250,000, an annual income of over five million dollars derived from dues and contributions, and an extensive list of claimed victories in Congress and the courts.[22]

Content

Four categories were devised to analyze the structures of news stories about Common Cause in the *Times*. ''Pronunciamento'' describes the direct transferral of information, ideas, and accusations from Common Cause to the readers. We do not contend that the material is transmitted unaltered by the reporter, only that no sources other than Common Cause are mentioned in the story. We categorized stories as ''Elaboration I'' when the major source was Common Cause but *one* additional source was included to elaborate or verify the organization's material. ''Elaboration II'' means two or more additional such sources were mentioned.

The figures are highly revealing: of the 149 major stories, 42.3 percent (63) were straight pronunciamento, 17.4 percent elaboration I, 24.8 percent elaboration II, and 4.7 percent not applicable. Only 10.7 percent (16) could be categorized as ''Adversary,'' meaning that the story contained any information, no matter how little, whether derogatory or not, from a source opposed to or conflicting with the Common Cause data or position.

An examination of the actual sources confirms the impression of Common Cause dominance over the content of *New York Times* stories involving the interest group. We divided sources into major and minor: the former provided the most paragraphs of information in a story; the latter were responsible for secondary material. In 66.4 percent of the stories, a Common Cause spokesperson was the major source; in an additional 14.1 percent it was John Gardner. The next highest categories were "other" and "not applicable" at 6.0 and 4.7 percent respectively. Non-elected government officials, candidates or their spokepersons, and non-campaigning elected officials all had negligible percentages.

Just because Common Cause official sources dominate *New York Times* news stories involving the organization does not necessarily mean that the stories are favorable. It is possible for reporters to treat information in ways inimical to their sources' interests and objectives. So we categorized the stories as favorable, neutral, mixed, and unfavorable. Some 96.6 percent of the "major" stories were favorable, 3.4 percent (a total of 5) were mixed. Not one was unfavorable. In almost every instance, Common Cause was presented as a champion of citizens' rights, a righter of wrong, a doer of good. It was also depicted favorably in 78.5 percent of the "minor" stories (where it appeared in a supporting or peripheral role). The remainder were mixed or neutral. There were no unfavorable minor stories.

Common Cause was further depicted in 98.0 percent of the "major" stories as "influential," with the power to influence governmental decision-making and decisions. In only 1.3 percent (2 stories) was it shown without influence. One story was categorized as "neutral." In the minor stories the percentages are 77.7 influential, 19.8 neutral, and 2.5 percent (3 stories) not influential. Considering again that Common Cause is a mere appendage in some of the stories, these figures are equally striking.

Finally, we tested how reporters and editors at the *Times* perceived and treated Common Cause by asking what they called it in their stories. Such phrases as "the civic group,"[23] "the good government group,"[24] and "the public interest organization"[25] are favorable on their face; others, such as "the very worthwhile people's lobby,"[26] "the reformist citizens' lobby,"[27] and "the citizens' lobby,"[28] contain the suspect word "lobby" but precede it with exculpatory language. We categorize them under the term "Conduit" and they compose 54.4 percent of the sample. Under "Partial Conduit" we put bland expressions such as "the new organization,"[29] and phrases in which the term "lobby" is not totally redeemed, as in "the public affairs lobby,"[30] and "the lobby group."[31]

Adding the conduit and partial conduit categories, we find that almost 90 percent of the phrases describing Common Cause were positive and supportive. A mere 9.4 percent (14) of the characterizations could be called skeptical—"the national organization that calls itself a 'citizens' lobby,"[32] "the self-styled citizens' lobby,"[33] "the self-described public interest lobby."[34] And a paltry 1.3 percent (2 references) were "antagonistic"—"the so-called citizens' lobby."[35]

A cautionary note: *Times* coverage seems to be changing. There appears to be a growing albeit almost imperceptible wariness, a slight increase in skepticism towards Common Cause in the press, manifest even in the *Times* coverage. The number of stories is decreasing; conduit referents show a consistent drop from 76.9 percent of all stories in 1971 to 18.8 percent in 1976; partial conduit referents have steadily increased from 23.0 to 75.0 percent over the same period.

Common Cause may be encountering the problems that beset successful groups once they achieve some of their objectives. A campaign finance law has been enacted. There is federal funding of at least presidential elections. There is no Nixon administration to kick around anymore. And in early 1977 John Gardner retired from active involvement with the organization.

Yet Common Cause spokespersons remain the source of over 80.0 percent of all major stories, few referents are in the skeptical category, and the last antagonist referent occurred in 1973. The group continues to be portrayed as influential; the stories remain overwhelmingly favorable.

Explanations

COMMON CAUSE MANIPULATIONS

The *New York Times* is far more a transmission belt, even a publicity agent, for Common Cause than the independent gatherer and dispenser of "the facts" it claims to be and which the dictates of responsible journalism seem to demand.[36]

In explaining the reasons, we focus first on the interest group. For, in contrast to marginal groups, Common Cause is both credible and legitimate. This stems from the prestige and background of its founder. A "liberal" Republican, John W. Gardner had been H.E.W. Secretary in the Johnson Administration, President of the Carnegie Foundation, Chairman of the National Urban Coalition, and on the board of directors of such corporations as the Shell Oil Company, Time, Inc., and the New York Telephone Company. He bestowed legitimacy and a patina of non-partisanship upon Common Cause when he founded it. His presence made it worthy of note; his pronouncements brought it attention; his participation gave Common Cause cachet and cartel with editorial writers and columnists.

Certainly Common Cause possessed legitimacy and credibility through its founder. It reinforced them by the number and social standing of its members who voluntarily joined and by its expressed purposes, which are widely viewed as desirable both by journalists and by the public. The result is regularized interaction. Common Cause does not have to struggle desperately to attract the attention of lowly reporters, the appearance of whose stories, if they write them, is problematic. Common Cause has the attention of reporters of repute whose stories, which they are likely to write, will probably be published. Being a story subject at all may confer status; being depicted both favorably and as influential raises status even more. Responses from Common Cause targets in the Nixon administration and Congress merely served as additional boosts for the organization.

This coverage was not automatic. There is a four-stage process involving the relationships of interest groups and the press. There must be an event or occurrence, brought to the attention of or covered by journalists, who in turn deem it newsworthy, and then transform it into a published story. Media-conscious staff members and officers at Common Cause were involved at all stages of the process: creating an event, giving it visibility, emphasizing the event's newsworthy details and, indeed, structuring them into a story for the press.

Common Cause's highly developed manipulatory skills were evidenced by the way it did most of the work for the media, thereby responding to their organizational demands. It continuously issued news releases, editorial memoranda, testimonies and speeches packaged for media consumption and publication. There was detailed information, highlights summarized, liftable quotes, and leads virtually composed. Trying to make its coverage convenient, the organization scheduled press conferences far enough in advance of deadlines and hand-delivered releases to the House Press Gallery. Ready to react immediately for the press, it called "impromptu press conferences," usually in response to a new development in Congress regarding an issue with which the group was concerned.

To insure adequate coverage, Common Cause maintained extensive press lists. List A, for example, contained the names of approximately thirty key reporters at the wire services, networks, news chains (Hearst, Gannett, Knight, Newhouse, and Scripps Howard), and the largest newspapers. Releases were usually hand-delivered to these reporters. This extensive compendium reflected in part the group's knowledge of the "beat" system of newspersons, particularly in Washington. Press List Q, for example, contained the names of all the reporters who cover military spending.

The public relations flair at Common Cause is attested to by the 1976 "Common Cause Guide for Judging the Candidates." The guide is particularly notable for achieving press coverage showing Common Cause as influential and equal if not superior to the presidential candidates. The *Times* story began: "Common Cause opened a pioneering effort today to introduce more truth and honesty into political campaigning by setting a code of standards for candidates and monitoring their compliance in the 1976 election year."[37] The public release of the code and accompanying press conference dominated the news. Lacking the code, the candidates could make no informed response. Consequently, the 23-paragraph story was devoted to the code and to Gardner's press conference, with the exception of one brief paragraph reporting the lack of response.

Subsequently, John Gardner wrote to some of the presidential candidates, asking if they would endorse the group's nine standards for "open, informative campaigns." Gardner's letter, the candidates' answers, including Ronald Reagan's and former Senator Eugene J. McCarthy's refusals to respond, and Gardner's reaction to their refusals ("this raises serious questions about these candidates") were, as intended, faithfully chronicled by the *Times* with the headline "Gardner Scores Two Candidates."[38]

THE TIMES

Common Cause did what it could to obtain extensive and favorable coverage from the *Times*. Why did the *Times* bestow it? The explanations reside in concepts of news, need for information, journalistic norms, and congruent values.

Common Cause was covered because it connected with the *Times*'s concepts of news. Its targets were "big" names: presidents, campaign finance chairmen, and the kind of congressmen whose length of tenure is usually commensurate with their arrogance, pomposity, and sense of security. These public targets were approached in the newsworthy terms of their derelictions, duplicity, and malfeasance, their efforts to conceal information which might lead to investigation and, perhaps, exposure. Individuals were attacked, accusations leveled, demands made. There was the tincture of scandal, of corruption. The press did not have to be cajoled; this is the stuff of daily journalism and its headlines.

Besides, Common Cause was adroit at selecting the right target to personalize and dramatize longstanding abuses for press and public, and was shrewd at identifying symbols of the need for reform. Consider its ultimately successful pressure on Congress to investigate and punish Congressman Robert L. F. Sikes (D., Fla.) for alleged conflict of interest. The subject contained such news ingredients as unscrupulous or unethical behavior by a powerful but little-known congressman, a struggle between a notoriously dilatory congressional committee and a reform organization sworn to uphold American values, and an orienting question—would the committee act? The conflict festered for several weeks and was the subject of four major and two minor stories in the *Times*, as well as an editorial. All portrayed Common Cause favorably, as an influential upholder of the standards of good government.[39] In one fell swoop, the group received publicity for its specific objective of unseating Sikes, for its general goals of establishing accountability and ending corruption, and for itself.

The press needs information; Common Cause provides it. This is the second reason for its success with the *Times*. It gathered and pried out information using several techniques. Suits were filed, disclosure sought, and data on financial contributions and election expenditures compiled. This is the very information which journalists seek but usually lack the time and resources to obtain. These hard, often statistical data, seemingly objective, accurate, and complete, are provided by an apparently non-partisan source with an aura of expertise on campaign finance shared by no other entity. And these data are neither immediately refutable nor refuted.

The norm of balance is rarely applied to statistics from authoritative sources. And even if reporters had sought other sources, none of them could expeditiously verify or rebut Common Cause figures. No wonder most such stories fell into the "conduit" category.

It is not only the information provided by Common Cause that was unquestioned. The *Times* usually transmitted the group's views untarnished or merely with additional explanatory material from supporting sources. The data indicate that the journalistic norms of balance and fairness need not be operative on most kinds of stories involving an authoritative, high-status, apparently nonpartisan group espousing widely shared values. Reporters and editors do not appear to regard these stories as controversial or as requiring the inclusion of opposing viewpoints. Even if journalists did want to be critical, they were inhibited by the norm of objectivity; prevented from including their own views in the stories, they could rarely find anyone to state them on their behalf. Common Cause did have antagonists, but most of these lacked credibility, lacked a case, had an impossible one (defending the exclusion of the public from the proceedings of congressional committees, endorsing unethical behavior), or were subsequently discredited.

Shared values is a final explanation for the *Times*'s coverage of Common Cause. They both shared in great part the "Progressive" movement assumptions that the American political system is basically sound; that there is nothing wrong with it that exposing corruption, reducing the influence of money in campaigns, and reforming some structures and procedures will not put right. Or at least they agreed on the importance of these endeavors. They shared, too, agreement on the desirability of the general goals espoused by Common Cause—a more "accessible," "accountable," "effective," and "responsive" government, to "open up the system." They may have agreed on the appropriateness of Common Cause's more specific objectives of public financing of campaigns, lobbying disclosure laws, conflict of interest laws, and financing disclosure laws. No doubt they also shared the dismal suspicion that many politicians are self-serving, disingenuous, and hypocritical. Asked to explain his paper's overwhelmingly favorable coverage of Common Cause, a *New York Times* reporter who had written some of it told us, while insisting he not be identified, "We agreed with them."

When values are shared by source and press and probably readers too, there is no felt need on the part of reporters to seek countervailing information elsewhere.

Effects

The *New York Times* is disproportionately read by public officials, foundation directors, the leaders of Common Cause, and the kinds of people who either join or are potential members of the group. These are "upper-middle class whites, well educated, middle aged, financially secure, with a disproportionate number of northeastern seaboard and Pacific coast residents." [40] The paper is a guiding light for many people in the media. What, then, were the probable effects of the *Times*'s portrayal of Common Cause and its leaders as active, influential, effective, non-partisan crusaders for good government?

Existing members were given public incentives to continue their allegiance even when their initial enthusiasm dissipated. They received a sense of purposes being fulfilled by an increasingly prestigious organization, and they encountered no damaging news of strain or conflict. Potential members were encouraged to join. No wonder a telephone survey conducted on behalf of the group revealed that more than half the new members were attracted by stories in the media. [41] The result was organizational maintenance and enhancement and the continued receipt of resources.

A concomitant effect was to affirm and reaffirm Common Cause's autonomy: "a distinctive area of competence, a clearly demarcated and exclusively served clientele or membership, and undisputed jurisdiction over a function, service, goal, or cause." [42] Media coverage in general and that of the *Times* in particular, the way the Common Cause data, claims, attacks, and successes were reported, bestowed national prominence on the group and its issues, bringing pressure on shrouded public officials.

For these reasons, supporters in public life were given additional reasons to believe Common Cause worth supporting. Actual and potential antagonists may have been persuaded to modify or mute opposition and actions which would otherwise expose them to a hostile press. With the *Times* as model, other newspapers, the television networks' news, and the weekly news magazines were reassured that their coverage of the group was responsible. And the leaders of Common Cause may have been emboldened to seek other targets and more difficult objectives.

Most important, the *Times* gave Common Cause the opportunity to imprint upon the public and public officials its definition of the woes of American politics and its prescriptions for those woes.

Thus (chain) links were constructed between money and political favors and corruption and Common Cause's solution—public financing of elections. But the hard data, the figures with which the links began, may not have been as neutral as they were taken to be by the *Times*. David Adamany points out omissions and exclusions in Common Cause's election receipts and expenditure data and "wonders whether these exclusions do not reflect a decision to publish less comprehensive information which somehow better serves the lobbying and litigation strategies of the organization." [43] Nor were the objectives sought by Common Cause invariably or necessarily desirable. Gerald M. Pomper argues that campaign finance reform has bad effects on the stability and viability of American political parties. [44]

Yet it was primarily through media coverage that these objectives were promulgated as desirable and desired. Other interest groups with quite different definitions and solutions were unfavorably depicted, while many went unheard and therefore unheeded.

Conclusion

Media coverage of interest groups helps to preserve the basic distribution of power in America by the way it presents organized demands for change. Organizations that accept establishment rules, and pursue incremental goals discreetly, benefit from journalists' needs and practices. Groups whose methods violate convention, whose objectives require a significant alteration of the structure of power, usually find their radical activities distorted or condemned, their radical analyses and proposals ignored or scorned. Any publicity they receive tends to isolate them from the mass of citizens, encouraging them to moderate their ways until they either fade from sight or shade into the establishment. The legitimacy of America's political, economic, and social system is preserved.

•

PART THREE

The Manipulated Public

CHAPTER NINE

•

Accepting the System

"I know of no safe repository of the ultimate powers of society but the people themselves, and if we think them not enlightened enough to exercise their control with a wholesome discretion, the remedy is not to take it from them but to inform their discretion by education."

Thomas Jefferson

WE HAVE EXPOSED THE ROOTS of news media content. We have analyzed the attempts of public figures to manipulate the media. We have explained why these self-interested efforts to achieve, retain or enhance power, to facilitate the achievement of policy preferences, are sometimes successful, sometimes not. Now we turn to the powerless: the vast mass of Americans who read newspapers, watch television, go to the movies. The content they absorb has distinctive, often unrecognized effects on them.

Despite the complications and exceptions, the general impact of the mass media is to socialize people into accepting the legitimacy of their country's political system (this chapter); lead them to acquiesce in America's prevailing social values (Chapter 10); direct their opinions in ways which do not undermine and often support the domestic and foreign objectives of elites (Chapters 11, 12, and 13); and deter them from active, meaningful participation in politics—rendering them quiescent before the powerful (Chapter 14).

Legitimacy

We begin with two concepts: legitimacy and political socialization. Legitimacy is the widely shared public belief that the political system is right for the society, and that governing institutions
and officials rightly hold and exercise power. Political socialization
is the process by which members of the society acquire political
norms, attitudes, values, and beliefs.

From the perspective of elites, political socialization should
encourage and sustain legitimacy. For children, it usually does so.
Such agents of political socialization as parents, schools, religious
institutions, and government, sometimes deliberately, sometimes
without conscious intent, help imbue young Americans with an
idealized image of their political system, its founders, functions,
and purposes.

But political socialization is a continuous process. Adult experiences can shatter childhood illusions. The activities of most
local governments possess the potential to destroy faith in their
representativeness and responsiveness. Watergate possessed the
potential to undermine faith in the legitimacy of the entire American political system. Vietnam possessed the potential to challenge
long-cherished myths about the innocence and nobility of America's aims as implemented by ruling elites.

The mass media are crucial in all this. Although other socializing agents remain operative, it is the media that bring Watergate
and Vietnam and local government—or do not bring them—into
American homes. What they communicate, how they frame and
present it, influences Americans' beliefs about the legitimacy of
their polity. In contrast to the situation in many other countries,
the American media are not the playthings of government. And
yet, the overall effect of their coverage of activities and events
which might undermine legitimacy is to sustain it.[1]

Journalists achieve this effect by doing their jobs: by following
the dictates of coverage discussed in Chapter 2. The socialization
effects are potent though usually unintentional. We illustrate our
argument with case studies of local newspaper reporting of a
city council and of national media coverage of Watergate. We will
end the chapter by evaluating the common elite complaint that,
far from helping to fortify underlying power relations in America, the mass media in recent years have encouraged disaffection.

Legitimizing a City Council

In Durham, North Carolina, the city council passes most of the legally binding ordinances and resolutions for the city and therefore occupies a central position of political authority in that community. The *Durham Morning Herald* is the only newspaper in the city which regularly covers council meetings. A comparison of what actually transpired at city council meetings with the way these events were portrayed in the *Herald* reveals that the coverage consistently reinforced the Council's legitimacy. The main explanation: the reporters' concept of professionalism.

By professionalism we mean a set of internalized norms that guide and structure the local reporters' stories. These canons of conventional journalism include condensing and summarizing; investing events with rationality and coherence (even though the events may be confusing to the participants, and the reporters themselves may not fully comprehend what has occurred and its meaning); emphasizing the council's decisions at the expense of its other activities; accurately conveying the specifics of these decisions; and treating the council and its members with respect. The implementation of these norms supports the council's authority in three general ways: by creating a sense of psychological distance between the authority and the reader; by rationalizing time and thereby reducing the reader's anxiety; and by providing symbolic reassurance.

CREATING PSYCHOLOGICAL DISTANCE

Psychological distance heightens the legitimacy of power holders. The *Herald*'s coverage of city council meetings creates psychological distance by using official language, referring to collective institutional decisions, using a respectful tone, depersonalizing, and giving minimum coverage to jurisdictional and procedural disputes. Some examples follow.

To achieve accuracy in reporting ordinances passed by the council, reporters sometimes quote directly from official language:

> Whereas there is a spirit of unrest and uneasiness now in evidence . . . be it ordained by the City Council . . . if any group of 25 or more persons desires to use any park, public street, or vacant lot facing a public street in the city for an assembly or group meeting,

that written notification be given to the Durham Police Department
at least 24 hours prior to the meeting.[2]

Quoting the actual law lends impact to the statements and may
impress the reader with the substance of the ordinance. It may
appear, however, to have been a decision made not by people but
by an authoritative collectivity which sits in a hallowed chamber
and hands down laws to protect the people of the city. Legal language adds a tone of legitimacy to the setting of council meetings
and to council decisions.

In fact, the *Herald* almost always speaks of decisions as being
made by "the council"[3] when in fact they are usually made by two
or three of the twelve council members who have particular knowledge of the question at hand. Although an article sometimes mentions who made the determining motion, this council member may
or may not be the same person who explained the details of the
problem to the other members and thus influenced their decisions.

Reporters further convey distance by writing stories in a tone
of respect. They infrequently mention personal jokes made by the
council members or describe individual idiosyncrasies. The articles are often simple accounts of motions and countermotions with
only cursory mention of the names involved. A typical opening
paragraph reads:

> The Durham City Council continued to hold a second demonstration
> control ordinance in abeyance Tuesday night by deferring action on
> the measure until the next regularly scheduled meeting. Two city
> laws aimed at controlling demonstrations were presented to the
> Council March 17. . . . A week later, the council by a nine-to-three
> vote approved an ordinance regulating use of Five Points Park "in
> promotion of public safety and welfare."[4]

To hold a decision "in abeyance" is formal and official in conno-
tation, and the image of the council presented here is highly impersonal.

When attending a council meeting, however, one was struck
by the distinctive personalities of the members exposed in revealing episodes. It was not rare to find one member dozing off to sleep
just as a vote was being taken on a crucial issue, or to see another
smacking on a large wad of gum while the intricacies of a public
housing dispute were discussed. The mayor, who wore a red car-
nation at all times, was inclined to add humor to the situation
whenever possible. After some elderly citizens requested that their

bus rates be reduced during certain slack ridership periods, including 7:00 p.m. to midnight, the mayor commented, "All I have to say is that if you plan to use the bus until midnight, you sure must have a bunch of swingers in your group." That the senior citizens made such a request was fully reported in the *Herald* the following day, but the mayor's comment was not.[5]

Finally, the *Herald* reports the substantial amount of council time devoted to jurisdictional disputes and bickering over procedures so briefly that those arguments do not diminish the council's distance from the citizenry. One example will show this and also illustrate the respectful tone and depersonalization just mentioned.

A large group of people went to the council meeting to protest a proposed public housing project. At this point in the design of the housing plan, the housing authority had control and it was doubtful that the council had any jurisdiction. The group of citizens, however, did not feel that they would be given the proper response to their protest if they took it to the housing authority, and thus came directly to the council. A long discussion over jurisdiction resulted among the council members, and when one suggested that it was not proper for the council to take any action at all, the audience booed and yelled. A motion was made to set up an investigation discussion committee. This resulted in another long discussion of who would comprise the committee. After this had been resolved, another question of procedure was raised as to whether the group should report to the housing authority or to the council. A suggestion by one councilman that it should be left up to the housing authority to consider the merits of the investigation findings resulted in more outcries from the audience, until it was finally decided that the group could report back to the council. The *Herald* report summarized this entire controversy quite neatly: "After much discussion of proper procedure, the offering of a motion, a substitute motion and a substitute for that, the Council voted overwhelmingly to look into the matter further."[6]

On the second page inside the paper, the account of the controversy over procedure is expanded, although still concisely and with no reference at all to the effect that the audience participation might have had in deciding the proper procedure in the case. The account of the controversy is at the end of the article, where it is susceptible to deletion.

This kind of coverage occurs because reporters have only a limited space in which to describe council activities. The most important of these activities, they believe (probably rightly), are the decisions reached and ordinances passed. Consequently, little space is devoted to the actions of individual council members, let alone their personal foibles and eccentricities. Moreover, the article cannot be filled with details of procedural and jurisdictional disputes. And to render complex ordinances accurately, it is useful simply to quote the formal legal language. The respectful tone which characterizes coverage of the council stems from the journalistic belief (still widely shared) that those in authority should be written about with respect (often whether they are worthy of such treatment or not). Reporters are therefore simply observing common journalistic norms as practiced particularly in small and medium-sized newspapers.

As a result, the city council is depicted as an authority-wielding body which is organized to deal with problems efficiently; which is responsive to the needs of the people without succumbing to pressure; and which reaches its collective decisions in an impersonal, depersonalized way. Consequently, psychological distance is maintained between the council and its members, on the one hand, and the public on the other; and the council's legitimacy is reinforced.

REDUCING ANXIETY BY RATIONALIZING TIME

One of people's greatest fears is that life may have no ultimate meaning or purpose. To overcome or at least to live and function within the overriding context of this fear, people order life around a concept of time as a progression of moments related to one another through some sort of continuum. Usually this sense of a time continuum is developed to harmonize with society's traditional sense of time. Meerloo observes that the "assimilation of self-time and tradition means the acceptance of authority"[7] and the reduction of anxiety.

The *Herald*'s articles on the council appear at regular intervals, invest the council's activity with meaning and coherence, and assert a temporal rationality. Consequently, they probably reduce the reader's potential or actual anxiety by complementing and facilitating his or her own attempts to develop a concept of time and to express it through verbal language. If Meerloo is right, this leads to a greater willingness to accept the council's legitimacy.

It is not, however, simply the regularity of council stories which reinforces the public's collective sense of time. To the *Herald*'s reporters the logical ordering of events is the demand of professionalism. One, who did not wish to be identified, commented that "often articles do not follow the order of the meeting itself. The reporter structures and orders the events artificially to try to make sense out of them. Often I join unrelated statements with things like, 'and X responded' when actually the statements are half an hour apart." In this way, the reader does not experience the council members' frustrations. Furthermore, the council appears capable of sifting through the complexity of issues to their very crux in order to reconcile difficulties quickly, easily, and gracefully.

Reporters sometimes reinforce this sense of rationality and temporal coherence by adding related material to the article when the story is unclear without it. In this way, no one moment is reported as being isolated from the mainstream. Life is depicted as essentially causal. That the final decision may not have been made for the reasons cited in the article but is rather a hasty "let's just settle this now and get it over with" action is rarely suggested.

Reporters further order time for the reader by summarizing the events of the meeting into a neat package. They find some incidents more important than others, highlight them in their articles, speed up time by omitting other events, and give readers the impression that, for the council, life is a continuous stream of important related moments. Since the existence of boredom and routine moments is not legitimized by recognition in the paper, it is as if they do not exist. The council, consequently, takes on an exceptionally vibrant and appealing image. Such is the result of professional reporting.

Symbolic Reassurance

Much governmental activity is essentially symbolic.[8] Myths, rites, and incantations reassure the public, leading to political quiescence and support of the prevailing institutions of authority. Often this works through what Lasswell calls the cathartic function of politics: the formulation of a resolution or law in no way specifically solves the substantive problem but somehow relieves the tension associated with the situation and directs the public's attention elsewhere.[9]

An example appeared in the *Herald* when the Chamber of Commerce concluded a study of housing in Durham and ceremoniously presented it to the city council. The *Herald* accurately reported the event, including the Chamber's recommendations and resolutions. But information extraneous to the specific ceremony was not adduced. For example, it was not mentioned that some of the people who made the study were allegedly the very individuals who build and maintain inadequate housing in the city. Thus the reader was probably left with the feeling of satisfaction that something would be done. Anxiety was diminished because plans for the solution of the problem had been presented in a neat package to the city council. Whether or not action was taken may have been irrelevant as far as the image of the city council is concerned because "people tend to judge a man by his goals, by what he is trying to do, and not necessarily by what he accomplishes or by how well he succeeds."[10]

The flow of symbolically reassuring actions from council to public is unwittingly facilitated not only by what is included in the *Herald*'s stories but by what is omitted. A survey of *Herald* articles revealed that the reporters rarely chose to write a story about an individual whose request was denied at a council meeting. Certainly it was news if a large group was denied its request, but the case of the isolated individual, often confused by administrative complexity, was not depicted.

An example: in one council meeting, well over an hour was spent deliberating over a sewage assessment that one man and his next-door neighbor had come to question. After much discussion, the council voted to keep the original assessment. The basic reason that the man had to pay a high fee was that he did not understand the procedure for petitioning the city to extend such service. He told the council that he had come to City Hall to find out the proper procedure, which he then followed, but that he had been given the wrong information. Nevertheless, he would have to pay because everyone else on the block suffered from misinformation and the council decided it would be too difficult to reimburse everyone. This decision came only after much discussion of laws which were not really applicable but served to confuse the petitioner, who was not very well educated. No mention of this discussion, which took one-third of the meeting to resolve, was made in the *Herald* article the next day.[11]

By adhering to the criterion of "interest to the most people," however, the reporter emphasized instead the actions of a senior citizens group. The headline read, "Group at Council Session Seeks Reduced Bus Rates for Elderly." [12] Thus the public is gratified that the city is considering helping its senior citizens rather than frustrated by the treatment the individual man received. The reporter simply chose to report the story which common sense decided had the most appeal. Because of his decision, the council's image as a highly authoritative, responsive governing body was undisturbed.

The newspaper's coverage would not be symbolically reassuring if the council granted requests from individuals and rejected them from groups. In practice, of course, the council is generally responsive to groups, or at least rarely explicitly negative (it tries to obfuscate when necessary). And some rejections of requests from groups (for example, of requests by blacks) are symbolically reassuring to substantial elements of the majority white population.

CAVEATS

Since the *Herald* study was conducted, cynicism about politics has increased substantially. As a result of the unsavory ambience that now envelops politicians, public attitudes toward council members as a class have no doubt soured. In addition, coverage in cities with a less politically inert populace and a more aggressive newspaper may differ.[13] Even in Durham, more controversies and demands have intruded upon the council, lessening its ability to appear as benevolently responsive to a consensual public interest. But the legitimacy of the city council as an institution endures; it is still thought the proper form of local governance.

There are two major reasons. First, the professional norms of journalists persist. They still inject legal and official language into stories, treat individual members respectfully (at least in print and to their faces), invest their depictions of meetings with rationality and coherence, and omit procedural disputes and small but potentially revealing council contacts with the idiosyncratic demands of individuals.

Second, perhaps more important, local government is not the source of most of the problems that have caused citizen disaffection—assassinations, Vietnam, recession, inflation. Nor is it perceived as the fount of solutions. Public expectations are low.

National government and officials have been the objects of the most intense disenchantment. Thought to be the most powerful, given to the most extravagant promises and pretensions (and media coverage), Washington politicians are the most vulnerable. The media have depicted their malefactions at some length, thereby contributing to political cynicism. The most publicized were the Watergate offenses of the Nixon administration. If anything should contradict our claim that the media faithfully uphold political legitimacy, it is Watergate.

Watergate

Because of the way they were reported by the mass media, the events collectively called Watergate never undermined the legitimacy of the American political system—and may have enhanced it. We shall show that there were four stages of coverage, to each of which the mass of the media reluctantly advanced when their prevailing focus was revealed as misleading. They began by neglecting the scandals, calling them a caper. Then, when events were thrust into prominence by investigations and hearings, the bulk of the press cooperated with Nixon's strategy of laying the blame on his associates—thereby preserving the legitimacy of the president and presidency. Then, as evidence of Nixon's guilt became overt, dramatic, and threatening, the media contributed to his downfall. But they then helped to resolve public disquiet without pursuing the underlying lessons of the corruption. They persisted in protecting the legitimacy of the presidency and of established institutions.

This media protection was not a racket perpetrated by a cabal of conniving journalists and class-conscious elites. As we have demonstrated throughout this book, such political effects grow out of the interaction of the media's conventional goals and practices with the manipulative efforts of power-holders and -seekers.

NON-EVENT (PHASE I)

Most of the baleful official actions together labeled Watergate occurred between 1969 and 1974. These events did not begin to be widely publicized until the spring of 1973. Had the press placed

Watergate on the public agenda sooner, subsequent events might have been different.

During the period July through October 1972, following the June break-in at Democratic party offices, less than 5 percent of television network news stories concerned government corruption. Many of these were not about the Watergate affair; a hot item was alleged profiteering from sales of wheat to Russia.

CBS was the only network that devoted more than passing attention to Watergate. The first extended ABC report was broadcast in April 1973. NBC and PBS took until May.[14] None of the networks did much original reporting. Most stories were brief mentions of charges appearing in the *Washington Post* or other papers, followed by Nixon administration denials.

Not that print journalism deserves much credit. Many of the *Post*'s scoops and those of the few other papers investigating the scandals were neglected by the rest of the country's press. Ben Bagdikian studied the nation's 30 largest papers. He found a third of the most important Watergate stories were not even carried, and most of the rest were not highlighted. Newspapers that had endorsed Nixon were particularly wont to ignore Watergate.[15]

Gallup polls revealed that around half the public had not heard of Watergate prior to election day; and a mere 3 percent mentioned government corruption as an important issue.[16] Watergate did not play a significant role in the 1972 election.

Why not? First, journalists then shared with most Americans an awe of the presidency. Av Westin, executive producer of the ABC Evening News at the time, later said that in 1972 he thought it "inconceivable that the scandal went to the Oval Office."[17] Presidents just did not do such things. Suggestions of presidential involvement were simply too discrepant to be accorded serious attention. Far easier to accept the administration's plausible explanation: a few overzealous underlings got carried away. Second, except for the obviously self-interested Democratic candidate, George McGovern (and Woodward and Bernstein's "Deep Throat"), no newsworthy member of the elite inside or out of government was voluntarily producing information on Watergate or manipulating the media in an effort to make the scandals a campaign issue.

The 1972 campaign did feature as a major issue the purported incompetence of the Democratic candidate. A study of voting in the election shows that public perception of McGovern's misman-

agement of his campaign was about as important as party identification as a direct influence on presidential voting.[18] This is
powerful testimony to the media's ability to create issues—and
non-issues. The press was full of stories about McGovern's poorly
run campaign and ill-suited, ill-starred, and just plain ill running
mate. Concurrently, Nixon and his staff were hatching and covering up buggings and break-ins, shaking down corporation heads for
contributions, and otherwise acting irrationally, given his enormous lead. And incompetently at that: they were caught. A year
later, Nixon's running mate, the hale, hearty, bluff, and relaxed
Spiro T. Agnew electrified the country and shocked an anxious
administration by copping a plea on a battery of felony charges
unrelated to Watergate.

WHAT DID THE MEDIA EXPLAIN AND WHEN DID THEY EXPLAIN IT?
(PHASE II)

The mass media began to cover Watergate extensively after
the election. But still legitimacy was preserved: guilt was laid not
on the political system, for a long time not even on the president,
but on Nixon's associates.

The Senate Watergate hearings are usually seen as the beginning of Nixon's end. They are portrayed as the epitome of the
virtues of the Constitution, with an independent legislative branch
combining with a free press to lay the truth before the court of
public opinion. Yet in many ways the media were remarkably
gentle with Nixon throughout most of 1973.

Certainly Watergate acquired all the qualities of a big news
carnival: conflict, drama, suspense, revelations, and polyglot personalities. Democratic elites began supplying Watergate information and other, Republican elites responded. Watergate finally
provided two-sided, partisan conflict. It had colorful clashing personalities: the feisty ethnic Judge John Sirica, homespun Senator
Sam Ervin, Jr. (D., N.C.), dourly foreboding John Mitchell.[19] Continuing new revelations were furnished by executive, legislative,
and judicial officials acting variously out of conviction, partisanship, ambition, and fear. These could all be pegged to the increasingly recognized Watergate theme.

In response, Nixon exploited other journalistic norms. As it
evolved, his strategy was to hide behind the symbols and legiti-

macy of the presidency and use his former aides, first John Dean and later John Mitchell, John Ehrlichman, and H. R. Haldeman, to deflect attention from his culpability. He knew that most GOP members would find the idea of presidential involvement unbelievable and threatening to their own interests. Given the media's norms of partisan balance and respect for the presidency, his own possible guilt would not be stressed until Republicans in official positions joined his accusers.

We have evidence from both the print and electronic media. One researcher examined *Chicago Tribune* and *Chicago Daily News* and the three networks' stories during the five weeks of key Senate testimony in 1973 by Dean, Mitchell, Ehrlichman, and Haldeman. He found "no evidence of a monolithic determination to convict the president in the press."[20] The most publicized Watergate stories were those with particularly dramatic appeal, such as Ehrlichman's quotable metaphors and emotional speeches by committee members.[21]

Our own analysis of CBS Evening News coverage supports these findings. A count was made of the number of times that stories contained direct, explicit assertions (by sources or reporters themselves) that Nixon or other administration officials were guilty of illegal acts.[22] A large majority of the assertions of criminal guilt were directed at Nixon's subordinates during the major Watergate events of 1973.

The polls indicate Watergate coverage during the summer of 1973, when the scandal received the most concentrated attention because of the hearings, had relatively little effect on public opinion. Findings of a June 1 Gallup survey—taken before any key witnesses testified—were nearly identical to those taken September 7–10, after all the major officials had appeared.[23] Other Gallup polls showed that in late June, 18 percent of the public favored Nixon's impeachment and removal. By mid-August this had increased only to 23 percent.[24]

The media reported the hearings and investigations. Following journalistic norms, they mostly refrained from making explicit judgments of guilt. They dutifully transmitted Nixon's assertions of his innocence. And that is precisely the point. Myths of a crusading and autonomous press notwithstanding, media protection of the public from official corruption relies upon and is limited to other officials' definitions of guilt. Reporting must give both parties' spokespersons equal play. Undermining of Nixon's personal authority was limited by the blindness and timidity of most Republican (and many Democratic) elites, who long refused to believe what the evidence indicated.

THE LIGHT DAWNS LATE (PHASE III)

The sheer number of accusations should not be taken as the sole measure of media handling of Richard Nixon. In the fall of 1973, questions about the Watergate break-in and spying were superseded by doubts about Nixon's willingness to comply with the Constitution. He resisted judicial orders, congressional subpoenas, and prosecutors' requests: he began convicting himself, and in eminently newsworthy fashion.

If journalists had persisted in treating Nixon with the total neglect of 1972 or the benign neglect of most of 1973, public opinion and elite pressures might not have changed. Instead, the media heavily covered the unusual events that his doomed and desperate defense inexorably required. His guilt loomed implicit in his creation of these events, which were compelling fare for the press. They were dramatic, involving high officials in unprecedented constitutional confrontation; they were threatening, displaying the chief protector of the political order in decidedly disorderly conduct. Yet, unlike the events in the previous two phases, they did not require investigation or even questioning of the president; they were public and overt.

The media did not suddenly start directly asserting Nixon's guilt or quoting those who did: our analysis of CBS showed most guilt was still being attributed to subordinates, right up until Nixon's resignation. But implication, innuendo, story placement, and repetition—even coverage of Nixon's protesting avowals of innocence (see Chapter 4)—propelled his downward spin in public and elite esteem. The major stories were the "Saturday Night Massacre," the IRS's realization that the president owed several hundred thousand dollars in income taxes, his release of expletive-deleted and doctored but to many people still incriminating taped conversations, and finally the House Impeachment Committee vote. Gallup polls show three large jumps in public support of impeachment: to 37 percent after the "massacre," 51 percent after the tax and tape publicity, and 65 percent after the committee decision.[25]

Sometimes the media's negative contribution was quite subtle. Under normal circumstances, public officials are dignified in two conspicuous ways by television coverage. First, they are usually shown in their work environments, engaged in activities purportedly benefiting the public. Second, in contrast to ordinary people, they are framed at a respectable and respectful personal distance by the camera—no tight close-ups or demeaning camera angles for them. Deviations from these visual conventions disrupt, even undermine, the aura of authority.

The stake-outs that were so prominent a part of Watergate coverage violated normal TV practices. As they rushed from house to courthouse, the options of the members of the Nixon administration were limited undignifiedly to evading questions, pleading to be left alone, refusing to respond, declining even to acknowledge the cameras and reporters, or fleeing. Whether the Nixon minions were polite or curt, the impression left by moving hand-held cameras, abrupt close-ups, long shots of rear views—of public officials as prey—were not authority-enhancing.

From Personal Tragedy to Collective Triumph (Phase IV)

Consider the event: the forced resignation of a president after two years' recitation of unethical and illegal acts. Then Gerald Ford became president: a man not popularly elected but appointed —by Richard Nixon. These events could have raised doubts about the legitimacy of the American political system. They did not. Mass media messages helped transform the nightmare into fantasy. The main themes were: Ford's goodness and his legitimate, fortunate accession to the presidency; Nixon's personal tragedy; and the marvelous functioning of the institutional mechanisms and governing values that led to Nixon's ouster. These themes were visible in both the words and the visual imagery that accompanied the transition.

Thus the *Time* and *Newsweek* issues published the week following the transition (August 19, 1974) contained 38 photographs of President Ford. Three of the photos in each magazine juxtaposed Ford with an American flag, prime symbol of the nation. Both magazines offered pictures of him as a young boy, in college football regalia, with the young Betty Ford, with former Senate Republican leader Everett Dirksen of Illinois, at his swearing-in by

Chief Justice Warren Burger, swinging on the golf links, bobbing in a swimming pool, smiling with his attractive children. Unlike all his predecessors, Ford had been elected neither vice president nor president. He might have been considered a usurper who represented only Nixon and a few hundred cronies in Congress. This coverage conveyed a different impression.

The magazine portraits gave his ascension continuity with prior transitions. New presidents are always honored with television and magazine pictorials showing the fresh leader's rise from boyhood to manhood to power. By evoking the aura of previous, normal changeovers, the coverage helped legitimize both Ford and his office. The depictions probably reflected habit, in part: it was a presidential succession, however peculiar. Lacking any other frame for illustrating it, the periodicals fell back upon prior experience. The treatment may also have been deliberate. Media owners were concerned to reinforce the legitimacy of the system—and of their own organizations, which had been charged with taking the Watergate story beyond the bounds of objectivity and patriotism.[26]

Newspapers and television were as blatant. In editorials published during the three days after Nixon's resignation, the *Washington Post* asserted five times that Ford's assumption of the presidency was "legitimate." It praised Ford's "candor" and "openness" twice; the *New York Times* did so four times. Wide public support for Ford was invoked (without benefit of survey evidence) four times by each paper. Both repeatedly praised the workings of the system, the continued vitality of its institutions.[27]

"Tragedy and Triumph" in the *Times* encapsulated the themes dominating editorializing in the mass media: hortatory rhetoric, dripping with symbolism:

> Irrespective of political differences, President Ford has the Congress and the people behind him during these difficult days of transition. While at this time there can be nothing but pity for his shattered predecessor, there is universally warm support for Mr. Ford even among his adversaries. . . . Mr. Ford has one supreme advantage. He took his solemn oath of office secure in the knowledge that the country stands firm, the structure unshaken, the genius of American democracy renascent. Out of the morass of Watergate, the nation has planted its feet on solid ground again. Out of the tragedy of Mr. Nixon has evolved the triumph of America.

CBS was no different. In the instant analysis after Nixon's resignation speech, Dan Rather said:

I think it may very well go down when history takes a look at it as one of Richard Nixon's if not his finest hour. It needs to be made clear and can't be re-emphasized too often, I think, as I think the president made clear in his speech, there is no joy in this for anyone. No decent thinking American could take any joy out of this. That sadness is tempered for many with awe, awe for the constitutional process, what we sometimes call the system, which worked magnificently. It was that constitutional process, it was a process of law which brought us to this moment. The president in his speech made clear that he respects that, he understands that, he has that appreciation and that awe for it. He did give, and I would agree with Walter [Cronkite] what you said, he gave to this moment a touch of class, more than that a touch of majesty, touching that nerve in most people that says to their brain: "We revere the presidency, we respect the president; the republic and the country comes first."[28]

CONCLUSION

No need now to dispute either the validity of these observations or the sincerity of the journalists—deeply committed to system legitimacy—who made them. But there are two questions which must be asked. First, were alternative explanations and analyses possible?

As one example, Americans could have been told by at least a few reporters, editorial writers, columnists and pundits that the Watergate scandal was not attributable only to Nixon's personal flaws but also revealed profound moral contradictions in American values; the fragility of constitutional freedoms and the flimsiness of many power holders' commitments to them; and the total inadequacy of elite recruitment mechanisms. Richard Nixon, a man of questionable moral and mental character,[29] was repeatedly nominated for high office; the media were derelict in not more forcefully and fully revealing his character earlier. From this perspective, Watergate was not Nixon's "fault"; it was the fruition of his character and the political system which nurtured him.

The second important question is whether the interpretation of events propagated by the mass of the mass media became prevalent among the public. The answer is yes. Many Americans saw the upshot of Watergate as a reaffirmation of the vitality of American institutions. Distrust of incumbent government officials in general (surface level political cynicism) did not increase much during

Watergate. New antipathy was balanced by a new sense of trust on the part of some people impressed with the way Nixon was handled. And there was no evidence that alienation deepened to include a rejection of political system legitimacy.[30] It appears that mass media coverage helped to maintain the legitimacy of American institutions in potentially threatening circumstances.[31]

The media are prime agencies of adult political socialization. Through them, the system is made to seem right and good even after it has been headed by illegitimate officials who commit illegal acts.

Mass Media and Public Disaffection

There are those who would dispute our analysis. The mass media, they claim, dissolve rather than cement citizen loyalty. They point to a new class of New York and Washington, D.C., journalists whose members encourage impossible demands on government, scornfully deride the legitimacy of power holders, and promote the views of malcontent groups of blacks and feminists. These critics cite as evidence surveys showing a precipitous increase in public cynicism about politics since 1964. Some also trot out studies purporting to expose an overwhelming liberal bias in television news.[32] These complaints overlook too much.

Citizen loyalty is not only based on ideas taught and reinforced by the media, but also on actual experience. Contradiction is therefore likely if the system fails to deliver on its promises; disillusionment may ensue.

Roughly between World War II and the early sixties, a generation was socialized to believe that America offers guaranteed liberty and justice for all based on limitless growth and the altruistic use of international power. Dissenting voices rarely reached news or entertainment media. Then reality intervened. Some blacks, some poor, some students, some women became unruly. Vietnam obtruded.

National officials faced enormous political and economic obstacles in responding successfully to the passions of the 1960s. Pleasing both sides of a sometimes polarized public was not easy, it was impossible. Government actions did not bring immediate equality to the downtrodden—or force them back into docility. Short of nuclear war, government could not provide both peace and victory in Vietnam.

Journalists for the major media, themselves similarly social-ized, were surprised, even dismayed by the inadequacies of their government.[33] Unable or unwilling to trace these failures to struc-tural limitations, they resorted to personalization. They blamed officials for being unresponsive or incompetent. This coverage pro-voked both left and right. Once the flurry of Great Society legisla-tion was blown away by Vietnam, liberals became frustrated by inadequate government responses to the causes of peace and equality. Conservatives reacted against permissiveness toward law-breaking demonstrators and welfare cheats. The mass media contributed to superficial cynicism about politics by indicting poli-ticians.

But it is one thing to believe that politicians are uncaring or bumbling or corrupt. Such views merely assert that the people occupying certain institutional roles are behaving badly or im-properly. These are surface level beliefs. There is a vast gulf be-tween that stance and rejecting the legitimacy of authoritative institutions and values—the deep level. Disaffection at this funda-mental level has not increased.[34] One reason: the mass media have never given powerless Americans the necessary information to link the ubiquitous rotten apples to the structure of the barrel. Nor do they offer alternatives to the reigning system.

The powerful should be grateful. Media practices helped pre-vent erosion of legitimacy despite the public's frustration and anx-iety. Instead of revolt, surface level alienation was constrained, issuing largely in apathy and resignation. Such feelings may lower voting participation, thereby even redistributing power to the pow-erful.[35]

Under certain conditions, such as a major depression, surface level disaffection may become virulent. With a discordant enough reality, it could deepen into mass rejection of the legitimacy of the political and economic system. But if the hordes ever do rise up, the mass media will not be in the vanguard.

CHAPTER TEN

•

That's Not (Just) Entertainment

"I believe television is providing quality across the board. Tune in any of the three commercial networks any day and you'll find quality. You'll find expertly produced program schedules responsibly meeting today's entertainment and informational needs in a contemporary, meaningful, and human way."

> NBC President Fred Silverman (former executive at both CBS and ABC)

"Thib loses his sight after a car crash, and two drug-crazed teenagers turn a gas station into a fiery inferno."

> *240-Robert*—ABC Network, October 15, 1979

"Barnaby attempts to foil a sinister plan to drive his wealthy but emotionally disturbed niece insane."

> *Barnaby Jones*—CBS Network, October 18, 1979

"Kate and her partner Det. Sgt. Varrick uncover an extortion racket which forces suburban housewives into prostitution."

> *Kate Loves a Mystery*—NBC Network, October 18, 1979

POLITICAL LEGITIMACY is not rootless. It is sustained and nurtured by support for the social system; by people's beliefs that the way they and most other Americans lead their lives—their habits, goals, self-images and general world views—are natural and right.

Otherwise they are likely to begin pressing disruptive demands upon government for social change. The mass media help perpetuate social legitimacy. In this chapter we explain why. Although similar arguments could be made of most Hollywood movies, popular music, magazine fiction and comic books,[1] we focus on commercial network television. For in the typical home, the television set is on for more than six hours each day. Over 40 percent of all free time excluding sleep, over three-quarters of all the time Americans devote to the mass media, is now spent in front of television sets.[2]

Saturation

To the casual viewer, television fare may appear as a relief from the rigors of the day, a diversion, an opportunity to watch attractive women and aggressive men cavort across the screen. In reality, all that "entertainment" and advertising is saturated with political meaning. Television teaches its audience about the options their society offers, the norms it enforces; about the expectations, values and standards of judgment Americans apply and should apply to life.[3] In this way, television goes beyond the provision of reassurance, vicarious participation, diversion, escape; it socializes.

Theodor Adorno penetrated the mystique of television politics well:

> The "hidden meaning" emerges simply by the way the story looks at human beings; thus the audience is invited to look at the characters in the same way [as the story] without being made aware that indoctrination is present . . . th[e] message is hidden only by a style which does not pretend to touch anything serious and expects to be regarded as featherweight. Nevertheless, even such amusement tends to set patterns for the members of the audience without their being aware of it.[4]

Consider the 1979 one-hour season premiere of *Kate Loves a Mystery* whose synopsis we gave in the chapter epigraph. The extortionists who blackmail the housewives into prostitution are a bartender and an obviously evil hood, both apparently unmarried. Of course, the victimized women should not have been in the bar in the first place; television condemns daytime drinking by both

sexes and solitary evening drinking in bars by women. The housewives profit little from their activity. One ends up murdered. The
male villains take most of the earnings of the rest. And it is made
perfectly clear that the women in no way enjoy their illegitimate
sexual experiences. Prostitution is certainly evil, sex outside marriage almost as bad.

One of the housewives persists in prostitution because her
husband is out of work. But his unemployment is caused not by
economic conditions but because he is waiting for "the job"—one
which pays $65,000 a year. When his wife confesses how she
makes her money, he, having been under the impression she was
working as a secretary, slaps her—hard. Then they embrace. We
assume he will give up his unrealistic aspirations and go to work.
She will return to hearth and home, or really become a secretary.

Vivacious and appealing, Kate Columbo is a reporter.
Through her individual efforts the villains will be apprehended.
She goes to the bar pretending to be a housewife prostitute. Going
to a bedroom with a laughably passionate, overweight man, she
uses her radiant feminine charm to stay unsullied and persuade him
to return with renewed love to his wife and family. The prime
villain kidnaps Kate, ordering her to drive to a destination where a
bad fate awaits her. She frustrates his plot by driving so fast she
attracts several police cars who pursue her as she returns to the
bar. The villain is confused, having apparently never seen this ploy
in old movies. After her exertions, Kate reaffirms her femininity
by collapsing in the arms of her policeman friend, who drives her
home. Meanwhile, the bartender has conveniently confessed. The
police get their men. Everything is happily resolved; traditional
values reinforced, but with a nod in the direction of a suitably
liberated woman.

Creed

Entertainment and advertising are created by individuals—
writers, producers, directors, actors and actresses, camera operators, et al.—working within bureaucracies at networks, production
companies or advertising agencies. Individuals' personal goals are
variously satisfied and frustrated, but usually bent into well-paid
service of organizational needs and practices. The overriding need:
to maximize profits. This does not mean that every show is aimed

at the largest, lowest common denominator audience; programs are often designed for different segments of the population. But once the demographic thrust is determined, the objective is to attract as many of its members as possible.[5] Other factors affecting production—technology, professional norms, individual beliefs—are largely shaped by the profit motive. Unlike the news, entertainment need serve no myths of community service or public interest; there are few obstacles in the way of unbridled profit seeking.

The result is a set of informally codified imperatives which define entertainment. Like their cousins, news definitions, they generally appear self-evident and non-political to those who, often automatically and unconsciously, act on and abide by them. They set the boundaries of expression and direct the kinds of appeals television entertainment and commercials make in their pursuit of the audience.

This basic entertainment creed is internalized by media personnel. It has two parts:

- Hew to the familiar social values and practices, long-socialized by all cultural institutions (including the media themselves). This awakens recognition and identification (and prevents disturbance) of the widest possible audience.
- Appeal to new trends in order to stay abreast or ahead of the competition but do not go so far as to violate the first principle.

These tenets translate into more specific guidelines and axioms for television producers: personalized conflict draws viewer interest; viewers seek to identify with characters and solutions and want a main hero around whom most action revolves; continuity of setting and character reassures viewers; the truly unfamiliar is disquieting, though "novelty" that basically conforms to established mores is titillating, intriguing and must be catered to; visual imagery must continually move and change to maintain attention.

How similar these are to news definitions! And underlying them all is a common assumption: television must appeal to the largest possible audiences or to the largest portion of the targeted audience subgroups.

These entertainment-advertising imperatives have three significant political effects. First, much television content simply reinforces the basic values on which American society operates. Competitive individualism, success, Social Darwinism, and consequent unequal status and wealth are embodied in the programs' characters, plots, and morals.

Second, in their striving to hold and expand audiences, television executives compulsively detect and inevitably spread new social attitudes, behavior, and trends. The social status quo is disrupted. Television is no stern purveyor of conservative morality, rigidly guarding against change in social mores. Instead it stimulates changes; but it renders them compatible with continued social legitimacy. For in a dynamic society like the United States, political legitimacy and an acceptable social system require continuous modifications and adjustments in the particular values and practices that at any one time comprise the accepted social order. Responding to the profit urge, the television production mechanism contributes to stable legitimacy by helping to alter social values incrementally, to take the oppositional bite out of social innovation.

Yet, third, television content rouses dissatisfaction. Implicitly, through the affluent homes, surroundings, and lifestyles of its characters; explicitly, in hectoring advertising; it tells viewers that their lives are insufficient and inadequate. But the discontent is apolitical, channeled into the acquisition of products.

To see how television manages superficial change in social values and practices while maintaining the social system's legitimacy, we shall briefly sample four of its major genres. They are sports, medical dramas, situation comedies, and commercials. We lamentably lack space to deal with religious programs, game shows, and soap operas—all of which blatantly purvey their social values.

Reinforcement

SPORTS

Sports seen in person are different from those seen on television. On the scene, a baseball or football game conveys contradictory impressions: competition and cooperation, individual striving yet also self-sacrifice, desire for victory but also joy in the very playing of the game. But because decisions about which events and players to show in a game, about which of the season's contests to cover, are determined by the aim of maximizing audiences, television puts individual games into contexts that emphasize competition, individualism, and success.

Each season sees the acting out of Social Darwinism, reinforcing many Americans' belief in the continued appropriateness of the "survival of the fittest" ethos. For each season starts with an array of teams from across the United States. They differ in strengths and weaknesses, in potential for success. There are last year's champion, leading contenders, dark horses. The teams' performances are a perpetual focus of media coverage, which includes polls purportedly gauging their standings. Tension and viewers' interest are stimulated by a series of contests, continuing throughout the season, which inevitably and inexorably eliminate the contestants. Indeed, the essential importance of each contest is defined for the audience in terms of its outcome, its bearing on the standings.[6] Primarily covered are the games bearing on the league championship, the ones involving high-ranking teams from major markets. The game of the week rarely includes the games of the weak.

At the climax, the champion is enshrined. One team reached the top, the others failed. Thus each season portrays Social Darwinism as surely as Greek tragedies depicted winners and losers according to the dominant values of that era. But if teams were populated by anonymous players rotated each week from team to team, win–loss records would be meaningless, championships absurd. Television would be deprived of its continuing theme, suspense, and budding climax. Viewers' interest would have to be engaged solely by the intrinsic merits of each game.

Although the stress on outcome over process in sports coverage has other sources in American culture (and in the need of the teams to attract a paying audience), the media foster and even increase this emphasis to maximize interest. The striking similarity between television coverage of sports events and presidential elections is not coincidental.

The ambiguous value implications of sporting events are also transformed into firm reinforcement of American individualism and competitiveness by the particular way actual games are portrayed by television. One close analysis of televised football found that the camera focused overwhelmingly on the ball carrier. The effect was to exclude the players not directly involved in advancing (or stopping) the ball. Viewers were infrequently shown the overall symmetry of the game—the dependence of the fleet backs and ends on the solid linemen. Football appeared less a team sport than a series of individual performances. Announcers underlined this picture by emphasizing individual personalities, especially stars', in describing the action. The game itself was made to appear more exciting and violent than it is by such visual techniques as cuts and zooms and by amplifying the roar of the crowd.[7]

American individualism and competitiveness triumph over team cooperation in football coverage. Our impression is that the same is true in most team sports. An exception may be basketball, where the team effort is visible even on television because there are only ten players confined in a small playing space. But even here, individual "stars" are highlighted.

With sports such as golf, tennis, and boxing, individualism becomes the major motif. Players' careers are often mythologized, elevated into Horatio Alger stories: hard work and a modicum of fortune yield fame, riches, glory. The vast majority of tennis professionals, golfers, and boxers who barely earn a living (if that) are omitted; losers are rarely entertaining. Again Social Darwinism reverberates. And there are always new stars rising to replace fading ones; competition is unceasing, the position at the top insecure, the best always getting better. And this, after all, is fair, for there would be no space for new winners if old ones refused to give way. The saga of individual athletes forms an unconscious allegory (and justification) for the mythical capitalist free market, where only the fittest corporations survive and prosper.

The pervasiveness of sports coverage in the conversation of most American males attests to the wide reach of this ritualistic support of the system's underlying myths. Watching sports on television consumes many male Americans' leisure time. It encompasses weekends and is expanding through the nights of the week. The more uncertain their lives, the more dolorous the country's economic circumstances, the more Americans seem to turn to watching television sports—which reinforce some of the very values helping to produce their economic woes.

MEDICAL DRAMAS

The glories of individualism glow throughout the disease and distress of the medical drama genre which, with one hero or another, survives on television. The makers of such shows take particular pains to achieve a semblance of realism. And audiences do identify; many people have undergone close personal experiences with serious illness. There is a built-in familiarity, a deep-seated emotional connection, that is missing from most other programs. The realism convinces many Americans: the "Marcus Welby, M.D." show received over 250,000 letters during its first five years addressed to the good doctor, most seeking medical advice.[8]

What impression of American medical care, its practitioners and institutions, do television viewers receive from such shows? Analyzing the "Welby" series, Michael Real concluded that there "emerged a view of health care in which fatherly concern and personal attention abound, bureaucracies and mechanical deper-sonalization do not exist, and every patient receives the best that money can buy."[9] Another scholar closely examined 15 doctor shows. Each contained a medical problem and a personal crisis of some sort. In 40 percent of the programs the medical treatment was successful, in 40 percent its results were unclear, and in 20 percent it failed. But in all cases, the doctor's help led to a satisfactory resolution of the personal dilemma.[10] And television's patients never seem to have to pay their doctors, let alone have difficulty paying them.

The overall portrait: doctors are generous, courageous, inventive, and attentive. They do everything humanly possible to cure physical ailments. Then they go beyond the call of duty to reduce the accompanying psychic malaise. Certainly they well deserve their enormous incomes, high prestige, and unbridled control over the American health care system. Individualism and free enterprise triumph again.

CONVENTIONS

Television's conventions also provide more subtle reinforcing cues that make the social hierarchy seem natural, thus legitimate. Scholars have found that women characters in television fiction are pictured as less smart, powerful, and stable than men; women are also younger than men, and more likely to be victims than perpetrators of violence.[11] Language used by characters mirrors hierarchy. Women in television shows tend to issue commands only about areas where females are usually authoritative, in traditional roles. Males give broader, action-oriented directives.[12] Program titles and dialogues reproduce the society's pecking order as well. Shows about working class or low status characters are usually called by first or last names alone ("Laverne and Shirley") and addressed by the same tags in dialogue. Doctors and lawyers are addressed by their formal titles; only peers, never patients, called Dr. Welby "Marc."[13]

Sanitized Change

SITUATION COMEDIES

Most situation comedies directly reinforce traditional stereotypes, roles, and values, and reduce personal conflicts and problems to the most banal level. And yet, beneath the laughs, some situation comedies do tend to reflect, foster, and sometimes foist social change more than most other genres of television and entertainment. Take Mary Tyler Moore. In her long-running, now widely syndicated series, she played an independent career woman whose life did not revolve around finding, keeping, losing, or weeping over a man. She was more liberated in this respect than television's typical females—wives or man-chasers all (but rarely both except in soap operas). There were suggestions she had occasional sex with the men she dated; her job sometimes involved exerting authority (though she was not in charge and called her boss "Mr. Grant"); she had genuine friendships with men and women, married and single.

In these ways, at least when the show first appeared on television, it reflected changing sex roles which were more characteristic of major urban areas than the rest of the country. The notion of female independence was introduced, legitimized, and restated week after week. Unlike much news coverage of feminism, with its negative, bra-burning symbolism, Mary Tyler Moore and her cohorts offered faintly political messages in ways women and men with unraised consciousness could understand. The show communicated new options to many women living more traditional lives.

But the show fit the new situation into essential conformity with the old society. Mary was no radical lesbian, nor even an admitted feminist; her stance against sexism was limited to demands for equal pay and respect. These goals are increasingly compatible with historic American values; their legitimacy is diffi-

cult to question openly (if easy to ignore in practice). More important, the problems Mary had as a modern woman, which provided
many of the laughs, were always resolved through Mary's personal
and quintessentially feminine good will and tact. Each week's conclusion implied that the conflicts which arise between and among
the sexes as women change are not serious, do not involve institutional oppression or personal suffering. Nor are the conflicts political in either source or cure: they are amenable to solution on an
individual, *ad hoc* basis. To have played it otherwise would have
transformed the show from comedy to controversy.

Even the challenge to traditional women's roles was meek.
Witness the supporting cast of characters. There were vain Ted
and his lame-brained girl friend, Georgette; macho boss man Lou;
conniving female rival Sue Ann; good-natured family man Murray;
and man-starved Rhoda. Every one fulfilled sexual stereotypes.
Joking about their peccadillos may have produced laughs; it also
trivialized serious problems caused by frozen attitudes and un-
changing behavior. The characters were funny because they fit
familiar cultural archetypes. Otherwise they would have been up-
setting or boring—and Mary might have lost her audience.

Indeed, Mary herself was nothing so much as a contemporary
earth mother, ministering to her flock of neurotics with infinitely
generous doses of wisdom and warmth. Grant Tinker, Moore's
husband and producer of the show, told an interviewer that Mary
"does come close, in her 1970s version, to the good old-fashioned
virtues. . . . The show appears to be rather hip on TV, but in fact
she and all the characters in that show—forgetting their comedic
eccentricities—are all four-square people." [14]

The show was one of many media products helping to channel
public understanding of women's liberation into relatively manage-
able directions.[15] As with the news, the redefinition or containment
of conflict emerges as a key function of the media, which protect
the overall order by discouraging a political understanding of personal experience and current events.[16]

Attempts to use comedy as vehicles of social comment, like
"All in the Family," similarly founder. Archie Bunker's supposedly radical son-in-law was a warmed-over 1950s liberal. The
"controversies" were usually over such barely burning issues as
open housing and whether women, Jews, and Italians are human
beings. Bunker's irascible bigotry, played for laughs, stripped his
attitudes of the fear, evil and hatred they cause in real life. Not

surprisingly, then, people perceive the program as supporting their values: racists tend to believe it endorses prejudice.[17]

COMMERCIALS

Because they want maximum sales, advertisers try to avoid annoying any substantial segment of the (target) audience. Network program officers are similarly cautious in order to maximize audience size and commercial fees. This common interest among advertisers and networks produces ubiquitous commercials that protect the dominant values of society—the ones which, by definition, are the most widely shared.

And yet commercials often reflect and promote new trends as sponsors and their advertising agencies seek to capitalize on fads and fashions. Thus advertisements tend to disturb the status quo by promoting new trends. The effect, however, is to incorporate change into traditional values. This can be seen in the ways television advertisements use sex and race.

Commercials often cater to sexual stereotypes. Women are usually pictured as dim-witted housewives or sex objects. They are used as sex objects in promoting products aimed at men because few appeals to the male subconscious can stir such deep, behavior-motivating associations as sex. Commercials featuring housewives, in turn, are pitched precisely to the many women whose careers involve the acquisition of household products.[18]

This use of women in advertisements follows the sexual division of labor and the consumption decisions in American society. Advertisers seek merely to make the most effective appeal to the group most likely to buy the product in the society as it now exists.[19]

But society is changing. From commitment or economic necessity or both, more and more women enter the gainfully employed labor force. Individually and through organized groups, more and more women assert their demands for equality of opportunity and treatment. Advertisers respond. Commercials show apparently independent women in increasing numbers. Yet the basic message remains the same: precisely because the female executive is so busy, she needs a particularly effective (but natural) hair dye or pain reliever to retain her allure. Television commercials announce that women's liberation has already been achieved. They define it to embrace the basic American value so dear to the heart of advertisers: the freedom to consume a wider variety of products. New opinions are channeled into compatibility with product sales. Advertising tames women's liberation, makes it safe for consumer exploitation.[20]

Commercial racism tells the same story. For many years, blacks were invisible in television advertisements. Advertisers believed that blacks constituted an insignificant market, raised dark associations among many white consumers, and looked unnatural in advertisements featuring middle class whites.

Realization of the black market plus political pressures have succeeded in making blacks quite common in commercials. They are usually shown as part of a group of typical, happily consuming, middle class Americans in some salubrious environment.

Their presence may contribute to social change in the form of the diminution of racism by showing that all blacks are not cops, crooks, or athletes (their principal entertainment functions). But by depicting blacks and whites the same way in advertisements, television promotes myths that have undermined black progress and legitimizes a social system in which blacks are still handicapped, in which most blacks still lag economically well behind whites. For television advertisements suggest that integration and equality have arrived under the umbrella of a consuming society. Omitted and ignored are the frustrated, economically deprived lower class blacks, and logically so from the point of view of advertisers, who are selling middle class products to a mostly-white audience. RCA is unlikely to promote the desirability of its products by showing angry ghetto blacks storming a store and carting off portable color televisions.

Each vivid, carefully crafted television advertisement—and all of them taken together—present the public with evidence of the truth of America's social and political self images applied to the market place. Commercials suggest that by competing for customers by advertising, corporations are responsive to consumers. With seductive visual techniques, commercials graphically show that Americans have numerous options to consume highly attractive goods that fulfill people's needs—choices that appear free and uncoerced.

Commercials redefine individualism in ways that would dismay the Founding Fathers. It becomes the consumption of material goods in conformity with the styles and standards set by advertising. No longer does individualism mean control over political decisions—or even personal ones; no longer does it involve altering or abolishing outmoded or oppressive structures. Advertising defangs American individualism, working against its socially and politically revolutionary meanings, channeling individual strivings toward easily controlled non-political outlets.[21]

Discontent

And yet, in ways barely comprehended and unintended, television provokes dissonance and may even undermine some conventional values. For many Americans are drawn and devoted to the world portrayed on television. They take it seriously. They use its fiction-based nostrums and homilies to try to deal with their personal problems. The result: television's reality puts the lives most Americans lead to shame.

The television world is a dramatic place, peopled by unusual characters living vibrant and, if they are protagonists, felicitous lives. Television drama, which is present in American lives to a degree unprecedented in human history, presents clear plots, clear conflicts, definite heroes and villains, and always resolution. Television's inhabitants do not wait in traffic or ticket or restaurant lines; cars do not break down; convenient parking spaces are invariably available. The shows' heroes, even when they are stereotyped uneducated working class ethnics, are facile with words and usually physically attractive. Most main characters are fiscally comfortable and live at a standard far higher than their income would allow. Exceptions are duly noted and derided, and become main sources of conflict or laughs.

Sadly, real life rarely offers the kinds of clear-cut conflicts and unequivocal solutions that are the staple of television. Nor are motivations as transparent, truths as fathomable, villains as evil, heroes as virtuous. People, processes, things, do not work so smoothly.

Before the advent of television, people rarely saw in their own homes so many moving images of extraordinary physical beauty or encountered thoroughly competent and well-adjusted heroes, or were familiar with families where father and mothers were always understanding with each other and their children. Now, television viewers behold a continual parade of pulchritudinous females and striking males, ideal families, or, more frequently, joyously swinging singles who have no family burdens at all.

In comparison, most Americans lead lives that are mundane, even drab. They may be brought invidiously to compare the quality of their sex, love, family, and personal possessions with those shown so persistently on the screen. Few doctors can best the deep wells of empathy and wisdom of their television counterparts. Few police are as tough and cool as television's heroic lawmen. To many men, nurtured and tutored by television in the make-up of female desirability, few women are as alluring as Charlie's Angels. Few children are as cute as the television moppets who romp through life under the benevolent if frenetic guidance of one or more parents. Few families are as resolute and united as the members of "Little House on the Prairie" and "The Waltons"—nostalgic invocations of a mythical American past.

The failure to measure up can result in shame, guilt, confusion, and frustration. They may even combine with other complex causes to increase social pathology: rising rates of child abuse, infidelity, divorce, and depression—and the concomitant vast consumption of prescription and non-prescription drugs which television fosters.

Television can also reduce people's self-esteem and feelings of control over their lives. There is a class component to this effect. The viewers most likely to feel inadequate as a result of televised pseudo-reality are the vast majority of Americans whose lives are not portrayed. With few exceptions, television is inhabited by white, upper-middle-class families headed by a professional. The lower classes and the poor appear—when they do at all—as delinquents, loafers, criminals, or objects of comedy. So working class people behold on television mostly an unobtainable middle class ideal with which to compare their own lives. They cannot meet the standards of dress and diction of these characters, share their aspirations, or afford the luxuries television takes for granted.

Reams of research show that self-esteem and a sense of understanding and control over one's environment are prime psychological bases for tolerance of diversity, equality, and change.[22] By reducing these qualities among the members of the lower classes, television may be contributing to the susceptibility of some viewers to autocratic or demagogic politicians.

Expectations roused by television entertainment about the solution and resolution of public issues compound the effects just described. For the definitions and forms of news and entertainment are similar. Both are dramatic, personalized, conveyed as narrative. Both have stars (anchormen and -women) and continuing characters (correspondents). But unlike entertainment, the conflicts and problems of politics, the public issues, are rarely resolved by the end of the news—or for many news programs, ever; they persist. Viewers who have just seen a conflict successfully concluded on "Monday Night Football," "Bonanza" or "Mary Tyler Moore," may become frustrated and discontented when the news so often fails to bring the same resolution.

But television channels as it foments discontent. Advertisements and entertainment programs lead viewers away from political awareness. When television characters do exhibit imperfections or experience problems, their misfortunes are linked to bad luck, laziness, ineptitude. The structure of power rarely obtrudes into their lives; economic injustice, class, race, or age discrimination, illness caused by workplace injuries or industrial pollution—these dilemmas are absent. On rare occasions a corrupt politician or venal businessman oppresses; inevitably he or she is punished, and right (in the person of the hero) ultimately vanquishes. The implicit lesson is that people are not constrained by the social order. If they do well, their skill or luck should be credited. If they do poorly, the onus is on them. If they are harmed by the caprice of the powerful, it is an exception to be remedied by removing the offending individual, not by altering the structure of power—or the social values under which it operates.

Conclusion

Some analysts suggest that people spend their time with the mass media because capitalism alienates them from each other and from themselves. In advanced capitalist nations like the United States, these very media also stimulate consumer demand for the system's abundant material products. They thereby help prevent severe economic disruption and stabilize the economy and the political order. The dialectic turns tragic. Capitalist structures alienate people, thereby driving them toward escape in the media and consumption of the products the media push. Yet it is precisely the public's loyal use of the media and continued purchase of products it might not otherwise buy that fortify those structures.

Contradictions do exist. Although materialistic commercials reinforce basic American values, even they could become attacks on the system. If an economic crisis develops and people are no longer able to purchase the goods, the long conditioning by years of entertainment and seductive advertisements could provoke profound discontent. Witness the frustrations of inner city residents who have never enjoyed affluence but do watch television, or the fulminations of the middle class whose standard of living is increasingly insecure. Besides, commercials convey to the perceptive an indictment of some of the moral and aesthetic qualities of our civilization better than any reactionary or Marxist tract. For they provide a continuing display of cynical manipulation of sentiment (Geritol); loathsome encouragement of alienation from and insecurity about one's body (mouthwash, deodorant, chemical douches); honest admission of widespread personal pain, anxiety, and depression (Excedrin, Sominex).

Personal discontent and limited social change could combine to catalyze major unrest. If economic shortfalls should ever become incurable depressions, if feminism and other unconventional values and movements receive endorsement by politicians in the news so that a linkage between personal life and politics is clearly made, the profit-seeking media's role in spreading even diluted social change and de-politicized discontent may come to haunt the powerful.

CHAPTER ELEVEN

•

Public Opinion

"Wrong opinions and practices gradually yield to fact and argument: but facts and arguments, to produce any effect on the mind, must be brought before it. Very few facts are able to tell their own story, without comments to bring out their meaning."

John Stuart Mill

THE PREVIOUS TWO CHAPTERS revealed how the mass media inculcate and preserve the fundamental values and assumptions that undergird and legitimize the political process—and elite domination of it. Now we turn from underlying values to the more superficial, specific, sometimes volatile opinions Americans express about public officials, events, and problems of the day. Journalists and politicians commonly call these responses to major ongoing political developments "public opinion."

Our argument: elites crystallize and define issues, provide supporting information; they substantially influence, if they do not establish, public opinion. Because of the way news is defined, gathered, and reported, the mass media are often the unwitting handmaidens of the powerful. When elites agree, media depictions tend to be one-sided, to relay and transform elite consensus into public affirmation. But when elites conflict, the mass media may influence public opinion in ways that favor one elite position over another, thereby redistributing power.

Caveats and Distinctions

We must interrupt our argument and analysis for some caveats and distinctions. First the caveats. The causes of public opinion are a complex combination of the different characteristics of source, medium, messages, and audience. The opinions themselves are often fickle, even contradictory; they defy simple summary. The commonest way they are measured—by surveys—is primitive and unreliable.[1] Because most studies of the media's impact on opinions contain data and hypotheses only tangentially relevant to the broad political effects with which we are concerned,[2] we are compelled to make this chapter even more speculative than its predecessors.[3]

As for the distinctions, we need to distinguish, more explicitly than heretofore, kinds of news media and types of audiences. In practice, there are three main kinds of media. They are the specialized press, consisting of business, professional, and technical periodicals such as *Barron's, Medical World News,* and *Platt's Oilgram News;* prestige print media such as the *New York Times* and *Washington Post* newspapers and the intellectual journals (*The Nation, National Review, New Republic, New York Review, Atlantic,* and *Harper's*); and the popular press (ABC, CBS, NBC, and most local TV stations and newspapers). *Time* and *Newsweek* are more like television than the prestige print media; we consider them part of the popular press.

The second distinction concerns the population hierarchy. Based on people's media use, sophistication and level of knowledge, and propensity to engage in politics, we identify four groups: elite, attentive, mass, and apolitical.

THE GROUPS

Elites are on top. Less than 1 percent of the population, they are the people who make public policy or whose preferences directly influence government. Public officials, corporation heads, major interest-group leaders, a few notorious professors and think-tank denizens, even some celebrated journalists, are in this category. They generate most original policy proposals in reaction to problems and events. Their views define the conventional wisdom and structure the public debate about politics. They provide the sources of most political stories in the national media.

Around 10 to 15 percent of the populace has a reasonably high degree of political information and a coherent way of viewing politics. These "attentives" follow politics closely and may participate actively beyond voting. They are the white-collar managers and professionals (and their spouses) who join voluntary organizations, organize pressure groups, coalesce around candidates and issues, and generally lead their local communities. Most congresspersons have a coterie of such people in their districts upon whose support and advice they rely.[4]

Roughly 60 percent of the public follows politics to a limited extent and votes at least sporadically. The mass citizenry, they peruse their local papers, watch television news occasionally, and rarely see prestige or specialized media. Their political preferences are unstable; their opinions fluctuate; their knowledge of politics is limited[5]; their numbers decide elections.

The bottom 25 percent or so of the public is apolitical. These people have only the most rudimentary knowledge of politics and little contact with print media or even the network news. Rarely voting, they are marginal to conventional politics.

These categories are neither immutable nor inevitable. It may be possible for a person to be a passionate attentive on an issue like abortion, an ignorant apolitical otherwise; or attentive in middle age only to retire into the mass citizenry later. Nonetheless, this classification does help us clarify the nature of public opinion, showing how it circulates among different strata of the population and connects to the media. We shall continue the distinctions between population groups where appropriate, using the term "public" to refer to all non-elite segments of the populace together.

Top Down

Political opinions flow downward. They originate among elites, are picked up and propagated among attentives, then reach and shape the thinking of the mass citizenry. Apoliticals are uninvolved, attracted only by a major controversy or dramatic event. The prestige and popular media are the prime conveyor belts.

The influence of elites on attentive and mass citizen opinions works through their sway over the content of all three types of media. This is because the media types are linked, affecting each other's content in a hierarchical fashion mirroring the hierarchy of audiences. The prestige media transmit (often conflicting) elite interpretations of problems and events, and preferences for dealing with them. Their content contains background, follow-ups, investigations on occasion; they frequently transcend the abbreviation and utter simplification that prevails in the popular press. Attentives are the ones who read the prestige press, contact and pressure national elites, and even hold modest power themselves on the local level. The interplay between and among contending elites and sometimes groups of attentive activists provides the raw material for the newsworthy political conflicts that dominate popular media reporting. The latter follow the lead of the *Times* and *Post* in selecting and highlighting stories, contain little detail on policies and problems, and tend to stress symbols and to personalize elite disagreements. For reasons discussed in Chapter Two, even this simplified news bears the imprint of the elite vantage.

The opinions of all three groups are influenced by the media, but to varying degrees.

Elites use the specialized press, the prestige media, occasionally even the popular press, but the latter two have less effect on elite preferences than on everybody else's. Elites obtain valuable political information from specialized and prestige print media. The rest comes from briefings with other knowledgeable people, and from direct involvement in policy making.

Elites use the popular press to keep abreast of newsworthy developments and conflicts within sectors of the elite outside their own sphere of influence; popular reports affect their thinking about current policy problems and shape their perceptions of the political climate among the rest of the populace.

Many attentives form preferences by orienting themselves around the positions staked out by the elites and conveyed in prestige papers and magazines. Attentives are also influenced by the popular media, but less than mass citizens because they have more sources of information, more time, and more sophistication. As for the mass citizenry, the skimpy information provided by television and local newspapers is generally all they possess; it heavily influences their opinions.

Linking

Linking is the key to the media effects on public opinion that we shall describe. It is an integral part of journalism. All stories contain information previously unknown to most people, plus an explanation in terms of things already known. Explanations not based on familiar material would likely befuddle the audience.

Perceptions are generally evanescent, vanishing with the click of a switch or turn of a page. Those that stick in the public mind (or craw) usually arise from the media's repetitive linking. The need for simplification, news pegs, emotional resonance and wide familiarity, encourages journalists to explain news items by associating them with known political celebrities, symbols, or thematic story clusters (Watergate, energy crisis, inflation). These provide intelligibility (of a sort) and an anchor for audience memory.

The perceptual links made by the media originate largely in the ideas and dialogue of journalists' elite sources. These links furnish the raw material mass citizens use in forming or changing their preferences. Fasten news of Vietnamese or Zairean or Iranian rebels to negative symbols of red peril and there will be unfavorable evaluations of the insurgents. Link the rebels with positive symbols (of resistance to colonial or Soviet tyranny as in Afghanistan) and different opinions arise.

To be sure, audiences often make their own connections or discover them in talking with friends. The linkages suggested by the media may be ignored or misinterpreted by the audience. But most bonds between new perceptions and old are joined by the media, the prime sources of political information for the attentive and mass publics.

We do not mean to overstate the importance of politics in most people's lives nor to suggest that the mass citizenry studiously attends to the popular press. But it is the very peripherality of political news that makes the media so important. Were politics a paramount interest, the mass citizenry would search out specialized and prestige journals, join groups, broaden their sources of information and be less susceptible to the popular media. No, the significance of the mass media lies precisely in the way they connect with elites to select and describe the relatively few issues and persons which at any one time dominate the news and the consciousness of the marginally interested majority. We outline the effects in the next section.

Effects

The media have five effects on public opinion: they stabilize prevailing opinions, set priorities, elevate events and issues, sometimes change opinions, and ultimately limit options.

Stabilization

One of the most conspicuous effects of the media is to stabilize perceptions, and therefore opinions. Different coverage might change these opinions, but such coverage is infrequent—we shall discuss its occurrence later.

Stabilization is a routine outcome of reporting because journalistic descriptions and explanations are heavily larded with the dominant social understandings that comport with widely held conventional wisdom. For the reasons we discussed in Chapter 2 and illustrate throughout this book, disruptive reporting that offers unconventional views or interpretations is a rarity.

One source of journalistic practices particularly significant in stabilizing opinions is the phenomenon we call incomplete resolution. In brief, psychological research shows that initial impressions of anything new are profoundly influenced by a person's pre-existing attitudes and expectations.[6] Encountering the new, we see what the familiar has taught us to expect. Thus reporters' earliest stories about developing events, inevitably based on their first impressions, will tend to conform to their preconceptions. Only later, after the events are clarified or resolved, will reporters know enough about breaking developments to correct their possibly oversimplified, stereotyped initial depictions. Often this information is available only after so much time has elapsed that the event has lost its currency and is no longer newsworthy. The media, especially the popular press, scorn old news, relegating updates and revisions—when offered at all—to brief blurbs buried, barely noticed, in the back pages or closing minutes. The audience is left mainly with the early reports that accord with reporters' and its own prior and prevailing attitudes.

Incomplete resolution solidifies existing public opinions by publicizing new developments in a way that fits them within the frame of existing beliefs and by failing to present a complete, complex picture that might challenge audiences' existing thoughts. Our discussion of the Zaire story in Chapter 13 is an example.

PRIORITY SETTING

The stories stressed by the mass media tend to provide the issues many Americans come to think of as important.[7] But these subjects which begin to take precedence, at least temporarily, in many people's minds are the stories of most interest to reporters and their sources. These sources are elites. The mass public may have strong opinions about whether Laetrile cures cancer and should or should not be banned; they may be concerned about the inadequate education provided by the public schools and the costs of private schools; they may be distraught over the rapid rise of mortgage rates. Certainly journalists do not ignore these topics, and some politicians seek to exploit them as campaign issues. But the press devotes far more attention to such topics as Afghanistan, American hostages in Iran, and electoral prospects of candidates in the next presidential election. These are the subjects of particular interest to elites. The primacy of these topics is reinforced by public opinion polls which pose questions of interest to the people who sponsor them—journalists and elites—rather than to the public. The questions tap public opinion which may at best be casual and tentative, ignoring issues on which many people have intense preferences or inchoate desires.

More important are the potential effects on voting and other behavior. Whatever the issues of greatest importance to some voters, they may be impelled by media neglect of candidates' positions on these issues to make voting decisions on the basis of positions that the media do link to candidates. The media may not provide these voters with the raw material to link their top issues to candidates. By default, media news priorities structure people's voting priorities. Thus people might be led to vote on the basis of candidates' stands on dealing with Afghanistan or Iran when they care more about Laetrile and education. In 1972, Senator George McGovern's campaign competence was elevated by media coverage and became for many Americans the prime priority in voting. Yet people had desires on issues not covered by the press from which McGovern might have benefited.[8]

ELEVATION

Closely linked to priority setting is elevation. Few people, actions, and events are elevated into news. Sometimes elevation results from deliberate actions by journalists or media manipulators. Other times the rise from obscurity stems automatically from normal media routines.

Consider nuclear power. For years, nuclear policy was made in cozy privacy by utility corporations and the Nuclear Regulatory (née Atomic Energy) Commission. The public was left in the dark about policy specifics, while atomic energy was radiantly portrayed and linked to super-technological symbols in an occasional puff piece. This was a complex scientific region, and there was little elite controversy over it. Most information was conveyed in highly specialized periodicals. The issue of the safety and cost of generating electricity this way was latent, submerged.

The issue first attracted significant journalistic attention when civil disobedience and demonstrating took place at some plant sites in the mid-1970s. Simultaneously, some reputable scientists began publicly criticizing the industry. Respectable environmental groups and Ralph Nader added their voices, as did a handful of politicians. By 1979, there had probably not been enough coverage in the popular press to impress the nuclear issue on the mass citizenry. But there had been enough articles in the prestige journals read by the attentive public, including editors and reporters, to alert journalists to the existence of a big story possibility should a mishap occur.

Then came a serious accident, of the sort long predicted by critics and pooh-poohed by proponents, at the Three Mile Island plant near Harrisburg, Pennsylvania. It posed a continuing threat of devastating disaster, dwarfing any earthquake or flood, in a city only 125 miles from Washington. The convenient location, potential catastrophe, suspense as the threat was battled, and human interest all combined to emblazon the story for several weeks on the front pages and give it prime placement on television.

Had the specific incident in Pennsylvania somehow been averted, the problems posed by atomic energy would have still existed—and would not have been covered extensively. The accident did not "prove" the dangers of nuclear power, but it did exemplify them at a moment propitious for media attention. Rather than a sudden unexpected increase in the inherent hazards of nuclear power stations, it was primarily media practices and priorities —especially the attraction to disaster—that first made this example a big story.

Changing Opinions

The media can change some people's opinions by the events they report, how they depict them, or the way they link symbols for emphasis. Thus Harrisburg was presented as much more than a mere disaster story. Officials from the NRC and the utility were shown to be uncertain and confused. Their bewilderment was graphically displayed in split-screen TV presentations alternating statements in direct contradiction to each other. Emergency plans were probed; the media showed they were not kept current. Unforeseen problems and dangers bubbled to the surface, to the well-publicized consternation of technical experts. In the cynical atmosphere of the times, these stories implicitly (and in person-on-the-street interviews, explicitly) linked nuclear power to the negative symbols of thieving corporations and lying or incompetent bureaucrats. For many people contradiction was palpable between previous (if shallow) preferences for nuclear power, with its image as exemplar of scientific progress, and the media-prompted perception of atomic energy as bureaucratic and technical nightmare.

Some opinions changed. Support for "building more nuclear power plants" dropped from 69 percent in 1977 to 46 percent in 1979, primarily in response to events at Three Mile Island.[9] The persistence of the new opinions is unpredictable. But certainly different coverage would have provoked less change. Events at Three Mile Island might have been portrayed as a major triumph for nuclear technology. After all, the accident was due largely to human failure, and nobody suffered immediate health damage. If it had been seen this way, the volume of reporting would have been lower (good news is less newsworthy). The nuclear accident simply would not have been elevated to public consciousness or linked to negative symbols enough to induce a significant change in opinions.

Why was the incident portrayed as such bad news? Certainly the press could hardly justify all that coverage if the accident was not both dangerous and symptomatic of some more general problem. Drawn to the scene by the scent of disaster and human interest, the media had a natural tendency to magnify its general import. The story of the shoddy products and evasive shenanigans of business and the ineptitude and negligence of government agencies fit into popular media themes. Having been alerted to the nuclear peril by prestige journals, some reporters were suspicious of the energy industry. They saw Three Mile Island as confirmation of their doubts.

LIMITING OPTIONS

People mainly respond to what is reported in the media. Significantly different stories and themes might encourage different responses. But it is the perspectives of journalists' elite sources which customarily define the options available to and chosen by the attentive and mass audiences.

Once the nuclear issue was elevated, a set of new policy options was laid before the public. Few among the mass citizenry, even among attentives, had genuine preferences about the matter before March 1979; we suspect that their previous responses to survey questions were not based on much thought.[10] The possibilities discussed by government officials and industry spokespersons dominated reports. Almost all of the representatives of the antinuclear perspective featured in the news seemed (from our informal viewing and reading) to be scientists from established national environmental groups. They were respectable sources; more radical local activists in Harrisburg or elsewhere were not visible. The most widely discussed nuclear energy policies in the wake of Three Mile Island ran from doing nothing new (voiced by industry flacks), to tightening regulation (government officials), to a moratorium on new plant construction (established ecology groups). The more radical idea of dismantling plants violated private property traditions and was neglected. Ability to evaluate that possibility or the others was undermined by the typical failure of the popular press to describe historical background and the total context of energy use and waste. As is usually the case, the definitions of acceptable sources combined with journalistic practices to exclude the provocative positions and delineate the range of feasible options for the attentive and mass publics.

The exclusion of views that might threaten the system of elite power does not arise from a conspiracy of leaders who agree to disagree only on superficialities. Even the manipulators discussed in Part II rarely concern themselves consciously with preserving deeper values. Most of the elites who serve as news sources simply do not see problems or solutions in system-threatening ways.

The preservation of consensus values and the guiding of public opinion on conflictive issues of the day by elites, through the media

—these are two aspects of the same continuing process of adult socialization. Maintaining legitimacy requires harnessing the ever changing topical beliefs that comprise public opinion, keeping them within the boundaries laid out by consensus values. The media help by limiting options.

Elite Control and Public Opinion

By granting elites substantial control over the content, emphases, and flow of public opinion, media practices diminish the public's power. The more elites can dominate the perceptions and preferences developed by the rest of society, the less autonomy the public will have. If "public" opinions are confined to the topics and options suggested by elites and conveyed by the media, public power is limited. The real power-holders are those who shape opinions.

Yet, elites may anticipate public reactions and modify their preferences before publicizing them. And their domination of public opinion is imperfect. Vast numbers of citizens may resist even an elite consensus. For example, though most elites seemed to agree that the gasoline shortage in the spring of 1979 was authentic, polls showed that the majority of Americans felt it was contrived by the oil industry or a hoax.[11] When the masses have other sources of information—in this case their own experiences of shortages that (like the ones in 1974 and 1979) suddenly disappeared—the media's impact and elites' influence may be limited. In the shortage case, both the liberal and the conservative wings of the establishment wanted the public to take the energy crisis seriously. Though the two sectors had different remedies, the failure of the public to accept the gravity of the situation stymied both solutions. Power, even elite power, never flows in only one direction; the powerful sometimes experience frustration in exerting domination.

This is particularly true when elites disagree. In that case media coverage may reallocate power among the powerful by swaying public opinion to one or the other side. Having public opinion on its side (or seeming to) is one of many resources leaders may use to get their way.

One elite group and its non-elite followers may lose and another contingent gain; but it is the elite combatants who dictate the arcas of disagreement and the terms of the ultimate settlement; it is the elites' skill in manipulating the press (combined with the serendipitous coincidence of media interests and practices with those of one side or another) that largely determines which group will benefit most from the impact of news reports on public opinion.

Members of the public are more often pawns of power than independent holders of it. The media more often expedite than frustrate the control of elites as a class over the rest of society's political ideas. The next two chapters illustrate and amplify the discussion in this one with case studies of media impacts on public opinions about domestic and foreign policy.

CHAPTER TWELVE

•

Domesticated Opinion: The Conservative Myth

"As men abound in copiousness of language, so they become more wise, or more mad than ordinary."

Thomas Hobbes

THREE TIMES DURING July 1975, the *Washington Post* published columns by its highly respected columnist David Broder that alluded to the conservatism of American public opinion. In the first he wrote, ".... the political mood of the country is surprisingly conservative. . . ."[1] In the next he said, "The dominant conservatism of the public mood is beginning to assert itself into the liberal Democratic Congress . . . legislators are getting the message of how conservative their constituents have become. . . ."[2] And then: "The country is moving in the conservative direction . . . surely. . . ."[3] By the following spring, the conventional wisdom was that American public opinion was moving rapidly rightward. After the 1976 Democratic primary in Massachusetts, according to the *New Republic,* a network commentator proclaimed that "The electorate is more conservative today than at any time since pre-New Deal days."[4] By June 1978, Bruce Morton of CBS could say that President Carter "like just about everyone these days" was for lower taxes and less government spending.[5]

There were a few exceptions. Both the *Post* and the *New York Times* offered stories suggesting the prevalence of liberal sentiments under conservative garb.[6] But this did not lead to a disavowal of the conservative myth the *Times* had perpetuated a month earlier with a story headlined, "Opinion in U.S. Swinging to Right, Pollsters and Politicians Believe."[7] Most reporters and many politicians routinely attributed conservative sentiments to the American people during the middle 1970s.[8]

This chapter shows that such assertions were, at the least, premature. Public opinion polls taken from 1968 to 1978 show very little evidence of a conservative mood or trend (see the appendix at the end of this chapter). For the period through 1978, with few exceptions, liberal or left-wing options were endorsed by majorities as large as ever—or larger.

A case study of the conservative myth demonstrates several of the media effects we described in Chapter 11: linking, setting priorities, elevation, changing opinions, and limiting options. It also reveals how media reports can guide the political behavior of the attentive and mass publics, and even of elites.

Public opinion is a power resource. It possesses the potential of constraining and even directing policy-makers, who otherwise spend much of their time responding to the blandishments of the well-organized. By misrepresenting public opinion, by emphasizing some opinions at the expense of others, the press deprives the unorganized masses of some of their potential power. The media short-circuit the process by which public preferences may otherwise be translated into government policy. We shall explain how and why.

Chimerical Conservatism

Conservatism is a slippery term, so we shall examine several of the ways it could have been expressed in public opinion. They will confirm or refute the two related but distinct journalistic claims. First, that the general mood of the public was conservative —we take this to be a claim that majorities held right-wing beliefs. Second, that the overall trend was to the right. Full enumeration of the data can be found at the end of the chapter. We offer highlights here.

We rely upon public opinion surveys. There is no need to reiterate their numerous shortcomings. The polls are all we possess. We enhance their reliability by using where possible identical questions asked over a number of years. The important consideration is the weight of the survey evidence, not any one, potentially questionable, poll.

What did people call themselves? Asked to describe their personal philosophies in 1978, "conservatives" outnumbered "liberals" by 35 to 21 percent. The mood was not liberal, but neither was it conservative: a plurality endorsed "middle of the road." Was there a conservative trend? No. In 1968, the conservatives outnumbered liberals by 43 to 22 percent. Fewer Americans called themselves conservatives a decade later. The middle of the road category grew at the expense of the conservative. This is a slight leftward drift if one accepts the validity of simple self-labeling.[9]

What about party identification? From 1968 to 1978, the Democrats gained adherents, going from 41 to 46 percent. The Republicans declined from 29 to 23 percent. Much of the populace can tell the parties apart—they know the Democrats are more liberal.[10] A conservative trend should have borne more Republicans despite Watergate.

Party label too is ambiguous. Specific policy preferences might tell us more about the public mind. Consider economic issues. Many commentators and politicians insisted during the 1970s that the public was strongly reacting against government regulation of "private enterprise." But only small minorities rejected government regulation over a range of issues. In the words of two respected conservative scholars who pondered the polls, the public thinks ". . . regulation is bad when it means telling people how to run their business or when it forces business to raise production costs or prices unreasonably. Regulation is good when it means protecting the public interest from the 'bad behavior' of businessmen who charge high prices, pollute, produce shoddy products, or indulge in corruption."[11]

Indeed, there was a strong trend of disenchantment with the behavior of private enterprise. Especially dramatic is the plunge from 70 percent (1968) to 15 percent (1977) in the percentage of people who believed business fairly balances profit considerations and the public interest. The legitimacy of capitalism as a system, however, was still not widely questioned.

Was there a decrease in support of government services? From 1973 to 1978 there was a drop in those wanting to spend less on the military and a slight decrease in support of spending on urban problems. Welfare (unpopular when so labeled, more accepted when dubbed "aid to the needy, disabled, and aged") became slightly less popular. But the percentage of Americans willing to say that the government was spending too much money on improving the nation's education system and protecting the nation's health and the environment remained very low—around 10 percent.

Similarly, over two-thirds not just of self-styled liberals but of conservatives too, approved liberal government activism: programs to help pay medical costs, guarantee jobs for all, achieve fair job and housing opportunities for blacks, and enforce safety standards for factories.

Judicious journalists made a distinction. They wrote that the public had become more conservative on social, if not economic, issues. But among all the social issues we researched, only two showed significant (though modest) rightward shifts. Between 1969 and 1978, support for capital punishment grew from 51 to 62 percent. Attitudes toward crime generally hardened. And, according to Harris, approval of the Equal Rights Amendment decreased from 66 to 55 percent between 1976 and 1978. Conservative activists won big and well-publicized victories on those issues in many state legislatures during the 1970s. Whether this was a cause or effect of the survey results is not clear.

On the other hand, the movement on many social issues was liberal. Approval of efforts to "strengthen and change women's status in society" rose from 42 to 64 percent between 1970 and 1978. Support for abortion held steady, although again conservatives enjoyed some legislative victories. At least in surveys, by 1978 almost everybody endorsed open housing for blacks. (Busing for racial balance remained unpopular as always.[12]) Public tolerance of marijuana reached an all-time high and gun control retained its popularity.

The ability of conservatives to mobilize effectively around some social issues should not be minimized. But the social mood was by no means conservative, and much of the drift was to the left.

As a last possibility, the public's putative conservatism may have displayed itself on foreign issues. Fewer and fewer Americans believed too much money was being spent on defense. And although a July 1978 Harris poll showed a 59 to 36 percent opposition to larger defense budgets, by December of the same year the figure was 50 to 47 percent in favor.[13] Perhaps this demonstrated the potency of the well-publicized scare talk of revivified Soviet expansionism in Africa, Asia and elsewhere. Yet in the December poll the public by 52 to 39 percent favored cutting defense spending rather than federal aid to education; and 54 as against 37 percent would cut defense rather than health programs. In 1978 growing majorities approved détente with the Soviet Union, a new Strategic Arms Limitation agreement, and diplomatic recognition of mainland China.

By 1980, however, hawkish attitudes on defense had increased somewhat. Perhaps there was a conservative shift in the defense-foreign policy area, but it transpired mostly in 1979 and 1980, well after the conservative mood reports began appearing.

We can best summarize the basic message of the data in the words of political scientist Everett Carll Ladd, Jr., a consulting editor for the journal *Public Opinion:*

> Many politicians, pollsters and newsmen assume that Americans are "moving right." The only problem with that assumption is that it is fundamentally wrong. . . . Despite a clamoring for tax cuts and a heavy dose of anti-Washington rhetoric, there is still no sign that the U.S. public wants to cut back substantially on the post-Depression spending habits of the federal government. In many instances, polls show just the opposite. . . . Over and over again, when asked if they want to cut back on spending for public services, the public today says no. . . . The underlying trends of the 1960s and 70s are clear enough. And they are not conservative, in any sense of that much abused term.[14]

Explanations

Then how to explain the notions of conservative mood and a trend to the right? One source: the rapid growth in public distrust of the leaders of most large social institutions, including government.[15] It was easy—though mistaken—for journalists schooled in traditional American ideological categories to confuse the disenchantment with government officials with a rejection of government activism.

Such a perception was encouraged by a genuine conservative shift and heightened activism among the right-wing Republican elites, who are major sources for national political news.[16] GOP media stars like John Connally, Ronald Reagan, and Jesse Helms delivered self-serving interpretations of the growing political discontent. They claimed it showed a revolt of the American folk against big (meaning liberal) government.

The hiring and syndication by the *Washington Post* and *New York Times* of fresh conservative columnists enlivened the opinion columns of many newspapers.

The politicians and columnists were supported by an unlikely set of new acolytes, the neo-conservatives. These were former liberals now energetically advocating smaller government in opinion journals and op ed pages.[17] The ideological center of gravity along the Cambridge-New York-Washington axis had clearly moved right. The liberal-left ardor of some prominent New York-based, intellectual magazines had chilled, even frozen. These periodicals are sources for some of the ideas and insights purveyed by columnists and editorial writers. Thus the mutually reinforcing musings of rising Republican stars, reborn social reactionaries, former liberals, and uninspired editorialists combined to give an illusory picture of public opinion.

Many liberal politicians collapsed before the rightist assault. There was a void (or an echo) in the places where journalists were accustomed to finding liberal responses to conservative voices. Farther left, the activist groups of the 1960s had ceased being newsworthy. No longer did the news feature a continuing crescendo of radical demands that made it seem to reporters that the country was moving rapidly left.

The conservative myth reinforced itself by affecting reporters' choices of sources. In a time of putatively surging conservatism, journalists may have perceived spokespersons on the left as irrelevant or naive. As these delegitimized sources were consulted less frequently, liberal proposals and interpretations received less coverage, and those on the right obtained relatively greater emphasis. Moreover, the location of the all-important center, to which editors cleave and by which reporters set their bearings, was perceived as having shifted rightward. Positions and politicians once thought too conservative became a part of the respectable mainstream; contrast the treatment of Barry Goldwater during the liberal heyday of 1964 with Ronald Reagan 16 years later.

PACK JOURNALISM

The propagation of the idea that public opinion lunged to the right between 1975 and 1978 is an archetypal case of pack journalism. Reporters, columnists, and editorial writers converged on the theme in interpreting events; with infrequent exceptions, their accounts coincided.

We mentioned pack journalism in Chapter 2. It is useful to dissect some of its more important causes here. First is competition. Spurred on by editors, reporters converge on the news. There is a great fear of missing a story that a competitor snares. So reporters congregate.[18] Physically concentrated in the same places, they interact socially, they share the perceptions and gossip that shape stories. The more intimate the physical space, the closer the social relationships, the more similar the news. Strong conformity pressures exist in small groups faced with common stimuli and tasks.[19] Thus pack journalism reaches its height in reporting from the presidential candidate's campaign bus (or jet), where reporters are cramped together continuously. The Washington journalistic community is almost as insulated, as claustrophobic, as the campaign bus.

Even without physical proximity, understaffing and shortages of time lead journalists to borrow ideas from other media. This opinion leadership is hierarchical. Subjects or themes treated by a David Broder in the *Washington Post* are deemed worthy of culling; news not fitting the *Post* (or *New York Times*) is neglected.[20]

There are more specific reasons for the packlike seizure on the conservative mood. The use of vague, simple, and culturally resonant symbols serves journalistic needs. It conserves space or time, always at a premium in newspapers or television. Unable to discuss the nuances of ideological conflict and change, reporters can attribute election or referenda results to a revolt against big government—a theme already familiar to audiences. Such simplifications are supposed to enhance understanding by audiences deemed to have little patience with abstraction or complexity. The shortcut labels also appear to link past and present, giving the audience a bogus but reassuring sense of continuity of politics. Symbolic pseudo-history aids journalists in processing information; it saves them from having to understand expressions of public sentiment that often perplex even scholars with more time and expertise. Finally, linking up a specific event with a thematic cluster story like "the conservative trend" helps reporters sell stories to their editors. Needing news pegs, reporters sometimes concoct dubious connections between their stories and currently popular symbols.

Amorphous symbolic themes receive repeated coverage and reinforcement by politicians and pundits. But detailed discussions of individual policy issues are few. This helps explain why, despite several years of constant assurance that they were turning conservative, the public stayed liberal on specific issues. Some, perhaps, came to agree that "big government" was a problem, and moving in a conservative direction the solution. But the mass media failed to link such vague notions to particular policies that might implement the right-wing analysis.

Effects

Through 1978, the conservative myth had had no appreciable effect on people's stands on policy issues as measured by polls. But to look only for identifiable changes in specific public attitudes is to miss more speculative and vital possibilities. We will describe several ways the conservative myth may have directly or indirectly affected politics without necessarily altering the public's policy preferences.

ACTIVATING CONSERVATIVES, DEACTIVATING LIBERALS

The perception of conservative renewal may have fostered the entrance of right-wing candidates for office. Their efforts might have been boosted especially by the belief among members of the attentive public in a favorable climate for the right: campaign volunteers join up, contributors pay up, party workers line up votes.

Would-be liberal politicians may have been discouraged from running. If they did announce themselves as liberals, they had to confront a widespread impression that leftish candidates were unrepresentative of the public, out of touch with reigning sentiment. They were susceptible to being cast at best as underdogs, at worst as arrogant and insulated pretenders to the public trust. Scenting defeat, volunteers, sugar daddies, party activists may have stayed away.

Perceived climate of opinion[21] might well have affected the campaign planning of those entering the fray. Hearing constantly of revolt against big government, advisers may have encouraged candidates to promise that they, and not their opponents, were the ones who could slash budgets. Given the nature of media campaigning—scarcity of time and space needed to dismantle conventional wisdom convincingly—candidates would have been hard pressed to demolish the conservative myth, even if their own private soundings showed it to be false. Few indeed are the candidates able to combat successfully the prevailing symbolic agenda. During the anti-communist scare of the 1950s, most politicians argued over who could best control the "Red menace," not over whether it existed.

Journalists amplified the situation by imposing their simplifying news pegs of big government, their story clusters of the conservative mood, on the campaign. They asked questions in these terms, which were thus picked up by more candidates. Both politicians and reporters may have found it expedient to orient their public dialogues around the same agenda. No wonder so few candidates called themselves liberals by 1978.[22]

Campaign advertisements, speeches, and news coverage shaped by the conservative theme affect the voting participation of the mass citizenry in turn. People with liberal issue priorities and preferences are discouraged from casting their ballots when Democrat and Republican both proclaim the rightist gospel. In the 1970s, off-year elections drew under 40 percent of the voting age population, presidential elections under 55 percent. The less-participating segment tended generally to be poorer and more liberal.[23] To win, Democrats had to attract as many of them as possible to the polls. Democratic candidates contributed to the deactivation of their own natural supporters among attentive, mass, and even apolitical publics when they pitched their campaigns to the phantom conservative mood.

Take Jimmy Carter. In 1976, his support peaked after the Democratic convention where he endorsed a liberal platform, made a populist acceptance speech, and chose a running mate widely identified with his party's liberals. Even discounting the usual post-convention halo effect, Carter's 2–1 lead in the July polls was remarkable. But there is a difference between endorsing a candidate in a survey and bearing the costs of voting for him. What happened in November was a very close election indeed. Over 45 percent of the potential electorate stayed home; many others switched to Ford. We suspect one reason (certainly there were many) was Carter's timid, even vacuous campaign that stressed symbols and the taming of big government.

Limiting Options and Setting Priorities

The 1970s were unnerving for many Americans: their purchasing power declined.[24] The increase of taxation as a proportion of income was one reason.[25] The costs of food, fuel, housing, medical care and clothing soared, too. The conservative myth proposed both a diagnosis in big government and a solution—cutting it back. Other ways of defining the problem—big technology, big capitalism, big sin—and of solving it—return to nature, nationalizing corporations, mass conversion—were passed over. The conservative myth thereby helped set public priorities; by limiting options, it may have guided political participation into the so-called tax revolt of 1978. It did not alter the public's policy preferences.

Eleven states passed initiatives in 1978 limiting taxation or spending. All but three were traditionally conservative states; and a further five initiatives were defeated. The most publicized was California's Proposition 13. Given the chance to control one aspect of inflation—taxation—a large majority of the 43 percent of voting age Californians who participated took it. But its supporters' motives were complex, not conservative. In a statewide poll, Californians endorsed by 2–1 the notion of limiting the 57 percent tax cut to homeowners and maintaining existing taxation on commercial property.[26] That radically redistributive tax reform was not on the ballot. Nor could the public decide on the prices of food and other necessities by referendum. They chose the only option offered. They reduced property taxes that had soared with the wildly inflating California real estate market.

Numerous national polls showed the public desired neither tax cutting *per se* nor slashing government services. The major targets rather appeared to be inflation and inefficiency. Gallup showed a 91 to 8 percent majority favored controlling inflation over cutting taxes.[27] A poll by the *Washington Post* found that a 64 to 31 percent majority approved making "government programs more efficient so that they do what they are supposed to do" over cutting government spending and reducing taxes.[28] Greater efficiency in the activist programs the public endorsed and an end to inflation seemed to be the dominant public preferences in 1978—not a return to laissez-faire.[29]

ELEVATION AND CHANGE

America's political culture provides a stock of ideological symbols. At any given time some are active, others dormant. In the 1950s, anti-communism loomed ominously. By the middle 1970s another symbol from the cultural heritage, distrust of big government, had resurfaced. In each case, the symbols furnished much of the material for public dialogue—centerpieces of editorials, rhetoric in election campaigns, standards for judging candidates and proposals. With an assist from elites, the news media elevated big government, brought it up from the dustbin of the

Hoover-Coolidge era to the post-Nixon public agenda, linked it with a symbolic solution, conservatism.

The notion that Americans were turning right enhanced the legitimacy of conservative policy proposals and politicians. The conservative myth (and other forces) may have led public officials by the late 1970s to become, both in their rhetoric and substantive policy decisions, less hospitable to liberal reforms, more amenable to business-oriented bills, even though, simultaneously, business was at a recent if not all-time low in public esteem.

Public opinion often follows elite opinion and actions. With public officials, editorials, and news stories alike identifying big government as the problem, and cutbacks as the solution, some citizens were bound to follow. This was especially likely in the absence of other prominent diagnoses of, and cures for, the nation's difficulties.

The likelihood of a genuine rightward shift by 1980 was magnified by that year's election campaign. Numerous, vociferous, persuasive conservative Republicans contended for their party's nomination in ideological harmony and then united around Ronald Reagan, the right's most effective communicator. Liberal Democratic principles, by contrast, had few national spokespersons, and suffered guilt by association with an incumbent president widely perceived as incompetent. Data from 1980 surveys provide some evidence of rightward drift, as do the Republican triumphs in the November elections. The media's conservative myth certainly encouraged—though it did not alone cause—the apparent change in some citizens' opinions between 1978 and 1980.

Elite Moods and Public Opinion

The surveys we relied upon are decidedly limited tools. None that we know of probe the respondents' opinions deeply enough to reveal actual public opinion, the complex amalgam of political feelings, fears, attitudes, and beliefs present among the American people. Nor do surveys ask the citizen to respond to the complicated policy tradeoffs that public officials must usually decide. Of course the public wants low inflation and taxes, high levels of employment and of efficient public services. When asked about these four sometimes incompatible goals in separate questions, respondents naturally endorse each. The important sentiments involve priorities and tradeoffs, subjects about which surveys offer little enlightenment. More deeply probing polls might have found majorities in 1978 that favored the more conservative choices among conflicting goals; or such polls might have found more definitive evidence of persistent liberalism than we uncovered; or they might have uncovered confusion, ambivalence, indecision in the public's thinking.

This uncertainty arising out of the rudimentary state of social scientific understanding of public opinion supports our concluding points. Real public opinion is perennially diffuse, contradictory, unsettled. It should not be summarized with an ideological label. Liberal and conservative, radical and reactionary strands probably coexist, inchoate, ready for crystallization and exploitation by contending elites. On balance, the evidence we were able to muster indicated that the liberal strand in public opinion was no weaker, the public no more conservative, in 1978 than earlier. But with the media's push, conservative sentiments were ascending, and they were certainly being exploited by Republican and other elites as the 1970s ended and the 1980s began.

Journalistic goals, practices, and limitations give elites the opportunity to define the "public" moods and trends for the media. Elites often select political problems for publicity; they propose the palliatives and panaceas that obtain coverage. Because they assumed their elite sources were cannily reading and responding to fresh intimations from the citizenry (and for all the other reasons we have explained), journalists depicted the public as more conservative during the middle 1970s.

With their tendency to simplify and summarize in a label, the media may always have denied the continuing complexity and contradiction of public opinion. Thus, when during the 1960s many elites were high on liberalism and the benefits of activist government, the press swayed that way, probably depicting the public as more unambiguously liberal than it was. The media thereby provided a power resource for liberal elites: the appearance (and perhaps ultimately the reality) of supportive public sentiment. Then in the 1970s they provided that power resource for conservative elites.

The powerful are themselves influenced by what they learn from the media. Some liberal leaders developed new opinions or changed their behavior in response to press descriptions of the new conservatism. Other, faithfully liberal elites, resisted. For reasons selfish or altruistic, they preferred that perceived and actual public opinion not move right. Yet they too had to grapple with the conservative myth.

The persistence of that myth demonstrated the mass media's independent ability to redistribute power among the powerful: the press helped shift the political advantage to conservatives. For the society as a whole, the media's conservative myth diminished the ability of ordinary citizens to influence power holders by distorting the true state of public preferences, inhibiting their translation into government policy, and compounding mass malaise.

APPENDIX
Survey Evidence on the Conservative Mood

I. Describe your personal political philosophy:

	LIBERAL	CONSERVATIVE	MIDDLE-ROAD
1968	22%	43%	36%
1972	26	35	38
1976	23	36	41
1978	21	35	45

Source: Harris polls cited in *Public Opinion* (September/October 1978), p. 33.

II. Party Identification.

	DEMOCRAT	REPUBLICAN	INDEPENDENT
1968	41%	29%	29%
1972	43	26	31
1976	46	22	32
1978	46	23	29

Source: Gallup and Harris Polls cited in *Public Opinion* (September/October 1978), p. 28.

III. Which party can best handle the most important problem facing the country?

	DEMOCRATIC	REPUBLICAN	NO OPINION/ NO DIFFERENCE
1968	29%	34%	37%
1972	29	39	32
1976	43	23	34
1978	33	19	48
1980	27	30	43

Source: Gallup polls cited in *Public Opinion* (September/October 1978), p. 32; and *Denver Sunday Post,* August 3, 1980, p. 22.

IV. It is worth the costs added by government regulation to:

	YES	NO	NO OPINION
Protect workers' health and safety	52%	12%	36%
Ensure equal employment opportunities	42	21	37
Protect the environment	42	19	39

Source: ORC poll, 1978, cited in Lipset and Schneider, 1979: 11.

V. The best way to get good quality products or services in the following industries at reasonable prices would be to:

	AUTOS	CHEMICAL	STEEL	OIL
Increase government regulation	39%	35%	42%	54%
Keep same level of regulation	32	31	23	16
Decrease level of regulation	18	12	21	15

Source: Roper poll, December 1977, cited in Lipset and Schneider, 1979: 12.

VI. Economic Issues.*

    A. Should government limit corporate profits?
    B. The rich get richer, the poor get poorer.
    C. Business tries to strike a fair balance between profits and the interests of the public.

RESPONSES		1968	1972	1975	1977	1979
A.	Yes	33% (1971)	40%	55%	55%	60%
B.	Agree	48 (1966)	61	76	77	—
C.	Agree	70	32	15	15	19

Sources: (A) ORC polls cited in *Public Opinion* (September/October 1978), p. 34, and (June/July 1980), p. 33.
        (B) Harris polls cited in *Current Opinion* (February 1973), p. 9, and (January 1978), p. 6.
        (C) Yankelovich polls cited in Lipset and Schneider, 1979: 9; and *Public Opinion* (April/May 1980), p. 29.

* To facilitate comparisons over time, data are displayed using surveys taken during five different periods, unless otherwise noted.

VII. Are we spending too much, too little, or about the right amount on the following problems? Percentage answering "too little" or "about the right amount."

	1973	1976	1978	1980
Improving and protecting the environment	92%	90%	90%	84%
Improving and protecting the nation's health	95	95	93	92
Solving the problems of the big cities	86	78	78	76
Halting the rising crime rate	95	92	94	94
Improving nation's educational system	91	90	89	89
Improving the conditions of blacks	77	73	73	74
Welfare	46	37	39	41
Space exploration	39	38	50	57

Source: NORC surveys cited in Ladd, 1979b: 132; and unpublished data provided by NORC.

VIII. Approval for various government programs among self-styled liberals and conservatives.*

	"LIBERALS"	"CONSERVATIVES"
1. Government help with medical costs	91%	82%
2. Government guaranteed jobs for all	81	71
3. Fair job and housing opportunities for blacks	79	67
4. Government safety standards for factories	77	69
5. Sex education courses	85	69
6. Government restrictions on handgun sales	71	55
7. Allow sale of pornography to adults	68	51
8. Remove government restrictions on marijuana	56	34

*Source: New York Times/*CBS polls, 1978, cited in *Public Opinion* (January/February, 1979), pp. 38–39.

* Middle of the roaders' approval percentages fell between those of liberals and conservatives in all cases.

IX. Social Issues.

	1968–69	1972–73	1975–76	1977–79
A. *Courts have not been hard enough on criminals: Yes.*	—	74%	85%	88% (1977)
B. *Death penalty for murder: Yes.*	51%	57	65	62 (1978)
C. *Abortion should be illegal under all circumstances: Yes.*	—	—	22	19 (1979)
D. *Equal Rights Amendment: Favor.*	—	—	57 (Gallup) 66 (Harris)	58 (1979) 55 (1978)
E. *Favor most of the efforts to strengthen and change women's status in society.*	42 (1970)	—	59	64 (1978)
F. *Would vote for woman for president.*	58	74	76	81 (1978)
G. *Blacks have right to live wherever they can afford to: Yes.*	63	—	—	93 (1978)
H. *Federal handgun registration: Support.*	—	—	77	80 (1978)

Sources: (A) Gallup polls, cited in *Public Opinion* (March/April 1978), p. 24.
(B) Gallup polls, cited in *Public Opinion* (September/October 1978), p. 35.
(C) George H. Gallup, *The Gallup Poll: Public Opinion 1979* (Wilmington, Del.: Scholarly Resources, 1980), p. 132.
(D) Gallup and Harris polls, cited in *Public Opinion* (January/February 1979), p. 35.

(E) Harris polls, cited in *Public Opinion* (January/February 1979), p. 35.
(F) Gallup and NORC polls cited in *Public Opinion* (September/October 1978), p. 36.
(G) University of Michigan and CBS/*New York Times* polls cited in *Public Opinion* (September/October 1978), p. 37.
(H) Harris polls cited in "Public Strongly Backs Gun Control," *San Francisco Examiner* (August 7, 1978), p. 3.

X. Foreign Policy and Defense Issues.

	1968–69	1972–73	1975–76	1977–78	1979–80
A. *Is the U.S. spending too much on defense and military purposes?* Yes.	52%	42%	36%	23%	14%
B. *Would you favor U.S. troop involvement if Western Europe were invaded?* Yes.	—	—	39 (1974)	43	67
C. *Do you favor détente with Russia?* Yes.	—	—	59	69	—
D. *Would you favor an agreement with Russia to limit nuclear weapons?* Yes.	—	—	—	67 (NBC/AP)	81
	—	—	—	78 (CBS/ NY Times)	63

Sources: (A) Gallup, Harris and CBS/*NY Times* Polls cited in *Public Opinion* (March/May 1979), p. 25, and (February/March 1980), p. 22.
(B) Harris, Roper, and NBC/AP Polls cited in *Public Opinion* (March/May 1979), p. 26, and (February/March 1980), p. 26.
(C) Harris Polls cited in *Public Opinion* (July/August 1978), p. 24.
(D) Cited in *Public Opinion* (March/May 1979), p. 27.

CHAPTER THIRTEEN

•

Domesticated Opinion: Foreign News

"The function of the press in society is to inform, but its role is to make money. The monopoly publisher's reaction, on being told that he ought to spend money on reporting distant events, is therefore exactly that of the proprietor of a large fat cow, who is told that he ought to enter her in a horse race."

A. J. Liebling

SOON AFTER FIDEL CASTRO came to power in Cuba and began indulging in anti-Yankee rhetoric, he was characterized as crazy by segments of the American press. A *New York Daily News* editorial was entitled, "The Guy Seems to Be Nuts."[1] The *Miami Herald* called him "as balmy as the tradewinds."[2] In early 1961, Castro started charging the United States with backing an invasion of Cuba. *Time* called the claim "wild,"[3] the *Detroit News*, "an utter absurdity."[4] The CIA-trained, U.S.-financed invaders landed at the Bay of Pigs in April of the same year.

After the military coup that removed President Salvador Allende from power in Chile by assassination, Eric Sevareid opined on CBS that the action was an example of Latin American "instability so chronic that the root causes have to lie in the nature and culture of the people. The policies of other nations, including this one [The United States] . . . have to be minor and fleeting influences in comparison."[5] The *New York Times* editorialized that the United States had "on the known record . . . only the most periph-

213

eral responsibility in the downfall of Dr. Allende. . . . To pretend otherwise is simply to obscure the basic reasons for the Chilean tragedy."[6] Earlier, the looming concern in both the news and editorial columns of the *Times* was the safety of American investments. Allende was pictured as a threat to democracy, his opponents as defenders of human rights.[7] At least for a while after the coup, *Times* coverage of the junta was generally positive.[8] Official government reports now show the United States covertly provided millions of dollars to subsidize the opposition to Allende —parties, demonstrations, newspapers, military hardware. The human rights record of this military regime has not been exemplary.

As opposition to the regime of the pro-American Shah of Iran grew more intense in 1978, the dominant theme of American press coverage was typified by this excerpt: "Much of the recent rioting has grown from demonstrations called by religious extremists opposed to the Shah's attempt to Westernize this oil-rich, anti-Communist nation and to loosen the traditionally firm grip of the Moslem clergy."[9] Repeated use of such words as "mobs," "riots," "anarchy," and "rampage" reinforced the picture of a minority of zealots. The Shah was virtually never identified as a "dictator." Instead, his "autocratic" ways were juxtaposed with descriptions of his royal jet-set lifestyle and his dynastic lineage. Rarely was it noted that the Pahlavi "dynasty" reached back only to 1921.[10] *Time* was not atypical in assuring its readers that: "Few believe that the Shah is in any danger of being overthrown. Iran's monarch still has the machinery of power firmly in his hands. The Shah also has a broad base of popular support . . ."[11] Several months later, one of the few effective general strikes in modern history forced the Shah's departure.

These three stories are typical examples of journalistic coverage of foreign affairs, even if they are among the most dramatic cases of faulty analysis and prediction.[12] At the minimum, they reveal a consistent failure to report important aspects of complex but not unfathomable foreign events.

The syndrome is significant. As the preceding chapters document, media–elite relations on domestic politics are often characterized by disagreement, suspicion, even outright hostility. Disputes abound; presidents and other public officials are hard pressed to use the media successfully and continuously to advance their interests and power.

Not so in foreign policy. Elites concerned with foreign affairs tend to agree on goals, to disagree intermittently only on tactics. The basic assumptions: America's diplomatic aims are honorable; American corporate profits and investments must be protected when threatened; revolutionary change is undesirable in most countries and must be discouraged. The reasons for this consensus are beyond our concern. But not the consequences for public opinion. On foreign policy, the mass media tend to speak in a monolithic voice, to report a narrow perspective, to limit rather than expand public knowledge of alternative possibilities. The consequences: the mass media are conduits of elites' visions of America's overseas interests in all but the most exceptional circumstances.

In this chapter, we analyze why the mass media speak with so much unanimity on foreign affairs and fail to provide a diversity of descriptions of foreign countries, their leaders and policies. We begin with the conventional criticisms of foreign news and then invoke the Central Intelligence Agency to introduce a more subtle explanation of the ways in which foreign news is defined, gathered, and reported. We present an illustrative case study of coverage of the Shaba province rebellion in Zaire, and conclude with the likely effects of the syndrome we have identified.

Conventional Explanations

When foreign coverage is criticized for being too brief, too simple, frequently distorted, and often misleading, the explanation is conventionally traced to the shortages reporters encounter overseas. There are four: time, knowledge, labor, and interest. Time: foreign news often concerns fast-breaking crises that do not allow reporters the opportunity to unearth and carefully confirm information. Knowledge: American reporters are frequently dealing with countries whose language and culture are unfamiliar; they cannot help misunderstanding some of what transpires; inevitably, they graft familiar concepts onto an alien reality that might otherwise baffle American audiences. Labor: profit-conscious media proprietors circulate few American reporters around the globe; there are fewer than 200 stationed outside Europe. Correspondents must cover diverse countries spread out over huge territories that often have poor communications and transportation. Interest: even if more and desirable foreign stories were being produced, they would be omitted entirely or cut down to fit the limited foreign news slot.[13]

The reason journalists give for these space limitations is the American public's uninterest in foreign affairs. Except in wartime, polls show foreign policy at the bottom of public priorities and knowledge.[14] Of course, as A. J. Liebling pointed out: "readers . . . who depend entirely on the [wire services] for their foreign coverage are in the position of motorists on a state throughway that is served only by Howard Johnson restaurants. What they get will not make them eager for more."[15]

Under these conditions, it is no surprise that certain kinds of foreign news are pre-eminent. Such news is closely connected to significant leaders (usually heads of state); is usually perceived as negative (the result of person-made or natural disasters), replete with violence and destruction; and, most important, concerns potential threats to American diplomatic and economic interests. Conversely, geographical and especially cultural distance of a country decreases the likelihood of events there being transmitted to Americans.[16] Ambiguous foreign events are likely to be reported to conform to familiar expectations and stereotypes; their ambiguity is underemphasized.

The bulk of foreign news thus originates from states where American cultural ties or diplomatic interests are strongest. A study of network foreign news from 1972–1976 shows 29 percent of the stories stemmed from Western Europe, 26 percent from Indochina, and 19 percent from the Middle East. Only 7 percent came from Africa, and 3 percent from Latin America. There are differences in the kind of news from region to region: 24 percent of the Latin American news concerned natural disasters, in contrast to only 1 percent of the Western European stories.[17] Perhaps nature is crueler to the hapless South Americans, inhabitants of a chaotic and threatening land. More likely, the lack of cultural ties and diplomatic threats south of the border means Central and Latin America must experience some form of destructive violence— mass murders, a revolution, an awesome natural calamity—to make news in the United States.

It could be argued that the mass media perform a valuable service. From the vast amount of data in the world, they select and condense a portion and make it widely available. Some distortion surely creeps in, but this is inevitable. In sum, the media inform public opinion, however imperfectly, and thereby help democratize foreign policy-making.

This is a valid argument, but it neglects very important questions. What precise form do the simplified stories take? Are the shortcuts, emphases, and omissions merely random and idiosyncratic, or do they fall into consistent patterns? If they are patterned, why? And what are their effects on foreign policy and on the possession and use of power in America?

The Central Intelligence Agency

To answer these questions, to delve below conventional explanations of the mass media's foreign news content, it is useful to begin with the Central Intelligence Agency. Carl Bernstein estimates that 400 journalists have had some kind of secret relationship with that organization. This figure excludes "even larger numbers . . . who occasionally traded favors with CIA officers . . ."[18] More than 20 journalists actually worked as paid intelligence operatives for the agency. Perhaps they thought they could keep the two jobs separate. The evidence encourages skepticism:

> The longtime foreign editor of the *Christian Science Monitor* said that he had been "happy to cooperate" with the C.I.A. in the 1950s, providing the agency with letters and memorandums from correspondents that contained background information not included in their dispatches, and occasionally assigning a story in which the C.I.A. had expressed an interest.
> But [he] said he had never known that one of his reporters in the Far East was also serving as a C.I.A. political adviser to the Asian head of state about whom he was writing.[19]

The agency had "paid agents in the foreign bureaus of the Associated Press and United Press International to slip agency-prepared dispatches onto the news wire."[20] Other agents managed press clubs in foreign countries which served as message and mail drops, rest and relaxation centers for correspondents. According to one agent, "some [reporters] are lazy." The manager-agent would "slip them things and they'd phone it in."[21]

At the same time, the CIA controlled or influenced the content of a number of English-language publications regularly read by American foreign correspondents and by journalists in America. Stories and ideas from these publications often appeared in American newspapers and magazines, transmitted by reporters lacking fluency in the local language.[22] The CIA also owned or financed some news agencies. "One, the Foreign News Service, produced articles written by a group of journalists who had been exiled from Eastern European nations. In the early 1960s the articles were sold to as many as 300 newspapers around the world, including the *New York Times,* the *Christian Science Monitor* and the *New York Herald Tribune.*"[23]

Cooperation and connivance extended far beyond individual reporters to news executives and publishers. *New York Times* publisher Arthur Hays Sulzberger arranged for some ten CIA employees to be given *Times* cover between 1950 and 1966 under a general policy to help the agency whenever possible. The publisher had a close relationship with CIA Director Allen Dulles. "At that level of contact it was the mighty talking to the mighty," a high-ranking CIA official said.[24] Indeed, Sulzberger promised Dulles that no *Times* staff member would be allowed to accept an invitation to visit the People's Republic of China without the director's consent. He kept his promise.[25]

CBS executives provided cover for CIA employees and supplied them with outtakes of news films. They "established a formal channel of communication between the Washington bureau chief and the Agency; gave the Agency access to the CBS news film library; and allowed reports by CBS correspondents . . . to be routinely monitored by the CIA. Once a year during the 1950s and early 1960s, CBS correspondents joined the CIA hierarchy for private dinners and briefings."[26] When the head of CBS news complained to CBS president Frank Stanton about having to call the CIA by pay telephone, he was instructed to install a private line bypassing the network's switchboard. He did so.

And when, in 1966, the *New York Times* published a series of articles on the CIA, they were first submitted to former CIA Director John A. McCone, who deleted some elements of the series.[27]

Underlying Causes

This may all seem passé, a carry-over from the Second World War, a relic of the Cold War—mindless patriotism which is no more. The symptoms may be gone: reporters and publishers no longer cooperate widely and well with the CIA; the 1977 *New York*

Times series on the CIA was reportedly not vetted by the agency. But some of the symptoms of the connection remain. They stem from the ways foreign news is viewed, gathered, and reported by journalists for the American mass media. The approach is best summed up by a former editor of *Newsweek*'s foreign section. Asked to explain his cooperation with the CIA, he replied: "We were all on the same side."[28]

In a sense, they still are. The news practices, the professional norms and values that editors and reporters live by, are rooted in the ideological perspective that most Americans share. The result is visible in foreign news; it can be seen by looking both at the content of these stories and at the recipe followed in their creation.

Of the ingredients of mass media content, three are particularly important for foreign news. They are sources, vantage point and language. Each reflects the "same side" view which once encouraged so much credulous cooperation among journalists, their publishers, and the CIA.

The sources upon whom the press relies for foreign news consist mainly of Washington officials concerned with foreign policy who comment on and react to events abroad. Many of the ostensibly foreign news stories in the American mass media emanate entirely from Washington, even though they may be about NATO, Chile, or South Africa. Occasionally, elite critics of administration policies are sought out. While they may criticize various specific decisions or proposals, they usually share and accept the official foreign policy premises and assumptions. They rarely endorse the conduct of states which are less than friendly toward the United States.

Excluded from consideration is the quite substantial body of theory and argument which does question the premises and intentions of American foreign policy. But, as Jerry Hough discovered: "The only spokesmen for such viewpoints which received coverage on the newscasts were either representatives of unfriendly governments (almost always addressing their own people rather than fitting their arguments to the American frame of reference), pacifists speaking in a framework of an idealistic opposition to war in general, or emotional Americans appearing in a setting (usually a wild demonstration) which labels them as extremists."[29] This was in 1967; the situation is little changed today.

People interviewed in a foreign country are frequently officials from the home country stationed abroad (the ambassador, press aides, intelligence agents) whose information often will be off-the-record. When foreigners are interviewed, the reporter's views of who is to be relied upon for credible facts and who is not are strongly influenced by American political values about how societies should work, who is and should be in charge, and what is a justifiable way of bringing about political change. Moreover, in many foreign countries, reporters are limited by language barriers (their own lack of facility with the language and the requirement that the people they interview speak English), restrictions on where they can go and what they can see, the unavailability of records, and censorship on what they transmit.

Consequently, foreign sources are predominantly high-ranking government officials presenting the official viewpoint or the officially sanctioned, not underground, opposition. The major exception is in reporting from communist countries, where anti-government dissidents are often cited. These are the very indomitable men and women whose values are most consonant with those held in democratic societies. Otherwise, groups thought to be communist, terrorist, religiously fanatic, or in any other way outside conventional authority are not the sources reporters rely on for the "facts" they use to build stories. If sought out, their views are usually denigrated.

Allied to sources is the reporter's vantage point. What one sees depends upon where one sits; reporters sit on the side of the States. A movie or television camera's or reporter's vantage point in turn influences audience reactions. As a simple example, television cameras pointed at demonstrators from behind police lines encourage viewers to identify with the predicament of law enforcers facing the hostile menace of militants. When the camera points at the police (a risky location), the identification is reversed. When cameras look down at demonstrators and police from above, audience identification with either side is discouraged, the reasons for the clash dissolved in a welter of violence.

A vantage point, then, is inevitable; and it determines the questions asked and problems posed by reporters. These usually revolve around the implications of the events for American interests as defined by the president and State Department. Questions that represent different definitions of problems and issues tend not to be asked—or answered. But it is the questions as much as the answers which inform the audience.

Finally, there is language. Words often become symbols that

transmit meaning beyond their mere definitions. The interpretations people make of foreign news, the attitudes they develop, are influenced by the ways the stories are written. The United States seems usually to have "allies" whose freedom it "defends." The Soviet Union has "satellites" which it "controls." A Russian-equipped army tends to be labeled "communist" though its American-backed opponents are rarely called "capitalist." The words chosen by sources, especially high-ranking officials concerned with foreign affairs in the reporter's own country, tend to be the words used by reporters. Thus is language imprinted with the vantage point of sources.

There are differences in foreign reporting. Because the countries of Western Europe are political allies of and culturally congruent with America, they are the best covered by the American media. Stories are more detailed, complex, and balanced than those from less industrialized states. Even so, the stories are usually confined to notable political events such as elections; stereotype-reinforcing, quirky occurrences; and economic, military, and diplomatic activities which bear on America. In contrast, most East European countries are barely covered. Communist governments' restrictions on journalists' access and their totalitarian control over their societies compound reporters' difficulties.

What follows is a case study of an instance of reporting from a less industrialized state. News from these countries tends to focus on communist involvement and negatively to portray the groups or events that threaten what American officials define as U.S. interests. Such coverage is important for public opinion and policy. These are the very states where American military power is most likely to be deployed, where public and official unfamiliarity with the countries leads them to rely most heavily on media accounts.

Reporting Rebellion in Zaire

This case involves a fast-breaking crisis in an out-of-the-way territory of an unfamiliar country. Zaire has few if any full-time American correspondents, poor transportation, worse communications. The shortages of time, knowledge, labor, and interest that generally afflict America's foreign correspondents were particularly onerous. They explain much of the coverage, the marked shortcomings early on, and the later improvement as time elapsed, knowledge accumulated, more reporters were assigned, and interest developed. Yet journalists throughout had some freedom to choose sources, perspective, and language. We focus on those choices, which heavily influenced Americans' impressions of events in Zaire.

Although foreign news coverage has improved considerably since the early, credulous years of the Vietnam war,[30] this case study indicates that some traits—those visible in the sources, perspective, and language that American journalists employ—linger on. In many respects there were at least two versions of events in Zaire; Americans received much of one, far less of the other.[31]

On May 15, 1978, the story first made front-page headlines. What were labeled "invading rebels" attacked the important mining center of Kolwezi in the southern Zairean province of Shaba. They ruled the town for several days. Then, with American logistical support, Belgium and France sent in troops on what was called a "humanitarian" mission to rescue the Europeans. The foreign troops, along with those of the central Zaire government headed by Mobuto Sese Seko, soon forced the rebels to retreat. The major themes of the reporting were the alleged role played by Russia and especially Cuba in arming, training, and leading the rebels; and the mass slaughtering by the rebels of the Europeans who owned and operated the mines.

We have performed a content analysis of coverage in the *Washington Post,* the *San Francisco Chronicle, Newsweek,* and *Time.* In most instances they used the same sources and language and stressed the same themes. There were two phases of coverage, reflecting changing opinions from American officials. Phase I consisted of the events themselves. Phase II was the subsequent three-week period, when there was a controversy in Washington about Cuban involvement.[32] For all the data, consult the accompanying table.

First the sources. During Phase I, in the *Washington Post,* U.S. or European officials were quoted or cited some 65 times, officials of the Mobutu government 15 times. People from the Congo National Liberation Front (FLNC), which was responsible for the rebellion, were quoted or cited 6 times. *Post* readers—including most American government officials—saw the events almost entirely from the vantage point of American, French, and Belgian officials. The ratio was almost as skewed in the *Chronicle.*

Press Coverage of Zaire

	Washington Post*		S. F. Chronicle*		Newsweek*		Time*	
	May 15–May 27	*May 28–Jun 15*	*May 15–May 27*	*May 28–Jun 15*	*May 15–May 27*	*May 28–Jun 15*	*May 15–May 27*	*May 28–Jun 15*
No. of times U.S. or European source quoted/cited	65	N.A.**	58	N.A.	N.A.	N.A.	N.A.	N.A.
No. of times FLNC quoted/cited	6	4	10	0	2	0	0	0
Ratio Eur./U.S.: FLNC quoted/cited	11:1	—	6:1	—	—	—	—	—
Cuban link affirmed	36	35	20	20	19	10	12	7
Cuban link denied	13	33	10	16	3	6	2	3
Ratio affirm : deny	3:1	1:1	2:1	1:1	6:1	2:1	6:1	2:1
No. of times Cuba(n), Russia(n), communist mentioned	167	179	71	89	41	18	59	29

* All *page one* stories and editorials about "rebel invasion" of Shaba. All counts are approximate.
** Not ascertained.

In *Time,* the FLNC was not used as a source even once, in *Newsweek* only twice. The Phase II disparity was even greater: only the *Post* quoted the FLNC at all. Phase II was mostly about the accuracy of charges of Russian-Cuban involvement during Phase I. The FLNC, with a press office in Brussels, was barely consulted on that issue. Assuredly the office issued incomplete and propagandistic information, but so did the Zairean government officials who were quoted.

THE CUBAN CONNECTION

Not surprisingly, given this vantage point, the questions asked and problems posed centered on the preoccupations of American officials. During Phase I those people were apparently convinced or wanted Americans to believe that the rebellion had been led by Cubans and Russians. This was the view propounded by the press. Denials came mostly from sources explicitly denigrated as illegitimate, like Fidel Castro, and were heavily outnumbered by accusations from high American and European office-holders.

The facts are unclear. Castro claimed he tried to dissuade the rebels because he feared their action would provoke Western intervention threatening Angola's sovereignty. Besides, most Cubans in Angola were in the southeast; the Shaba rebels were in the remote northeast. This explanation was largely ignored, discounted, or rejected. A *Chronicle* editorial was entitled, "Fidel Castro's Big Lie on Africa."[33]

Carter administration spokespersons were the most important sources of the claim of Cuban involvement. These claims commenced on the day of the American-assisted Belgian-French intervention. Whatever the reasons behind the administration's public position—an attempt to portray President Carter as an implacable foe of predatory communism, simple confusion, genuine belief in the accuracy of its version—it was the administration's perspective that was conveyed by the press during Phase I. Yet two days before the first public charges, Castro had privately advised the administration that he was trying to quell the rebels and had told his troops not to cooperate with them. Castro may not have been truthful, but when his confidential assurances were leaked from the Senate three weeks later, the administration charge changed dramatically. Then it was claimed not that Cuba had led the invasion, but that Castro could have done more to stop it.

Thus, during Phase II, as legitimate sources in Congress (not Castro) started publicly disagreeing with Carter, coverage became more balanced. Additional background information was available to reporters. The shortage problems had decreased—there is a journalistic learning curve that usually makes later coverage more accurate than early-breaking crisis stories.

Now language. The UPI lead in the *Chronicle* on the first day of Phase I began: "Cuban-led, Soviet-backed Zairean rebels invaded the copper-rich province of Shaba. . . ."[34] The words "Cuba," "Russia" and "Communist" appeared repeatedly in the stories—dozens of times more often than "FLNC" or "Mobutu," the two major parties to the dispute. The language was a drumbeat of threatening verbal symbols, conjuring up Cold War images of the international communist conspiracy. The word "invaded" implies that the rebellion was outside aggression against a legitimate government. In fact, the rebels had earlier been forced to flee their homes in Zaire by President Mobutu, who had good reason to eject militant opponents. But they were "invading" only because they were exiles. The Mobutu government and its European and American backers perceived them as invaders. The rebels probably saw themselves as returning; the CIA-backed Mobutu[35] and the European mine operators as the invaders.

The words "invading rebels" were used instead of "FLNC." It was the same in Vietnam, where the term NLF was rarely used by American journalists to refer to the southern opponents of the Saigon regime.[36] The press used the labels supplied by American allies, rather than the group's self-designation. The power of labeling is consequential: calling it the FLNC grants the group some status as a political organization with reasons for trying to topple Mobutu's government.

Often foreign news concerns unconventional political opposition (anything beyond voting) to rulers the American government recognizes as legitimate. Media coverage of the opponents tends to concentrate on their methods rather than their political grievances. This is precisely what American officials usually see as the immediate political problem—the unauthorized activity and accompanying instability. So the conflict is defined from the standpoint of the American and foreign leaders who serve as journalistic sources: restoring order is the problem, not righting wrongs.

The words reporters use are emblematic. In the Zaire stories there were many references to the problem of making towns "stable," of restoring their "security." The American audience was encouraged to identify with this point of view. But to the FLNC, security and stability in Zaire could only be achieved by the removal of Mobutu and his supporters. By centering the story on the struggle to reassert orderly obedience to existing rulers, the media often rob movements of their political essence and depict their followers as outlaws.

Certainly Russian and Cuban involvement in training and equipping the FLNC implicated those nations deeply in the events. But the media stressed and stretched that one facet of a complex story beyond its genuine import. Too much was left out or glossed over.

Phase II did convey doubts and rebuttals from legitimate sources about the claimed Cuban connection. These stories rendered the Phase I charges of the Carter administration and others less believable; they reflected the continuing disputes over how to interpret and handle specific foreign problems that have bedeviled America's elites since Vietnam. Such disagreements have made the management of public opinion on particular foreign policy choices more difficult for recent administrations. But there are four reasons to think the most significant effect of both phases of the Zaire story was to maintain public support of the underlying assumptions and goals of American foreign policy, and thereby to increase the likelihood of public acceptance of the specific actions that elites finally agree upon.

First, the total number of assertions of direct Cuban participation far outnumbered the denials. The original chargers were the most sensationally portrayed and prominently displayed. Other subtle, less quantifiable aspects of coverage such as language and perspective strengthened the legitimacy of the claims. And, illustrating the stabilization of attitudes by incomplete resolution (see Chapter 11), the assertions fit the long-held expectations of reporters, officials, and ordinary citizens about the expansionist aims of communism. Reinforcement of this fundamental ideological tenet of American foreign policy was probably the main consequence of the Zaire story.

Second, the study reveals the continuing tendency to overlook the complexities and independence of nationalist revolutionary groups, to paint them as monolithic puppets of communist masters who can command their perfect obedience. Yet the ideological leanings of the FLNC are unclear. Some say they are only slightly to the left of Mobutu, and they have been roundly criticized by the leftist leaders of Mozambique and Angola. The media's frequent view is that "to have Russian guns is to have Marxist ideas."[37]

Third, crucial historical background was missing, just as it was from Vietnam reporting.[38] There was very little reference to the rebellions that had recently taken place in other parts of the country; to the Mobutu government's suppression of human rights; or to statistics indicating a steep decline in real income levels of the average urban resident of Zaire since Mobutu seized power.[39]

Finally, the coverage was never balanced by a full depiction of the geopolitical context. Like Russia and Cuba, the United States, Belgium, and France also train and arm African soldiers, overtly and covertly. The involvement of all five countries is rooted in a mélange of diplomatic, economic, ideological, and even ethical ambitions. But press coverage subsumed this complexity, emphasizing the good intentions of Americans and Europeans and the hostile gropings and graspings of the others. For example, the economic aims of the European troop landing—protection of their countries' lucrative mines—were whispered, while the humanitarian aspect was trumpeted and juxtaposed with portraits of FLNC looters. And in the storm over external support of the FLNC the media overlooked Zairean president Mobutu's history of handsome support by the CIA, the agency that helped to overthrow his predecessor. Such information would have provided a more realistic picture of the way international affairs are conducted, and of the full range of geopolitical sources and stakes of the Kolwezi developments.

SAVAGERY

Besides the purported Russian-Cuban link, the main Phase I theme was the killing of white civilians. The story was reported in sensational language that again gave only a part of a complex picture.

The *Chronicle* wrote of "a frenzy of killing and looting by rebel forces."[40] (An AP story we came across began similarly: "Rebel tribesmen slaughtered as many as 200 persons in a 'hunt for the white man' during the weeklong Kolwezi siege."[41]) The *Chronicle* included such phrases as "hordes, men of an extremely low level, full of hate and savagery"[42]; "left on their own, they went out of control"[43]; "bloodbath of terror."[44] The first *Chroni-*

cle report of the number of black casualties (far in excess of those suffered by whites) came four days after the white death stories.

Time claimed that "drunken guerrillas ran amuck, shooting, killing, wounding, maiming, and raping." [45] It also referred to the retreating FLNC force as the "largest and best organized stolen-car ring in history." [46] *Newsweek* wrote that the rebels "went berserk" [47] and that around their leader's neck "hung a radio-cassette player loaded with a Ray Coniff tape." [48]

The *Post* reported less sensationally, with more complexity and depth. Yet like the other three publications it described the retreaters as "loot-laden." [49] And its ethnocentrism was more veiled. For example, it described Kolwezi as a "once-prosperous city of small, neatly-kept villas and bungalows surrounded by trim hedges and flowering bougainvillea shrubs." [50] That description actually applied only to the white enclave, not the far larger, poverty-filled sections inhabited by the black majority.

Alternative facts, language, and interpretations were available but mostly unused. Stereotypes often prevailed. The word "frenzy" suggests that intoxication or going berserk are the only conceivable explanations of the black assaults. Perhaps years of festering resentment toward the effects of neocolonialism had something to do with the tragedy; but again this political aspect of the event was hidden. The rebels may have stolen cars to escape quickly from the technologically superior European forces, not for joy-riding. They may have used the "loot" to trade for food along the path of retreat. The number of white deaths was later estimated at under 100. The AP story called the rebels "tribesmen," thereby suggesting primitivism. But the FLNC, President Mobutu's forces, even the Belgian (Flemish and Walloon) army consisted of people from assorted "tribes."

This distinction among members of the FLNC, local blacks, and Mobutu's troops was obscured in the press, where the Africans were lumped together, labeled "drunken guerrillas" and smeared with the guilt for despicable acts. It now appears possible that some of the terror resulted from the spontaneously unleashed anger of black residents, not FLNC rebels; and some of the rest may have been committed by Mobutu's troops. The truth is hazy, indeterminate; but depictions of the FLNC's behavior obscured the ambiguity.

Besides being undifferentiated, black victims of the Kolwezi events were neglected. Television and the press contained numerous pictures of distraught Europeans arriving at Belgian airports with horror stories. The *Post* and *Chronicle* carried interviews with white victims, describing their ordeals in the compassionate, personal detail that encourages reader identification. There were few such personalized depictions either of black victims of violence or of the daily hardships endured by black residents of Kolwezi.

Much of this reporting stemmed from the sources used by the journalists involved. Officers in the European forces and white inhabitants of the area spoke reporters' language and provided the perspectives, the experiences, the facts for the stories. Moreover, the suffering of the whites, the deaths of missionaries, gave reporters a news peg on which to hang their stories for the American audience. And some coverage may have been attributable to the residue of racism to which reporters, like most other Americans, are susceptible. Whatever the reasons, the misleading coverage was scarcely corrected. In contrast to the issue of Cuban involvement, there was no Phase II. No alternative version was leaked from the U.S. Senate. Incomplete resolution was especially marked for this aspect of the Zaire story; audience stereotypes about savage communism and primitive Africa were stabilized.

Public Opinion

Although the Zaire story probably helped resurrect fears about the international communist menace and to reinforce white Americans' racial worries, it would be misleading to overemphasize its influence on opinions, especially of the mass citizenry. Zaire was all but forgotten by them a year later. Rather, the coverage should be seen as part of a stream of events and messages that establish a general perception by attentive and mass publics of the international political climate. This perception is used by elite power wielders and seekers to garner support for policies or candidates.

The Zaire story came amid reports of Russian and Cuban penetration in Angola, Ethiopia, and elsewhere in Africa. As part of this confluence of events and stories, Zaire probably helped to elevate defense issues to the public agenda. It made more visible the concern of some elites with the purported escalation of Russian arms budgets and deterioration of Western military potency. The lurid details of Zaire evoked a gruesome image of the consequences of one instance of ostensible Russian expansionism. Perhaps this made defense a higher-priority voting issue for some mass and attentive citizens; the reports may also have activated members of the attentive public to write Congress or join a pressure group.

The coverage may in addition have contributed to a change in opinions. Only indirect evidence is available. CBS/*New York Times* polls taken in 1977 and June 1978 (after Phase II) found that approval for "reestablishing diplomatic and trade relations with Cuba" fell from 55 to 43 percent; opposition rose from 29 to 45 percent.[51] A poll in 1975 showed a 52–21 percent majority opposed to sending supplies to the American-backed side in the Angolan civil war. By summer 1978, after Zaire, 56–34 percent approved sending supplies to American allies in Africa, and 53–40 percent endorsed sending U.S. military advisers to African countries threatened by communism. Pollster Louis Harris wrote that this was the "first time since Vietnam" that a majority had favored overseas military advisers.[52] And so we come full circle from the lessons of Vietnam.

Subtly and overtly, racial fears were reflected and probably reinforced by the coverage. Stereotyped vocabularies called forth archetypal fears of "savagery," left over from tales of the "dark continent." Imagery was remarkably reminiscent as well of the stories about the U.S. ghetto riots of the 1960s: drunkenness, looting, outside agitators, and a situation devoid of political meaning. The Phase I stories left the impression that African political organizations can have no independent will. Only if stirred up and led by Cuban guides will they move.

The framework of the Zaire coverage was Africa as a superpower battleground. This reflects the American media's habit of depicting events outside Europe and English-language countries in terms of their impact on U.S.–U.S.S.R. competition. But this approach may be only marginally relevant to understanding what transpired, thereby misleading policy-makers and misdirecting public opinion. Even when the perspective has a modicum of validity, a clearer understanding of American stakes would be obtained if coverage encompassed more fully the vantage points of the indigenous inhabitants involved in the events. The tragic results of epistemological ethnocentrism in Vietnam teach no less.

Impacts on Power

The foreign news formula gives high American governmental officials privileged access to the media. When they agree on an interpretation of a foreign occurrence, news stories will lopsidedly favor it. The coverage will not be subject to "balance" in the way domestic issues sometimes are. When public officials are in disagreement over a foreign policy issue, mass media coverage may present a wider range of information and alternatives for public consumption. But even in such cases, as in Vietnam and the Panama Canal and SALT II treaties, the perspective, language, and policy alternatives are still set by official sources.

Among all high officials, presidents are especially adept at manipulating public opinion by creating foreign media events. These include bogus or real crises, state visits, and dramatic diplomatic initiatives. The media love crises. And presidential visits, like Nixon's 1972 China excursion, fit mass media, especially television, interests beautifully.

A president whose popularity is in decline can take unfavorable news off the front page, as Jimmy Carter did with his Camp David Middle East peace initiative, thereby reshaping the whole news agenda temporarily. A president who has violated majority preferences on domestic policy can distract media attention from this fact during re-election campaigns, as did Nixon by his foreign travels. This ability to divert lessens presidential accountability on domestic policy and reinforces the power of elites who prefer the domestic status quo undisturbed by informed public opinion or debate. Much better if the citizenry is told about the China (or Berlin, or Wailing) Wall, or "Russian and Cuban aggression" in Zaire, when unemployment, inflation, and the rest persist.

Lower-level officials also manipulate foreign coverage. Bureaucrats may try to slip stories into the news in order to promote policies they or their agencies favor; to create a positive atmosphere—prestige—for their department; or to advance their personal careers.[53] The CIA has a long history of effective news management, only briefly exposed. The agency has planted fake stories on far-off places, for example, to affect American public opinion and foreign policy, and even to alter the internal policies of other nations.[54]

Foreign leaders now realize that to overcome the media's wall, they must scale it themselves and address Americans directly in as unmediated a way as possible—if necessary, come to this country. No one in recent years has understood this better than Egyptian President Anwar Sadat, followed, at some remove, by Israeli Prime Minister Begin. Sadat relishes exploiting the media's susceptibility for grand gestures (his trip to Israel), emotional displays (his embrace of Begin), rhetorical flourishes (too many to need instancing), and drama based on secrecy (the Camp David summit).

The media–elite relationship works both ways. Except for those who serve on foreign affairs committees, most members of Congress (and their staffs) rely on a few specialized and prestige media, especially the *Washington Post* and the *New York Times*, for most of their information about the state of the world. Cohen maintains that newspapers have enormous impact on congressional perceptions of foreign reality, and that those ideas shape their responses to foreign policy proposals.[55]

Thus Zaire coverage might have contributed to the renascent hawkishness on Capitol Hill in the late 1970s. This new thunder on the right arose from the direct effect of the Zaire story (and similar ones) on congressional perceptions, and from the impact representatives thought the stories had on public opinion. Often, too, news stories supply the rhetoric and arguments legislators use in defending their votes on defense appropriations and other foreign policies;[56] those statements in turn can attract media coverage and sway public opinion.

Foreign policy bureaucrats may have little information outside their own bailiwicks. Media stories tell them what is happening in the rest of the world. And officials often learn from the press what other agencies in Washington are thinking about a situation. As Cohen observes, the media provide officialdom with a common pool of foreign data, a pool that helps coordinate—and perhaps mislead, as in Zaire—agency decision-making.[57]

Corporate executives use foreign news as well. Leaders of multinationals employ media information in making investment decisions. The same people, as interest group leaders, may use media reports as a basis for deciding on the policies they will lobby Congress to enact.

For the mass citizen, rarely attentive or knowledgeable about foreign affairs but usually aware of major upheavals (like Zaire), four likely effects stand out. First, because news emanating from the less industrialized countries consists primarily of violence, conflict, and disaster, Americans may believe life in these countries to be more strife-ridden, less desirable, than life at home. Foreigners are seen as less willing to compromise, more irrational than Americans. The mass media show ideology and fervent religious convictions as dangerous, animating violence in Iran, Lebanon, and elsewhere. Americans can easily conclude that sectarian or just strongly held beliefs inevitably lead to disastrous conflicts and should therefore be avoided.

Second, the mass media infrequently display viable foreign alternatives to the American system. The Scandinavian way of life rarely appears; certainly social experiments in Eastern Europe do not—unless demonstrating oppression and failure. What about Western Europe? Of 164 television stories analyzed by one scholar, only four dealt with new programs. All four (gambling control, narcotics control, marriage law in Italy, and the introduction of the decimal coin system in Britain) proposed changes that would bring their countries more closely into conformity with American practices.[58]

Third, foreign news provides pseudo-participation, an illusion of public discussion, a symbol of democratic input and power in this most elitist of policy areas. But, fourth, while the mass media do sometimes promote opposition to current policies when legitimate elite sources are opposing them, as for a time was true with Vietnam, they maintain the public's support of the underlying long-run goals in international politics.[59] The media contribute to stabilizing public acceptance by allowing the perspectives, language, blind spots, and prejudices of their elite sources to inform overseas reporting. Unintentionally, often unconsciously, or even against their will, journalists—severely hampered by the four shortages and tightly hemmed in by the conventional news practices we have described—write stories that assist America's foreign policy elites. In the main, foreign news reporting helps the powerful mobilize public opinion (or quiescence) behind the basic goals of policies on which most Americans have little information and less control.

CHAPTER FOURTEEN

•

Participating in Politics

"Our job isn't . . . to give people what they're interested in. Our job is to provide people with the basic data that make democracy work. . . . We are engaged in a great moral enterprise." [1]

Richard S. Salant (former president of CBS News)

By PARTICIPATING IN POLITICS, ordinary Americans can try to exert power and influence the foreign and domestic decisions of public officials. Forms of participation include voting, the most common; contributing to a campaign fund or other political cause; writing an official; helping out in a campaign; working with a party, citizens' or other interest group to lobby, petition, organize; taking part in a demonstration; rioting; terrorizing; and running for office.

Neurosis,[2] boredom, sexual desire, career advancement, and fad—one or all of these can motivate involvement in politics. But our main concern is with participation whose objective is seeking and exerting power—the expression, facilitation, and achievement of political preferences.

How infinite are the ways the mass media could stimulate political participation! Their stories might and occasionally do demystify leaders and expose corruption; recount disastrous governmental policies; link problems and issues with the suffering or gain of specific groups; associate particular political acts with definite outcomes; tell audiences who gets what, when, how, and why.

But we have already shown that the mass media socialize Americans to accept the legitimacy of their governing institutions

and mold public opinion in substantial conformity with the perspectives of elites. Now we shall argue that, on balance, the press
diminishes the ability and inclination of ordinary Americans—the
mass citizenry—to participate effectively in politics, to advance
their interests by pressuring elites.

To Vote or Not to Vote

FOR PRESIDENT

Electoral participation requires two decisions: whether to vote
and for whom. Since 1964, even presidential elections have mus-
tered barely more than half the voting age adults.

People decide whether to vote by considering the following:
whether one party would, in office, benefit them more than the
other; whether their vote might affect the outcome because the
election is predicted to be close; whether they obtain personal
gratification from being part of the ritual of voting; and the costs of
voting—taking the time to gather information, register, make a
decision, and go to the polls. These costs can easily outweigh
benefits because the impact of any one vote on the election result
is minimal.[3]

In some ways, the mass media encourage voting in presidential elections. They report obvious party differences, cover the
candidates, and highlight the closeness of the contest. The elections consist of a year-long or longer media campaign in which
drama, conflict and suspense over the eventual outcome promote
interest and reaffirm the value of the voting ritual.

The abiding love of journalists for the election rite surfaced in
early reporting on the vote turnout of November 2, 1976. Pollsters
had projected a low turnout. Yet on election day observers at the
polls discerned long lines and claimed a tremendous outpouring of
civic spirit. Exulted Walter Cronkite on the CBS Evening News:
". . . it could even be a modern record." Said John Chancellor,
more understated as usual: "It looks as though we have a big story
on our hands tonight. The voters are going to the polls in what may
turn out to be record numbers . . ." The *New York Times* led an
edition with this headline: "Carter Leads in Heavy Vote." Most
journals with early deadlines echoed the *Times,* including *Newsweek.*[4] That people still cared enough to vote was a big story. It

confounded the doomsaying prophets—many of whom had blamed the media for inducing cynicism and apathy.

But the turnout was the lowest since 1948. Reporters and editors trusted the exaggerated perceptions of harried election day clerks and put out an erroneous story. Journalistic gullibility stemmed from a genuine desire to transmute doleful predictions that would confirm the desultory state of American democracy into a reaffirming ritual. Once upon a time, elections had been just that.

But the mass media treat the electoral process ambivalently. Accompanying the civics-book naiveté that inspires the enthusiastic reminder to "get out and vote" is the cynical perspective pervading campaign news. Reporters explain most candidates' actions as motivated by the search for votes. Stories focus on candidates' strategic plotting and personal styles at the expense of issues and positions.[5]

Journalists tend to denigrate the policy implications of elections because they believe, often rightly, that candidates evade or respond with generalizations to meaningful policy issues. Madison Avenuized candidates are themselves much to blame. As we explained in Chapter 3, politicians have reasons publicly to fudge significant conflicts. These incentives and inclinations are not created, only magnified, by the need to serve journalistic interests. The nominees' advertising campaigns, patently manipulative, do little to dignify the act of voting.

At the same time, reporters neglect policy differences between the candidates expressed not in public rhetoric but in the specifics of the parties' platforms, candidates' position papers, and in the specialist press. These sometimes fugitive policy positions are not always easy to pin down. Reporters may also believe that promises will be re-examined and re-evaluated by the victorious candidate when he is forced in office realistically to confront limited resources and competing priorities. And certainly policy stands lack glamor and immediacy; they cannot compete for audience attention with the clash of personalities, candidates' flubs, campaign strategies, and horse race prognostications as news.

As consumers of news, audiences may be uninterested in discussions of candidates' policies toward the Federal Reserve Board, multinational corporations, and the automobile industry—news which would help them as voters. Perhaps it is not possible to present policy issues in ways uniting public fascination and understanding. We suspect, however, that people would welcome exposure of the likely effects of the Fed's decisions on their incomes, of multinational corporations on their jobs, of Detroit on the energy shortage. They are usually not accorded the opportunity.

Coverage that centers on horse race and hoopla consequently depresses the quality—the rationality—of voting, and perhaps the turnout level as well. It does so by submerging policy differences among the candidates and obscuring the real effects the candidates' goals (if achieved) and their debts (if paid) would have on citizens' lives.

There is another way in which media coverage tends to compound confusion about, even hostility toward, the candidates among the electorate. For many people, a presidential campaign is experienced through the media as a bombardment of disparate and incompatible claims. Although coverage has a narrative thrust climaxing on election night, daily campaign events appear disjointed, confusing, and conflicting. In part this is accurate: candidates contradict each other, and the meanings of events are sometimes hard to discern. But the way the media report the campaigns adds to the confusion, leading to a "plague on all the candidates" attitude among many members of the electorate.

At the same time, by portraying the election as a saga, the presidency as a sort of holy grail, the media establish expectations of capacities and performance which no candidate can fulfill. Then by sheer excess of coverage, by persistent and detailed scrutiny of the candidates, by emphasis on their strategies, media coverage confirms the candidates' inadequacies for the job. The contenders are unworthy. Again voting is discouraged.

Most people use just one power resource: their vote. The lower the voting participation, the more politics is left to the "haves," who take other forms of action, and the less influence the "have nots" can expect. As voting levels drop, power is redistributed toward elites.

In Other Elections

The same overt encouragement and implicit discouragement of voting colors the news of non-presidential elections. An editorial in the morning daily *Harrisburg Patriot* the day before a local primary election typifies encouragement. It urged people to involve themselves in electing officials whose decisions "can affect our daily lives more than the political super-stars—candidates for President, Governor, or U.S. Senator. . . . there is a qualitative value in our system when compared to others. Unfortunately, it often isn't appreciated until the voting privilege is denied."[6]

Yet from an analysis of the newspaper's coverage during the seven weeks prior to the elections, Christopher Sayer claimed to find a total of less than a page on the local races. All but three of these items were straightforward rewrites of candidates' press releases. Even these stopped appearing almost three weeks before election day. Of the three staff-originated stories, two were brief pieces about a legal challenge to the ballot, while the third, a Sunday wrap-up, merely listed all the candidates.[7]

Harrisburg's *Patriot* may be typical. Mary Ellen Leary examined the coverage on six of California's major metropolitan television stations of the 1974 gubernatorial election. It was Jerry Brown's first run for the office. Of a total of 257 hours of news shows between September 4 and November 5, 2 percent (six hours) was about the campaign for governor. Two hours were aired on one station. Five of the stations averaged 48 minutes each over two months. Leary's explanation for this neglect: news managers found the campaign a bore and thought viewers agreed. They cut coverage in fear of losing rating points.[8]

Local media cannot provide exhaustive descriptions of all the dozens of candidates who run in state and local primaries and general elections. The information shortage is inevitable. The media merely compound it, with two main effects.

First, the failure to provide useful information raises costs of voting. Citizens wanting to find out anything about the candidates have to dig energetically—a task for which few powerless Americans have the background, time, and inclination. Under these conditions, especially in the absence of other guides to voting, it may be wiser to stay home rather than cast ballots in virtual ignorance.

Second, the media procure some political power for themselves. Given the ignorance under which most citizens labor, almost any morsel of information can have a significant impact on local voting; hence the finding that editorial endorsements are highly correlated with local electoral victories.[9] Republican and conservative incumbents and initiatives are the main beneficiaries, given the editorial position of most newspapers.

Voting

TRADITIONAL PERSPECTIVE

Despite or because of the mass media, a fair number of Americans go to the polls. What are the effects of media coverage on their voting decisions? The traditional perspective may be summed up as the "law of minimal consequences." The media are described as without effect on or as reinforcing the existing views of voters.[10] Conversion of a voter from support of one candidate to his or her opponent is rare, if it occurs at all.[11] Most Americans vote consistently, year after year, for the same party; their minds are made up before the campaign begins; shifter-doubters usually end equivocation by returning to their original preference. Undecided voters, those who change their opinions most during an election, are a very small minority of the electorate, one least exposed to the media.

The traditional view is that most people's voting intentions are set in advance of election campaigns by long-standing party and group loyalties. These assumptions apply no longer. In the years since the research cited above, a precipitous decline in party identification and loyalty has occurred. More voters now identify themselves as independents than Republicans. The undecideds are now often the most, not the least, educated and informed members of the electorate. With the breakdown of party and other allegiances, voting intentions are not pre-determined and people are susceptible to alternative influences. Nie, Verba, and Petrocik write that changes since the 1950s "add up to an 'individuation' of American political life. . . . The individual voter evaluates candidates on the basis of information and impressions conveyed by the mass media, and then votes on that basis. He or she acts as an individual, not as a member of a collectivity."[12]

But two distinctions are vital. We must distinguish the pre-election period from the campaign, and differentiate types of elections.

DISTINCTIONS

In previous chapters, we showed the mass media at work socializing Americans and shaping their opinions. As a result, the media influence voting intentions well before an election year is under way. All sorts of news stories—about crime, business derelictions, inflation, unemployment, and presidential excursions— have numerous, subtle, and interrelated effects on public opinion before, during, and after elections. The news elevates and submerges politicians and issues, links undeclared and declared candidates to policy positions or symbols thereof, creates new and changes old policy preferences and priorities. These effects impinge on and may even determine people's voting decisions.

It is also necessary to distinguish among elections. Some elections are far more structured for the electorate than others. By this we mean that they contain many guides for voting. These cues include the candidates' political parties, race, and perhaps even sex. For a male, black voter, a member of the Democratic party, a decision between a candidate with his characteristics and a white, wealthy, female Republican candidate is unlikely to be changed by media coverage of the election. But if the election is a Democratic primary and all three candidates are black and male, none of them incumbents, then voters have a far more difficult choice; media coverage of the election may be their only guide.

As further complication, there is usually more than one contest on a ballot. Voters not only decide whether to go to the polling booth or not but, once there, whether to vote for all the offices (from president to local board of education); and to vote for all the candidates of one party or divide their votes among the parties.

DECISIONS

Voting decisions result from a complex combination of attitudes including: party identification; perceptions of candidates (their personalities, ideologies, honesty, sincerity, leadership ability, and competence); and stances toward issues (their nature, solution, and relative importance). People vote for candidates they believe to be closest to their more intense preferences in these areas.[13] Although many people form impressions about the candidates and their issue positions from friends, acquaintances (occasionally enemies), and other personal contacts, the mass media are their main sources of information.

The media directly shape perceptions through the news they transmit about candidates' issue stands, ideological philosophies, and personal qualities. This news is rarely comprehensive, sometimes inaccurate. Nor of course do voters necessarily interpret media messages correctly. The result is often a great deal of public misperception. In 1972, Mr. Nixon's personal qualities were widely misapprehended; George McGovern's policy stands were viewed as being farther from those of the voters than they actually were.[14] Nixon and McGovern contributed to these disjunctions; so did the press.

The media influence the public's beliefs about which issues in a campaign are important. This priority setting[15] can favor one candidate and party by bringing their "issues" (e.g., the other candidate's "corrupt" associates) to public consciousness.

Information provided by the media also shapes voters' criteria of judgment—their standards. For example, when election news focuses on the candidates' ability to administer their campaign organizations effectively,[16] audiences are inclined to start judging the contestants' competence and leadership on this basis. And what the media omit is just as important, especially the difficult to obtain details on the business dealings of the candidates with their more dubious associates.

In sum, the attitudes and beliefs which Americans bring to an election campaign have been molded by the media. Once the campaign is under way, the media continue their impact by shaping people's perceptions, criteria of judgment, and agenda of issues. The cumulative effect of all this coverage is to influence the formation and expression of voting intentions—even if such effects are difficult (impossible) to measure directly. Furthermore, the media influence the electorate's behavior and election results in ways which are usually overlooked. They have direct effects on turnout, roll-off (voting for all the offices on the ballot or just a few), and split ticket or straight party voting.[17] They also indirectly affect election outcomes by stirring (or deterring) people to donate (more) funds to a party or candidate, solicit funds for them, canvass on their behalf, and promote them with friends and acquaintances.

Participation Beyond Voting

PRACTICAL

Voting is an important but limited way for an individual American to try to exert power. The vote conveys little information about preferences to its recipient. Even if the victorious candidates want to do their constituents' bidding, they may not know what it is. Practical participation, such as contacting public officials by letter or in person, contributing to an interest group, instituting a court suit, or forming a block association, is more effective. Directly or indirectly, it can communicate specific desires, demands, rewards, and threats in conventionally acceptable ways.

The mass media could alert and arouse members of the attentive and mass publics to these more potent forms of political participation. Sometimes they do so. One of the more striking examples came when President Richard Nixon fired Watergate Special Prosecutor Archibald Cox, Attorney General Elliot Richardson, and Richardson's deputy, William Ruckelshaus. His action was quickly dubbed the "Saturday Night Massacre." The thinly veiled outrage of radio and television commentators at this apparent violation of democratic norms, their barely disguised excitement over a constitutional crisis, helped generate a deluge of telegrams to the White House and Congress. How different the public reaction would have been if the "massacre" had been treated as a tolerable shift in government officials. Instead it justified dramatic interruption of regular programming, and the opening of the airways to Cox. This media-inspired contacting of officials affected policy: it helped to fortify a timorous Congress, which, even at that late date, had not begun seriously considering impeachment.

Such dramatic explosions are rare. Yet every day the press is full of stories about public officials, policies, and politically active groups and individuals. The news surely provokes occasional concern, outrage, even fear about some government actions and inactions. These reactions can move attentive and even mass citizens to practical political participation. But the mass media infrequently realize such an effect on mass citizens. We explain why.

Much of the information which might inspire political participation by ordinary Americans never appears in the news media. Part II of this book offers many examples of powerful politicians and groups whose activities might provoke, even outrage the public, but which rarely make news. The subcommittee and behind-the-scenes behavior of members of Congress discussed in Chapter 5 are one example. Moreover, much of the participation-provoking news that is aired is not given the prominence and repetition required for it to stand out from the competing morass of trivia. It fails to attract and retain public attention.

Even when actions and occurrences are controversial enough to merit full and continuing news coverage, the stories rarely inspire political participation by the mass public. People are not informed where, how, and on whom they might act to influence the events described. Lemert et al. suggest that this crucial "missing information" is excluded because journalists view it as too dull or biased.[18]

Through intensive coverage that links an issue or government decision to people's needs or interests, the mass media can stimulate practical participation without even suggesting it. But news stories mainly spur the involvement of the already knowledgeable and active members of the attentive public who do the bulk of the contributing, organizing, and contacting of officials. These people already know where the levers of power lie.[19] As a result, the media's scarce or non-existent coverage is less of a deterrent to their participation than to that of the less informed majority.

Timing also deters participation. So often, news stories are about governmental decisions reached, about things accomplished. The public may be told of the conflict over which route a new highway should follow; the decision to build a highway has already been determined. The press could subvert this pre-emption technique so common in government; it rarely does so. Neither bureaucratic deliberations nor possible plans for the future have much currency as news—until decided. And the bureaucrats who make the decisions are the sources reporters primarily rely on for specialized information from government. Officials are therefore often able to conceal their conclusions in the bowels of the bureaucracy until it is in their interests, or they are legally obligated, to make them public.

PSEUDO-PARTICIPATION

The mass media do encourage a vacuous form of political activity—we call it pseudo-participation. This is accomplished through public service advertisements.[20] PSAs are sponsored by government and private non-profit agencies, run about a minute or less each, and are aired without charge by broadcasters. Transmitting messages from America's elite to the public, they use the panoply of tried and persuasive commercial advertising techniques in an explicit and conscious effort to exhort people to social action.

At a rate of some 47 billion television impressions annually, they are a significant but unobtrusive part of media content. Consider:

- Give to the College of Your Choice
- I Mind Very Much if You Smoke
- Don't Be Fuelish
- People Start Pollution, People Can Stop It
- Only You Can Prevent Forest Fires
- America: It Only Works as Well as We Do
- VD Is for Everybody

Because these advertisements are purportedly directed at viewers' best interests, they are less liable to evoke the conventional defenses with which people try to protect themselves against product commercials.

PSAs expose Americans to national and international problems, sometimes lay blame, usually propose solutions. The effect is to deter effective participation in politics by denuding the subjects of their political significance. We explain briefly.

Problems are typically revealed through their effects on individuals (actors or non-actors) who are the subjects of the PSAs. They often concern people in unfortunate circumstances who need help—children, foreigners, victims of natural disasters or disease. Having nothing to do with politics, the causes are individual carelessness, incapacity, bad luck, affliction, or fate.

Problems are raised, victims and sufferers depicted or described. Is any blame placed? Not often. Of all the PSAs in our extensive sample that identified problems, 62 percent assigned no blame at all. The 38 percent remaining laid blame on the individual (29 percent), society in general (6 percent), and business (3 percent). Not a single PSA blamed government or any public official. The government-advertising nexus that produces so many of the PSAs is able to use them to exonerate itself of responsibility for societal problems by neglecting to discuss the causes or by pointing to the individual American as the source.

There are primarily three kinds of "solutions" to societal problems which appear, either singly or in combination, in PSAs. They are solicitations for support, recruitment, and personal admonitions. Solicitations for support ask viewers for funds or, much less frequently, some other help, such as volunteering time for charitable activities. Recruitment PSAs attempt to persuade viewers to volunteer for service in organizations such as the military, the Peace Corps, or VISTA.

Personal admonitions vary from general to specific. There are vague exhortations—actor Robert Young as Dr. Marcus Welby urges us to get to know our local hospital; our Lung Association tells us that alert citizen action can reverse air pollution; the American Bar Association instructs us to support court improvements (which appear to mean more judges and more work for lawyers). There are suggestions that viewers obtain information about problems from government or private agencies. There are specific courses of action—the Mormon Church (Church of Jesus Christ of Latter-Day Saints) instructs us to spend time with our children (presumably building a tree house, as does the father in the PSA); and the Department of Transportation tells us to fasten our seat belts.

Contributing, contacting, and joining are examples of practical political activity. They involve interaction with public officials and issues, the making of claims, assumptions of accountability, and responsiveness. But as defined by PSAs, they are more likely to deflect from than lead to greater political power for most citizens. Charitable organizations may characterize themselves as "Your" Lung or Heart Association, but they stand aloof and relatively immune from detailed public scrutiny. PSAs encourage the ordinary viewer to donate but not to join or play any meaningful part in their affairs. Certainly, donations are not solicited for political parties or candidates, or for advocates of policy stands that might be divisive.

Similarly, viewers who respond to PSAs by writing to governmental agencies for information are not expressing policy preferences in a way that will be acted upon by government. They are not establishing meaningful two-way communication. They are not insuring that policy-makers will make decisions consistent with their preferences. And they are not developing the personal skills or resources conducive to future practical participation.

As for admonitions, a Keep America Beautiful PSA is typical. The spot shows a majestic American Indian paddling his canoe down a river that becomes progressively more polluted. Factories and smokestacks are depicted at a considerable distance, virtually unnoticeable. The Indian then comes ashore near a highway littered with refuse. A bag of trash is thrown and lands at the Indian's feet. As the camera focuses on a tear running down his cheek, the slogan appears: "People Start Pollution, People Can Stop It." The slogan defines the problem as litter and the blame as individual, thereby relieving economic institutions and public officials of responsibility. Criticism of industry's role in causing pollution is deflected by emphasizing the extent to which pollution is the responsibility of individuals. The fight against pollution is equated with anti-litter efforts rather than with auto emission controls, smokestack filters, or prohibitions on non-returnable containers. Keep America Beautiful, Inc., is a privately funded organization with Pepsi-Cola a major contributor. Other contributors are reportedly Continental Can, Ford Motor Company, American Can Company, United States Brewers Association, and the Glass Containers Manufacturers Institute.

The only explicitly practical political activity in which viewers are sometimes encouraged to participate by PSAs is voting. Such exhortations occur around presidential elections (the general elections, not the primaries). They are studiously nonpartisan, simply urging viewers to register, "to go out and help someone vote," or to vote for the party of their choice.

Otherwise, the public service nexus is organized to deny air time to groups or organizations which could present different perspectives, which might introduce political considerations, urge practical or provocative political actions, or define political activity so as to legitimize it in schools and work places. The public service advertisements that are shown beguile the American public on behalf of the siren of pseudo-participation. They exhort Americans to act in a limited and predetermined manner. Defining both the problems and the solutions, PSAs also define the methods by which the solutions are to be achieved. Implicitly and explicitly, they deny the need for meaningful and active individual and group participation in the institutions that dominate peoples' everyday lives. They promote the delusion that social and economic problems should be dealt with apolitically—that is, without resort to unbecoming, provocative, or even practical political activity, conflict, and controversy.

PROVOCATIVE

Demonstrators are unpopular.[21] One reason: the way demonstrations are reported.

The press tends to judge demonstrators by the degree their goals are representative of what journalists think is public opinion. This creates a no-win situation for most demonstrators. If they represent majority sentiment, there is no logical reason for them to take to the streets—officials should do their bidding once pressured in practical ways. If they demonstrate without first trying more acceptable methods, their behavior is irresponsible. If they are an unrepresentative minority, as defined by journalists, the demonstrators are depicted as seeking policies they could not achieve through the normal, majoritarian process—at best, as nuisances; at worst, as threats to the social fabric.[22]

News reports center on the costs and dangers of demonstrations rather than their political goals. This reporting prevents the policy preferences of protest groups from being widely, let alone favorably, ventilated. It thereby limits the degree to which the media can be used to enhance the political power of demonstrators. If the preferences are mentioned, they are associated with negative symbols of deviancy and threat. Demonstrations may have hurt the anti-war cause among the bulk of the public.[23] Better to be ignored, as happens when the group is small and no violence occurs.

The mass media generally discourage protest participation. But they are not wholly negative about peaceful demonstrations. When journalists think public officials have willfully refused to acknowledge a legitimate grievance, and protestors are expressing an increasingly popular goal, the demonstration may enjoy neutral or even favorable treatment. If the assembly is large enough, coverage may be extensive. Certainly the mass media enhanced the legitimacy (and power) of the civil rights movement of the early 1960s, as we discussed in Chapter 8. More recently, anti-ERA demonstrators and anti-nuclear marchers benefited from a relatively benign press. And even unfavorable coverage may stimulate involvement by those whose peer groups endorse action or who are oblivious to the opprobrium associated with an unpopular minority and cause.

Beyond demonstrations and marches are riots. The mass media's record on riots is clear: unequivocal opposition combined with occasional accidental assistance. Riots are covered from the vantage point of those whose major goal is restoration of order—usually the police (see Chapter 7).

Local media were once accused of unintentionally fueling

1960s ghetto rebellions by their detailed, virtually play-by-play descriptions of urban riots. They responded with alacrity. In one study, 80 percent of the radio and television stations admitted to a policy of deliberately withholding information to prevent any firing up of city residents.[24]

Others may condemn this unusual elevation of civic responsibility over sensational and profitable news; we merely point to its effect on the political power of rioters. Participation in the 1960s ghetto riots was often a politically motivated act, not merely hooliganism.[25] But if rioters have any sway over public officials, it is the threat that the behavior will persist and spread. Curtailment of coverage dims the rioters' fire; news blackouts diminish rioters' power.

Conclusion

If ordinary Americans tried to participate more practically, actively, and effectively in politics, they might realize their powerlessness, as well as provoke serious problems for ruling elites. The mass media thus contribute to the stability and legitimacy of the reigning order by dampening whatever urge to participate exists among the powerless. Meanwhile, attentive Americans, who participate most, are disproportionately drawn from "those with higher income, higher education, and higher status occupations."[26] These are the people to whom the government is more responsive—"participation helps those who are already better off."[27]

CHAPTER FIFTEEN

•

Conclusions

"Pas de monstres, pas de héros."

Flaubert

WE HAVE DISSECTED THE ROOTS of the Alice in Wonderland world depicted by the mass media, and chronicled that world's political effects. Now we briefly summarize our six interrelated themes and contemplate the future.

The Present

First, the evidence is indisputable and overwhelming: the media influence the decisions and actions of politicians and officials, change their priorities, and can reduce their ability to control events. This book is a catalogue of such effects. Jimmy Carter organized his 1976 campaign for the presidency around a shrewd understanding of the media's imperatives. He used the media to cement his presidency in the months following his election. Then press coverage helped diminish his public support and his capacity to manipulate events. Other examples abound: the hearings held by members of Congress are often designed for or conducted with the media in mind, as our excerpt from the House Select Committee on Assassinations' off-the-record deliberations reveal. Even the Supreme Court may be brought to reinterpret or modify its more burdensome First Amendment decisions in response to press coverage and reactions.

249

Yet, second, a prominent media effect is to facilitate the insulation of many power holders from public accountability. This effect stems from the ability of the members of an institution virtually to exclude the press from their deliberations and decisions—witness the Supreme Court. It may result from skewed coverage: Congress is disparaged, but its individual members often manage to manipulate their local media to insure favorable or at least minimally unfavorable stories. And insulation may emerge from omission: the media failure to seek out the perspectives of Zaireans and other foreign peoples whose views conflict with those of American officials, the simple failure of the press to cover the activities of powerful corporations because of the public–private distinction. True, no institution is eternally immune—even the derelictions of the Federal Bureau of Investigation were eventually revealed—but, too often, too little is exposed too late.

As a result, when the media reallocate power, they do so among the already powerful. This is the media's third significant effect. The reallocation stems from stories recounting the actions and inactions, the alleged derelictions and accomplishments of power holders and seekers; from the way the media cover elections; from journalists' captivation by and promotion of persuasive illusions such as the conservative myth. Philandering legislators, buccaneering businessmen who enter government as presidential confidants, effete liberals, all can attest to the power of the press over their fates. Press freedom is central to the American creed; within limits, some members of the elite pay a genuine price for it.

But the *sine qua non* of power reallocation is elite disagreement. Elites are the main news sources. When powerful and newsworthy people develop new preferences, the media pay respectful, careful, sustained attention, offering up stories that can create new or change old opinions. Avarice, accident, ambition, uncertainty, inherent contradictions in consensual values—all lead elites to conflict over specific governmental decisions. These clashes are quintessentially newsworthy. They contribute to the creation or increased power of some authority holders and agencies, the decline or demise of others—in other words, the reallocation of power among the powerful. Erstwhile President Richard M. Nixon is a monument to this media effect.

Fourth, the media tend to limit the ability of mass citizens to comprehend and respond intelligently to the political events, issues, and power holders that compose the news—to wield power successfully. The conventional products of journalism reduce the power of much of the public below the level it might reach with different reporting and content. The framework of presidential election coverage generally inhibits informed voting choices and may discourage any voting at all. As coverage of the events in Zaire vividly reveals, the structure and processes through which journalists gather foreign information gives elites predominant say over the content of the popular press, thus over the media's effects on public opinion about such governmental decisions.

The opinions of the general public are ubiquitous in the news: invoked by politicians, described and dissected by reporters. But often as not the invocations are misleading, the descriptions mistaken, the dissections misdirected. The conspicuous case of the conservative chimera is a not uncommon instance of media reportage that diminishes the public's power by misinforming mass citizens about their own preferences and options.

Fifth, the media's coverage of governmental debate and delay, irresolution and confusion, the implicit and invidious comparison of politics and entertainment on television, do eventuate in public distemper, dismay, dissatisfaction, and discontent. However, the discontent is either unfocused, or concentrated on non-political sources, or personalized in individual politicians. Connections are not made between widely publicized official corruption and system values; between unresponsive government and the problems of personal life; between corporate misdeeds and practical political participation. The major consequences of media depictions are frustration, misdirected anger, and apathy, not insight and political activism. The structure of power persists, sporadically tarnished but fundamentally unchallenged.

Finally, the media help preserve the legitimacy of America's political, economic, and social system, both through the process of socialization and by the way they change the status quo. We documented these effects in Chapters 9 and 10. Performance of this mission is built into media goals, practices, and limitations. The media's routines, content, and impacts on the public are deeply imbued with consensus values and elite perceptions, perspectives and opinions. For this reason, the media help to bend into conformity with the basic order any new demands that arise from the conflicts and changes they so compulsively cover in news stories and use in entertainment programs. Automatically, stories omit, disparage, or dilute proposals and critiques that undermine the

American ideology; they promote those moderate innovations most compatible with the system as it is. Automatically, entertainment shows incorporate and subdue novelty and change. Consequently, although faith, trust and confidence in most public officials has declined severely in recent years, there persists an "unshaken belief in the institutional arrangement of society, both politically and economically."[1]

The consequence is quiescent mass loyalty. As Dahlgren puts it, this means: "moderate levels of *formal* political participation; non-intrusion with the political and administrative activities of the state; non-interference with the power of capital to shape the basic contours of society; cooperative involvement in the economic sphere as a docile labor force and predictable consumers; acceptance of the prevailing social definitions to interpret their experiences and define their needs; and lack of genuine political power to challenge the dominant social arrangements."[2]

The Future

Our analysis is based on prevailing media content. Major alterations in the structure or technology of the communications industry may produce different content with different effects on the distribution and uses of power.

First, structure. The mass media are highly concentrated and are becoming more so. Only about one-fifth of all daily newspapers are under single ownership. The larger resources of press conglomerates and profits of most newspapers have not been used to improve political coverage. Indeed, news makes up less of the paper than it did in the early 1950s.[3] And even though most newspapers have grown in circulation since then, they have not added reporters to serve their more populous markets but instead have extracted greater productivity (and profits) from existing staffs.[4] Moreover, papers that are parts of chains may lose some of their editorial autonomy to profit-minded central offices.[5]

The television networks each own five stations in leading markets that give them direct access to 33 percent of the homes in the country. They also own book and magazine publishers, record companies, movie theaters. Many non-network-owned stations are controlled by groups. Their broad investment portfolios suggest that television corporations use their large profits to branch out into related pursuits, not to enhance news quality.[6] Nor has rating competition between wealthy networks produced a proliferation of program offerings. Since the introduction of television, there has been a decline in types of shows, an increase in repetition and in imitation.[7]

The trend toward concentration portends less diversity, more homogeneity, probably even more concern with profit. Threats to the structure of political power are on balance less likely when sources of information and opinion are fewer and narrower in perspective.

But technological changes in the industry offer countervailing, competitive pressures. These changes include cable television, which can offer instant opinion polls and shopping at home for advertised goods; fiber optics, which increases potential channel capacity by up to 100 times; satellite transmission, which makes linking stations outside the four major networks relatively inexpensive; home video recorders; video discs; and electronic data transmission.

There could be up-to-the-minute news and weather bulletins, local advertising, highbrow cultural events, in-depth political discussions and documentaries, ethnic features, and other minority-audience fare readily available soon. The networks' share of audiences will drop; newspapers may eventually become obsolete. But just how diverse the new offerings will be, how willing viewers pressed by inflation will be to pay for expanded choice, is difficult to assess.

Assuming a significant increase in audience fragmentation as options open up, one political effect might be to widen the gap between the attentive and mass publics. Under the pressure of cable and other offerings, the commercial network news may become even more "entertaining," even less substantive. If newspapers are replaced by electronic data transmission and over-the-air local advertising and home shopping, the average member of the mass public will have even less contact with detailed political information. On the other hand, the competition among "free" network news, newspapers, and cable and its offspring may spur investigative reporting and muckraking. New revelations could impel the interest and involvement of the attentive and even mass publics.

The future is murky. Essentially the same people who own and manage newspapers and television now control the new technologies. They are guided by the same elite-sanctioned values, the same desire for profit. New journalistic and entertainment practices and effects will flourish, but technological innovations are unlikely significantly to disrupt the structure of power or undermine its legitimacy.

And yet, even though power redistribution through the media is constrained, the media's effects may ultimately transcend the limits of the elite consensus.[8] Media content does not have a single meaning for audiences, or simple effects on the powerful or powerless. Media messages interact with each other, with previous attitudes, with historical conditions. The final political consequences of media coverage of an event, official, or action may never be precisely isolated—they exist in a continuing stream of developments that constantly alter their meaning and implications for the distribution of power. Small reforms and incremental adjustments promoted by media coverage can combine with each other or with changing circumstances over time to bring about opposition to the power structure.

Elites cannot fully control how people will use the media.

Notes

Chapter 1. In the Beginning (pp. 3–8)

1. Bentley, 1967: 199.
2. Miliband, 1969: 19–20, 47, 64–65; and Lindblom, 1978: 123, 172–176, 190–192, 228, 232.
3. Dolbeare and Edelman, 1979: 95.
4. The phrase is Sir Eric Ashby's.

Chapter 2. The Sources of News (pp. 9–25)

1. Cited in W.F. Harris, 1978b: 23.
2. *Congressional Quarterly* 39 (July 22, 1978), p. 1863.
3. Lemert et al., 1974: 241
4. Hester, 1978: 89; cf. Larson and Hardy, 1977: 246; Almaney, 1970: 501.
5. Hofstetter et al., 1976: 192; Patterson, 1977: 3; Crouse, 1973.
6. Personal communication.
7. Owen, Beebe, and Manning, 1974: 5; cf. Friendly, 1967: 183, 267, 272.
8. Owen, Beebe and Manning, 1974: 120.
9. Townley, 1971: 46.
10. "Broadcast and Cable: Future Is Bright Says Commerce," *Broadcasting* 96 (February 12, 1979): 23.
11. Noll, Peck, and McGowan, 1973: 16.
12. Bagdikian, 1973b: 23.
13. J. Klein, 1979: 30.
14. See Wackman et al., 1975: 411.
15. Halberstam, 1979: 713.
16. James Aronson, "The *Times* is a-Changing," *In These Times*, March 2, 1977, p. 24.

17. Sobel and Emery, 1978: 146, 148.
18. Goldenberg, 1975: 99–100.
19. Frankel, 1971: 16.
20. Gans, 1979: 204–206.
21. Tillinghast, 1980: 19.
22. Ibid.
23. Sigal, 1973: 18.
24. See the tales throughout Schorr, 1977, and Halberstam, 1979.
25. D. Bowers, 1967: 45–52; see also Donohew, 1967; Goldenberg, 1975: 68.
26. Gans, 1979: 9–10.
27. Safire, 1975a: 44.
28. Westin, 1975: 3.
29. Sigal, 1973: chaps. 5 and 6.
30. Gans, 1979: 282–84.
31. Sigal, 1973: 119–26.
32. Lippman, 1922: 158.
33. Sigal, 1973: 54.
34. Tuchman, 1978: 152.
35. Kempton, 1971: 32.
36. Dunn, 1969: 56.
37. Bagdikian, 1975: 5.
38. Cited in Hall, 1972: 4.
39. Epstein, 1973: 258.
40. Altheide, 1976: 76.
41. An argument elaborated in the forthcoming book, *A Farewell to Journalism,* by Paletz.
42. This discussion is taken from Paletz and Pearson, 1978.
43. Lori Ann Haubenstock suggested this concept to Paletz.

Chapter 3. Presidential Candidates: 1976 and 1980
(pp. 29–53)

1. Arterton, 1977: 4; see also Barber, 1980.
2. See Paletz, 1978, for an early version of part of this chapter.
3. Paletz, 1971.
4. See Froman, 1966; Leuthold, 1968; and Kingdon, 1966.
5. Walters, 1973.
6. Dean, 1976: 306, 326.
7. A. Miller and W. Miller, 1977: 82.
8. Siegel, 1966.
9. W. Miller, 1979: 11.
10. Wyckoff, 1968: 47.

11. M. Schram, 1977: 57.
12. Patterson, 1977: 5.
13. *Broadcasting* 92 (January 3, 1977): 74.
14. Patterson, 1977: 4–5.
15. M. Robinson and McPherson, 1977: 180; cf. *Broadcasting* 92 (January 3, 1977): 38.
16. *CBS News,* February 24, 1976.
17. Patterson, 1977: 6.
18. Ibid.
19. Auletta, 1976: 20.
20. Patterson, 1977: 7–8.
21. A. Miller and W. Miller, 1977: 83; cf. pp. 71, 121 fn. 65.
22. Patterson, 1977: 11.
23. *Congressional Quarterly Almanac,* 1976: 873.
24. *Public Opinion* (April/May, 1980): 30.
25. "Making the Opponent the Issue," *The Washington Post,* June 9, 1980, p. A9. This is an illuminating series by *Post* staff writer Martin Schram based in part on interviews with and confidential documents obtained from high-ranking Carter aides.
26. Ibid.
27. Ibid., p. A8.
28. "Carter's Campaign," *The Washington Post,* June 8, 1980, p. A16.
29. "A Big Boost for Bush," *Newsweek* (February 4, 1980): 33.
30. CBS/New York Times surveys cited in *Public Opinion 3* (April/May 1980): 39.
31. Arterton, 1977: 11.
32. On the use of media in political campaigns see Wyckoff, 1968; McGinniss, 1969; Nimmo, 1970; and Patterson and McClure, 1976.
33. Cf. Sherrod, 1971–1972: 558–561.
34. Schwartz, 1973: 82–88.
35. Despite the tendentious questions used, some indication of the reliance upon and credibility of television news for the majority of Americans can be found in Roper Organization Report, 1979.
36. Arterton, 1977: 24.

Chapter 4. Presidents Ascendant and Descending
(pp. 54–78)

1. Halberstam, 1976: 65.
2. Neustadt, 1960; cf. Edwards, 1976.
3. Morgan, 1979: 6.
4. Peters, 1973: 6.
5. Cited in Grossman and Kumar, 1977: 32.

6. Wolfson, 1975: 13.
7. Grossman and Kumar, 1977: 13–14.
8. Kumar and Grossman, 1977: 22.
9. Lukas, 1977: 68.
10. Rothchild, 1971: 25.
11. Ibid., 26.
12. Grossman and Kumar, 1977: 26 (from the LBJ Library).
13. Memo from Alvin Snyder to Jeb Stuart Magruder, February 24, 1971.
14. Thomson, 1973: 53.
15. Fryklund, 1966: 174.
16. Wise, 1973: 248–50.
17. Baus and Ross, 1968: 313–14.
18. Chester et al., 1969: 375.
19. Kumar and Grossman, 1977: 17.
20. Wolfson, 1975: 7.
21. Nimmo, 1978: 208.
22. "Some of the Presidents' Men," PBS, May 16, 1978.
23. Wolfson, 1975: 5.
24. Kempton, 1971: 33.
25. Halberstam, 1976: 71.
26. Peters, 1973: 6.
27. Cited in Kumar and Grossman, 1977: 29.
28. Cf. Wilhoit, 1969: 318.
29. The study is a revised and abbreviated version of Paletz and Vinegar, 1977–1978. Richard T. Campbell helped analyze the data.
30. Minow et al., 1973.
31. "Squeeze Play by Pres. Ford Cues Web Time," *Variety*, October 16, 1974, p. 35.
32. Rutkus, 1976: 2.
33. Nixon, 1974: 337.
34. Ibid., 345.
35. All quotations in this paragraph are from a videotape of CBS news analysis of President Nixon's News Conference, March 19, 1974.
36. Nixon, 1974: 339–40.
37. Is it just coincidence that instant analysis is so often sponsored by such products as Renuzit air freshener; or a hair spray for men whose slogan contains the phrase "it's hard to believe"; or by Bufferin, offering fast relief for headache without upset stomach? Certainly a president's performance must be powerful indeed to withstand the effects of such a mordant juxtaposition.
38. Grossman and Kumar, 1977: 21; cf. Morris, 1977.
39. Lukas, 1977: 22.
40. Kumar and Grossman, 1977: 24.

41. "Adman Called In to Polish Carter's Tarnished Image," *Los Angeles Times,* July 10, 1978, p. 1.
42. "Carter Image Being Remodeled," *International Herald Tribune,* August 29, 1978, p. 3.
43. *Durham* (North Carolina) *Morning Herald,* May 19, 1978, p. 2A.
44. *Los Angeles Times,* July 10, 1978, p. 1.
45. Cf. Wolin, 1978; Entman, 1981.

Chapter 5. Congress and Its Members (pp. 79–98)

1. We thank our friend and esteemed colleague, scholar and novelist Roberta E. Pearson, for drawing Holmes's observation to our attention.
2. Balutis, 1976: 513; but cf. S. Miller, 1977.
3. Matthews, 1960: 97–99.
4. Bagdikian, 1974: 5.
5. This helps explain, incidentally, the refusal of the House of Representatives' Democratic leadership to permit the networks to control the televising of House debates. Those who make the news shrewdly intend to control the news, even though the repercussions may limit the promotional potential of coverage for both the institution as a whole (as against the presidency) and individual members. Speaker Thomas P. O'Neill, Jr. (D., Mass.) is justifiably wary of putting members' fates in the hands of network executives whose values and objectives do not correspond with his and his colleagues'. Arguably, though, just showing what takes place on the floor of the House, irrespective of who controls the cameras, can change the behavior of members, the chamber's procedures, the content and tenor of debate, and voting outcomes. See also M. Robinson, 1975.
6. S. Miller, 1977: 464.
7. Matthews, 1960: 207, quoting Carl Hayden (D., Ariz.), *Hampshire* (Mass.) *Gazette,* Nov. 8, 1956.
8. Kingdon, 1973: 204–206.
9. But cf. Matthews, 1960: 95.
10. S. Miller, 1978: 659.
11. Matthews, 1960: 203.
12. S. Miller, 1977: 464.
13. Schorr, 1977: 287.
14. Truman, 1951: 382; quoting from Robert D. Leigh, "Politicians vs. Bureaucrats," *Harper's Magazine,* January 1945, p. 102.
15. R. Harris, 1964: 67.
16. Halpern, 1972: 154–55.
17. Kuttner, 1972: p. 46.

18. Cf. Mayhew, 1974: 52–61.
19. Bagdikian, 1974: 5–6.
20. Manley, 1977: 15.
21. Dawson and Zinser, 1971; Jacobson, 1978.
22. See, e.g., Bagdikian, 1974: 8, 10; Carey, 1976; cf. Freedman, 1974.
23. McConnell, 1966; Lowi, 1969.
24. Cf. Mayhew, 1974: 130–31.
25. Cf. Fenno, 1975; Fiorina, 1977; M. Robinson, 1977.

Chapter 6. The Supreme Court (pp. 99–109)

1. Johnson, 1967: 94; cf. 95.
2. Morison and Commager, 1962: 489.
3. Grey, 1968: 107–108, 119.
4. Johnson, 1967: 95.
5. Cited in Edelman, 1964: 108.
6. Schubert, 1974.
7. Leslie, 1976: 26–29.
8. Ericson, 1977: 607.
9. Leslie, 1976: 23.
10. National Center, 1978: 2.
11. Ibid., 12.
12. Ibid.
13. Ibid., ii.
14. The people running the National Center for State Courts are shrewd in the ways of media management. The "special seven-member advisory task force . . . formed to help provide guidance in the drafting of survey instruments and to provide linkage between the survey and other activities related to the conference" (National Center, 1978: i) was a useful publicity device. Its chairman was Fred W. Friendly, Advisor on Communications at the Ford Foundation, and it contained journalists from the *Los Angeles Times* and *Newsweek*.
15. Johnson, 1967: 149.
16. Sanford, 1979: 59.
17. Hale, 1979: 46–47.
18. Weinberg, 1978: 129–41.
19. Woodward and Armstrong's (1979) revelations of the personal relations and behavior underlying the decisions of the Warren Burger court may have damaged respect for the institution, particularly among journalists, whose stories might become more critical. But as long as reporters lack the investigative time, resources, contacts, and skills Woodward and Armstrong exploited, the Court's control over

reportorial access will likely yield coverage that remains generally legitimizing, if only by omission.

Chapter 7. Law Enforcers (pp. 110–123)

1. For these data see *Sourcebook of Criminal Justice Statistics,* 1979: 62, 225, 478, 623–624; and *Statistical Abstract of the United States,* 99th ed., 1978: 168, 434. See also Hacker, 1977 for the idea of making such comparisons.
2. Chatten, 1978: 12.
3. Drummond, 1971: 8.
4. Chatten, 1978: 17.
5. Ibid., 19.
6. Ibid., 15.
7. Ibid., 6.
8. See *Statistical Abstract of the United States,* 99th ed., 1978: 177, 185, 197.
9. This is a revised and truncated version of Paletz and Dunn, 1969.
10. "Benton Foresees No Racial Violence," *Winston-Salem Journal,* August 3, 1967, p. 1.
11. Ibid.
12. "Gangs Riot, Loot, Set Fires Downtown; Police, Patrol and Guard Check Rioters," *Winston-Salem Journal,* November 3, 1967, p. 1.
13. "A Rifle Shot . . . and Mixed Feelings," *Winston-Salem Journal,* November 4, 1967, p. 1.
14. "Souvenirs Almost Deadly," *Winston-Salem Journal,* November 6, 1967, p. 6.
15. "City Hall—Armed Fortress at Dusk," *Winston-Salem Journal,* November 6, 1967, p. 6; see also November 4, 1967, p. 5 and p. 6.
16. U.S. Cong., Comm. on the Judiciary, Subcomm. on Civil and Const. Rights, *FBI Oversight Hearings,* 1975–1976: 602–603.
17. Navasky, 1976: 2.
18. Kruger, 1978: 11.
19. *First Principles* 3:9 (May 1978): 4. See also pp. 1–5. This information is taken from 50,000 pages of COINTELPRO documents released by the FBI. Another 12,000 documents were withheld by the Bureau. The files released were not in usable order and press coverage was sporadic, unsystematic and superficial. The staff of the Center for National Security Studies analyzed and synthesized the data. Their work is invaluable.
20. Wall, 1972: 14.
21. Rintels, 1972: 17.

22. Quoted in Chesebro and Hamsher, 1976: 7.
23. Rintels, 1972: 17.
24. Ibid.
25. University of Michigan, Institute for Social Research, *Newsletter* 1:15 (Summer 1972): 4.
26. "Report Cites Trouble Attorneys General Had in Reining FBI," *Washington Post,* February 20, 1977, p. A7.
27. "Understanding the FBI," *Washington Post,* October 3, 1976, p. 6.
28. Lazin, 1978.
29. See also Peek et al., 1978.

Chapter 8. Interested Groups: Uncommon and Common Causes (pp. 124–146)

1. Goldenberg, 1975: 135.
2. Ibid., 141.
3. Lipsky, 1970: 79.
4. Goldenberg, 1975: 135.
5. Tuchman, 1978: 21–25.
6. "Writs against Reporters Arouse Debate," *New York Times,* January 7, 1973, p. 1.
7. Garrow, 1978.
8. "Talk of the Town," *New Yorker* (May 8, 1971): 30.
9. Lipsky, 1970: 174.
10. Morley, n.d.: 19; cf. Tuchman, 1978: chap. 7; Gitlin, 1980.
11. See Foss, 1969; Freeman, 1955; Lowi, 1969; and Lindblom 1978.
12. Wardell, 1978: 101. See also Chapter 12 ("The Conservative Myth").
13. Truman, 1951: 251.
14. Ibid., 228.
15. Fritschler, 1969: 133.
16. "How Business Is Misusing the Media," *New York Times,* December 18, 1977, p. F14.
17. Mareth, 1976–1977: 16.
18. Cited in Gergen, 1979: 4.
19. Gardner, 1970: 4. This case study is a streamlined version of Paletz, Chandler-Henry, and Gardner, 1977.
20. "Response to Lobby Gratifies Gardner," *New York Times,* October 13, 1970, p. 37.
21. Glass, 1972.
22. See McFarland, 1976; Fleishman and Greenwald, 1976; Lutzker, 1973; Topolsky, 1974; and "Public Interest Lobbies: Nader and Common Cause Become Permanent Fixtures," *Congressional Quarterly* 34:20 (May 15, 1976): 1197–1205.

23. *New York Times,* March 19, 1974, p. 74.
24. Ibid., February 13, 1975, p. 38.
25. Ibid., March 1, 1972, p. 20.
26. Ibid., July 10, 1976, p. 22 (editorial).
27. Ibid., May 16, 1972, p. 36.
28. Ibid., January 28, 1973, p. 63.
29. Ibid., September 18, 1970, p. 19.
30. Ibid., March 29, 1974, p. 1.
31. Ibid., April 28, 1975, p. 63.
32. Ibid., October 8, 1974, p. 43.
33. Ibid., January 17, 1975, p. 29.
34. Ibid., March 20, 1974, p. 30.
35. Ibid., October 2, 1972, p. 30.
36. Paletz is severely critical of the contents and effects of "responsible" journalism, as his forthcoming book *A Farewell to Journalism* will make clear.
37. "1976 Code Offered by Common Cause," *New York Times,* November 6, 1975, p. 11.
38. *New York Times,* January 11, 1976, p. 39.
39. For the *Times* stories see "Common Cause and 45 Representatives Petition the House to Investigate Sikes for Conflict of Interest," April 8, 1976, p. 13; "House Unit Votes Inquiry on Sikes," April 29, 1976, p. 35; "Ethics Inquiry on Sikes Embroiled Over Secrecy," May 7, 1976, p. 16; "Panel Votes Inquiry Into Ethics of Sikes," May 13, 1976, pp. 1, 16; "House Panel Seeks Reprimand of Sikes on Interest Conflict," July 2, 1976, p. 17; "Sikes Faces Loss of Key House Job," July 3, 1976, p. 18; and "Sluggish Ethics," July 10, 1976, p. 22. The congressman was eventually found guilty of misconduct by the House Ethics Committee and stripped of his subcommittee chairmanship by the House Democratic caucus. He subsequently retired from Congress having been there for almost forty years.
40. McFarland, 1976: 4.
41. Telephone survey conducted by Richard Gibson and Jim Chamberlain for Common Cause between November 1972 and January 1973 (pages unnumbered).
42. Wilson, 1973: 263.
43. Adamany, 1977: 292.
44. Pomper, 1977.

Chapter 9. Accepting the System (pp. 149–167)

1. We do not have the space to delve into other aspects of socialization, such as the acquisition of party identification and other important

political attitudes. For an overview of the field, see Dawson, Prewitt, and Dawson, 1977. For a call to concentrate, as we do in this and the next chapter, on system legitimacy and consensus values, see Prewitt, 1977–78.

2. "City Council Defers Action on Demonstration Ordinance," *Durham Morning Herald,* April 9, 1969, p. A-1. Henceforth all dates refer to *Herald* stories. This section is based on Paletz, Reichert, and McIntyre, 1971.

3. For example, "Council Passes New Sunday 'Blue Law' Effective Oct. 1," September 2, 1969, p. A-1; and "Committee of the Whole to Consider Changing Eno Park Plans Today," February 12, 1970, p. C-1.

4. "City Council Defers Action on Demonstration Ordinance," April 9, 1969, pp. A-1, 2.

5. "Group at Council Session Seeks Reduced Bus Rates for Elderly," March 17, 1970, p. B-1.

6. "Housing Project Site to Get Further Study," April 7, 1970, p. A-1.

7. Meerloo, 1954: 108.

8. Edelman, 1964.

9. Lasswell, 1930: 195–98.

10. Edelman, 1964: 78.

11. "Group at Council Session Seeks Reduced Bus Rates for Elderly," March 17, 1970, p. B-1.

12. Ibid.

13. A once notorious California city hall reporter took umbrage at our analysis. In a personal letter (June 1971), he responded: "I always treasured any sign of life at a meeting, whether an angry crowd—whose epithets and arguments I would quote at length—or a character on the council. (We had one veteran with a real knack for quotes: at one budget session, he snarled, 'My platform is to get everybody at City Hall an electric typewriter and an assistant.' We made a box out of that.)" Michael Kernan is right. Not all reporters are as hidebound as the ones whose reporting we have described. Some relish the cut and thrust of council meetings—when it occurs. As he puts it: the *Durham Morning Herald* may very well not be "in the mainstream of local journalism." But it is. As in most cities, the newspaper has a morning monopoly; the evening paper is owned by the same company; the readers are relatively unsophisticated (at least they were when the research was completed); and there is a strong sense of civic pride or boosterism which the newspapers perpetuate. Besides, this disagreement does not vitiate our main argument.

14. Frank, 1973: 40–41, 51, 58; Barrett, 1975: 4.

15. Bagdikian, 1975: 5; cf. Woodward and Bernstein, 1974: 79.

16. *Gallup Opinion Index* No. 111 (September 1974), p. 7; Gallup, 1978: 64.
17. Personal communication.
18. A. Miller and W. Miller, 1975: 416. McGovern's removal of his first vice presidential nominee contributed to his image of incompetence: Popkin et al., 1976: 799–803.
19. See Paletz, 1976.
20. Larson, 1974: 447.
21. Ibid., 445–47.
22. Lawrence Carnevale, David Robertson, and Richard Willstatter carried out the content analysis under Entman's supervision while they were students at Dickinson College. The dates analyzed were: April 30–May 1, 1973; June 25–July 2, 1973; July 27–30, 1973; October 22, 1973; April 29–May 2, 1974; July 29–July 31, 1974; August 5–6, 1974; August 8–9, 1974. Audio tapes were provided by the Vanderbilt Television News Archive. The events covered were Nixon's dismissal of Dean and the resignations of Ehrlichman and Haldeman; Dean's Senate testimony; Ehrlichman's detailed exculpatory Senate testimony; the "Saturday Night Massacre"; the release of the White House tape transcripts, the vote of the House Impeachment Committee; the release of the "smoking gun," indubitably felonious tape transcripts; and Nixon's resignation.
23. Gallup, 1978: 128, 184.
24. Ibid., 133, 170.
25. *Gallup Opinion Index* No. 111 (September, 1974), p. 8.
26. Cf. Halberstam, 1979: 703; Entman, 1975; Schorr, 1977: 115–19.
27. Editorials examined were, in the *Times*, "The Nixon Resignation," "President-Designate Ford," and "Transfer of Power," August 9, 1974, p. 32; "President Ford," August 10, 1974, p. 28; "Tragedy and Triumph," August 11, 1974, Section 4, p. 16. In the *Post:* "The Resignation of the President," August 9, 1974, p. A-30; "The Transfer of Power," August 10, 1974, p. A-22; "The Unfinished Business," August 11, 1974, p. C-6.
28. From an August 8, 1974, audio tape provided by Vanderbilt Television News Archive. Roger Mudd mildly disagreed with Rather's comments and the similar ones of Eric Sevareid and Walter Cronkite. For explanations, see Entman, 1975: 173–174; and Schorr, 1977: 115–119.
29. Cf. Mazlish, 1972; Barber, 1977: 345–442; Halberstam, 1979: 332–33, 335–36, 350–51, 594.
30. See, e.g., Entman, Prothro, and Sharp, 1974; Sniderman et al., 1975: 443, 450, 453–56.
31. The mass media's failure throughout the Watergate period to analyze underlying causes of corruption or to draw lessons beyond "the system worked" is discussed, *inter alia*, in A. Miller, Goldenberg and

Erbring, 1979: 72; Hurwitz, Green and Segal, 1976: 120; and Entman, 1975.

32. For these criticisms see M. Robinson, 1976 (but cf. 1977); Kampelman, 1978. Documentation of increased cynicism is in A. Miller, 1979. On the "new class" of journalists: Ladd with Hadley, 1975: 186–91. Studies of alleged liberal bias include Efron, 1971 and Lefever, 1974; critiques of these are Hofstetter et al., 1976 and Frank, 1975. More rigorous studies of journalistic responses to black, student, and ecological activism refute the notion that authority was denigrated: Paletz and Dunn, 1969; Pride and Richards, 1974, 1975.

33. See Wicker, 1975.

34. Ladd, 1976–77: 546, 552; Lipset and Schneider, 1978: 41–42, 47.

35. Berelson, 1952: 317, and Huntington, 1975: 37 explain the usefulness of apathy and low expectations for elitist democracy.

Chapter 10. That's Not (Just) Entertainment (pp. 168–183)

1. Studies that lend support to our argument include: Entman and Seymour, 1978, on popular movies; J. Robinson, Piskaln, and Hirsch, 1976, on rock music; Franzwa, 1974, and Berelson and Salter, 1957, on magazine fiction; and Dorfman and Mattelart, 1975, on comic books.

2. J. Robinson, 1979: 43.

3. Cf. Gerbner and Gross, 1976; Fearing, 1972.

4. Adorno, 1954: 224.

5. See DeFleur and Ball-Rokeach, 1975: 177–80; Tuchman, 1974: 26, 28–29.

6. Goldstein and Bredemeir, 1977; cf. Paletz and LaFiura, 1977.

7. B. Williams, 1977; Wawanash, 1977; cf. Hall, 1975: 109; Real, 1977: 115.

8. Gerbner and Gross, 1976: 178.

9. Real, 1977: 241.

10. McLaughlin, 1975: 184; cf. Chesebro and Hamsher, 1976.

11. Tedesco, 1974; Gerbner and Gross, 1976; for comparisons of the portraits of women and blacks, see Northcott, Seggar, and Hinton, 1975.

12. Turow, 1974.

13. Goldsen, 1975: 44.

14. Chesebro and Hamsher, 1976: 7.

15. Cf. Fass, 1976: 40–45; C. T. Williams, 1976; Chesebro and Hamsher, 1976. On women's magazines, where similar changes have occurred: Ehrenreich, 1978; and Tuchman, Daniels, and Benet, 1978.

16. For example, take soap operas, with their catalog of personal distress accompanied by thorough obliviousness to world affairs (Katzman, 1972).
17. Vidmar and Rokeach, 1974: 37, 45–47; Tate and Surlin, 1976.
18. Courtney and Whipple, 1974; O'Donnell and O'Donnell, 1978, found that 93 percent of voiceovers were by men, in a sample of programs in November 1975. For household items, 86 percent of the product representatives (who demonstrate and extol the product) were women; for non-domestic goods, 78 percent of the product reps were male. On possible subliminal sexual messages in commercials, see the remarkable (if frequently dubious) work of W. B. Key (1973); cf. Adorno, 1954: 221–22.
19. Busby, 1975: 110.
20. Cf. Warren, 1978; Ewen, 1976: 159–84.
21. See Berger, 1977: 148–54; Ewen, 1976: 87–89; Gitlin, 1972: 352–53.
22. For example: Adorno et al., 1950: 421–33; Lefcourt, 1976: 92–94; Sennett and Cobb, 1973: 271; Lane, 1962: 168, 246, 367, 411. Although we cannot offer empirical proof of the connection between the television habit and personality, there are indications that heavy users have less self-esteem (Gutman, 1973: 394, 397) and are less trusting of others (Gerbner and Gross, 1976).

Chapter 11. Public Opinion (pp. 184–195)

1. Wheeler, 1976.
2. The predominant focus has been on media-induced change of pre-existing attitudes. While we consider attitude change, we also discuss other media effects on political thinking. Space limitations prevent a full account of the research in this area; the existence of insightful, comprehensive literature reviews and textbooks makes such a survey of the field unnecessary. Readers should consult such works as: Klapper, 1960; Weiss, 1969; Sears and Whitney, 1973; DeFleur and Ball-Rokeach, 1975; Davison, Boylan and Yu, 1976; Kraus and Davis, 1976; Nimmo, 1978; Graber, 1980. For critiques: R. Williams, 1974; Hall, 1973a, 1975; Gitlin, 1978.
3. The study of the effect of the external environment and of personal differences on the impact of media messages has been a prime concern of communications research. Its major point: identical media messages may have different effects on different people under varying circumstances. The process of forming and changing beliefs and attitudes is complex; this means there will be many exceptions in practice to our generalizations in this chapter—messages that affect some people in one way may have the opposite effect on others.

Moreover, causes and effects in the study of media, messages, sources, and audiences seem to us so thoroughly intertwined that the effects we suggest may not be empirically verifiable at this stage of the development of the social sciences.

4. Fenno, 1977: 886–89.
5. Converse and Markus, 1979: 43, 48–49; cf. Converse, 1964.
6. Cf. Jervis, 1976: 143–54; Steinbruner, 1974: chap. 3 and *passim;* Holsti, 1976.
7. Cf. McCombs and Shaw, 1972: 182–83, 186; A. Miller, Goldenberg, and Erbring, 1979: 68.
8. Popkin et al., 1976: 799–803; cf. W. Miller and Levitin, 1976: 139–59.
9. "Poll Shows Sharp Rise Since '77 in Opposition to Nuclear Plants," *New York Times,* April 10, 1979, pp. 1, 16.
10. Schulman, 1979: 8; see also Converse, 1974.
11. "How Americans Are Reacting to the Latest Energy Crunch," *Public Opinion* 2 (June/July 1979): 14–15.

Chapter 12. Domesticated Opinion: The Conservative Myth (pp. 196–212)

1. "Mr. Ford's New Confidence," July 6, 1975, p. C6.
2. "The New Focus in Congress," July 16, 1975, p. A14.
3. "A Hunch about Reagan," July 20, 1975, p. C6.
4. Quoted in "Primary Symptoms," *New Republic,* March 13, 1976, p. 9.
5. On a CBS instant analysis of Carter's June 14, 1978, televised press conference.
6. "And the Voters," *Washington Post,* May 16, 1976, pp. A1, A9; "More Conservatives Share Liberal View," *New York Times,* January 22, 1978, pp. 1, 30.
7. *New York Times,* December 4, 1977, pp. 1, 73.
8. Detailed evidence of the repeated claims of a conservative renaissance is present throughout the media of the middle and late 1970s. Agreeing with our characterization of media depictions of public opinion are Levitin and W. Miller, 1978: 5–7, 47 fn 8; A. Miller and W. Miller, 1977: 38–40; cf. Ladd, 1978. Some of the arguments herein were originally made in Entman and Koenig, 1976.
9. Some surveys used different wording and found increases in self-labeled conservatism. But they also found little ideological meaning could be inferred from those polls. Cf. Levitin and W. Miller, 1978.
10. Pomper, 1975: 171; Nie, Verba, and Petrocik, 1976: 196–97.
11. Lipset and Schneider, 1979: 10.
12. "And the Voters," p. A9.

13. "Budget Hikes for Defense, HEW Wanted," *San Francisco Chronicle,* December 18, 1978, p. 3.
14. Ladd, 1979: 74, 78; cf. A. Miller and W. Miller, 1977: 38–40.
15. W. Miller, 1979: 11; Ladd, 1976–77.
16. See Levitin and W. Miller, 1978.
17. See Entman, 1976.
18. Crouse, 1973; Dunn, 1969: 35; cf. Fedler and Taylor, 1978; Breed, 1955.
19. Janis, 1972.
20. Cf. Cohen, 1963: 129; Rivers, 1965: 52; Gans, 1979: 180–81.
21. Cf. Noelle-Neumann, 1974, 1977.
22. Cf. Salzman, 1979: 131.
23. Verba and Nie, 1972: chaps. 15 and 16.
24. Ladd et al., 1979: 130.
25. Ibid., 129.
26. Field, 1978: 4.
27. *Public Opinion* 2 (January/February, 1979): 27.
28. " 'More for Our Money!' The Real 'Revolt'," *San Francisco Sunday Examiner and Chronicle,* October 15, 1978, "World" Section, p. 28.
29. Cf. Ladd et al., 1979: 133–34, and especially Peretz, 1980.

Chapter 13. Domesticated Opinion: Foreign News
(pp. 213–233)

1. Francis, 1967: 262, quoting *New York Daily News,* January 22, 1960.
2. Ibid., 263, quoting *Miami Herald,* July 8, 1960.
3. "Cuba, the Breaking Point," *Time,* January 13, 1961, p. 29.
4. Francis, 1967: 264, quoting *Detroit News,* January 7, 1961.
5. Morris, 1974b: 24, quoting CBS Evening News, September 13, 1973.
6. "The Chilean Tragedy," *New York Times,* September 16, 1973, p. 14E.
7. Morris, 1974b: 16, 18.
8. Pollock and Guidette, 1977: 16–17.
9. "Thousands of Iran Troops, Tanks Enforce Martial Law," *Los Angeles Times,* September 10, 1978, Part 1, p. 4.
10. Dorman and Omeed, 1979.
11. "The Shah vs. the Shi'ites," *Time,* June 5, 1978, p. 39.
12. Cf. Knudson, 1977; Morris, 1979.
13. G. Robinson and Sparkes, 1976: 206–207; cf. Gerbner and Marvanyi, 1977; Hester, 1978; Almaney, 1970; Warner, 1968.
14. Schambra, 1979: 47.
15. Liebling, 1961: 185.

16. Galtung and Ruge, 1965: 81.
17. Hester, 1978: 94.
18. Bernstein, 1977: 58.
19. "CIA Established Many Links to Journalists in U.S. and Abroad," *New York Times,* December 27, 1977, pp. 1, 40.
20. "The CIA's 3-Decade Effort to Mold the World's Views," *New York Times,* December 25, 1977, p. 12.
21. Ibid.
22. Ibid.
23. "Nationwide Propaganda Network Built and Controlled by the CIA," *New York Times,* December 26, 1977, p. 37.
24. Bernstein, 1977: 60.
25. Ibid., 61.
26. Ibid. cf. Schorr, 1977: 274–80.
27. "The CIA's 3-Decade Effort to Mold the World's Views," p. 12.
28. Bernstein, 1977: 63.
29. Hough, 1967: 23.
30. See, e.g., Arlen, 1969; Epstein, 1975; Knightley, 1975; Braestrup, 1977; Hallin, 1980.
31. Our alternative explanations in this section of events in Zaire come from *Africa News,* May 29 and August 21, 1978; Manning and Talbot, 1978; Talbot, 1978; *West Africa,* 1978. We vouch only for their plausibility, not their accuracy. Information also came from Charles Ebel, editor of *Africa News.*
32. Phase I lasted from May 15–27, 1978; Phase II, May 28–June 15, 1978. May 27 was the first day after May 15 that a Zaire story did not appear on page one of the *Post.*
33. *San Francisco Chronicle,* May 28, 1978, p. B-2.
34. "Foreign-Backed Rebels Invade Zaire Again," *San Francisco Chronicle,* May 15, 1978, p. A-1.
35. Weissman, 1979.
36. Bailey, 1976b: 322.
37. Charles Ebel, personal communication.
38. See Hallin, 1980.
39. *Africa News,* May 29, 1978, p. 9; Cooper, 1979.
40. "Legionnaires Reportedly Killed Whites," *San Francisco Chronicle,* May 22, 1978, p. A-22.
41. "White People Said Hunted for the Kill," *Durham Morning Herald,* May 23, 1978, p. 2A.
42. "Americans in Zaire Escape from War Zone," *San Francisco Chronicle,* May 18, 1978, p. A-16, quoting a French diplomat.
43. "60 Europeans Reported Slain by Zaire Rebels," *San Francisco Chronicle,* May 20, 1978, p. A-1, quoting a Belgian.
44. "Paratroops Rescue 2500—Full Zaire Horror Unfolds: 10 Americans

Missing, One Feared Dead,'' *San Francisco Chronicle,* May 21, 1978, p. A-1.

45. "Inside Kolwezi: Toll of Terror," *Time,* June 5, 1978, p. 34.
46. Ibid., p. 32.
47. "Operation Dove," *Newsweek,* June 5, 1978, p. 54.
48. "The Fallout in Zaire," *Newsweek,* June 5, 1978, p. 48.
49. "Loot-Laden Rebels Move Homeward Across Zambia," *Washington Post,* May 24, 1978, p. A-1.
50. "Belgian Troops Leave Kolwezi as Dispute Grows," *Washington Post,* May 23, 1978, p. A-9.
51. Cited in *Public Opinion* 1 (July/August 1978): 25.
52. Schambra, 1979: 48.
53. Cohen, 1963: 187–91.
54. Loory, 1974; Wise, 1973; 16–18, 32, 108.
55. Cohen, 1963: 215, 232.
56. Cf. Braestrup, 1977, vol. I: 671.
57. Cohen, 1963: 244.
58. Hough, 1967: 33.
59. On the essential continuity of American foreign policy premises from the late 1940s through the Kissinger years, see Hoffmann, 1979; cf. Halperin, 1974: 11–12.

Chapter 14. Participating in Politics (pp. 234–248)

1. Speaking at taping of "Inside CBS News," Harrisburg, Pa., October 8, 1977.
2. Lasswell, 1930.
3. Frohlich et al., 1978; cf. Downs, 1957.
4. All these quotes come from Rosenstein, 1977: 37–38.
5. Graber, 1976; Patterson and McClure, 1976.
6. Sayer, 1977: 1, quoting *The Harrisburg Patriot* of May 16, 1977.
7. Sayer, 1977.
8. Leary, 1976: 18; cf. Kaid, 1976; Windhauser, 1976; Carey, 1976; see also T. Bowers, 1972.
9. McClenghan, 1973; Hain, 1975; J. Mueller, 1970.
10. Lazarsfeld et al., 1944; Berelson et al., 1954; Campbell et al., 1954 and 1960; cf. Klapper, 1960.
11. Schramm and Carter, 1959; Simon and Stern, 1955.
12. Nie, Verba, and Petrocik, 1976: 347.
13. W. Miller and Levitin, 1976: 47–48; A. Miller and W. Miller, 1977; Levitin and W. Miller, 1978.
14. Popkin et al., 1976: 799–801.
15. Cf. McCombs and Shaw, 1972.

16. Cf. Carey, 1976.
17. DeVries and Tarrance, 1972; Glaser, 1965; Hofstetter and Buss, 1978.
18. Lemert et al., 1977: 725.
19. Verba and Nie, 1972: 95–101.
20. This section is taken in part from Paletz, Pearson, and Willis, 1977.
21. See, e.g., Converse, Miller, Rusk and Wolfe, 1969: 1087–88; A. Miller and W. Miller, 1975: 413.
22. See also Gitlin, 1977: 792, 797–98.
23. Schrieber, 1976: 226–30.
24. Krieneman and Wright, 1975: 674.
25. Fogelson, 1971: 18–25; Sears and McConahay, 1973: 52–54, 68.
26. Verba and Nie, 1972: 12.
27. Ibid., 338.

Chapter 15. Conclusions (pp. 249–254)

1. Gergen, 1979: 4.
2. Dahlgren, n.d.: 15.
3. Bagdikian, 1973c: 16–17.
4. Bagdikian, 1973b: 23.
5. Wackman et al., 1975: 419–20; cf. Gormley, 1977.
6. Cf. Bunce, 1976: 105.
7. Dominick and Pearce, 1976: 77.
8. Some of the ideas in this chapter are discussed at greater length in Entman, 1978.

Bibliography

Books and articles consulted plus complete
references for footnoted items.

ABELSON, ROBERT P., et al., eds. *Theories of Cognitive Consistency*. Chicago: Rand McNally and Company, 1968.

ADAMANY, DAVID. "Money, Politics and Democracy." *American Political Science Review* 71 (1977): 289–304.

ADAMS, WILLIAM C. "Local Public Affairs Content of TV News." *Journalism Quarterly* 55 (1978): 690–95.

ADAMS, WILLIAM, AND FAY SCHREIBMAN, eds. *Television Network News: Issues in Content Research*. Washington, D.C.: George Washington University, 1978.

ADORNO, THEODOR W. "How to Look at Television." *Quarterly of Film, Radio, and Television* 8 (1954): 213–35.

ADORNO, THEODOR W., ELSE FRENKEL-BRUNSWIK, DANIEL J. LEVINSON, AND NEVITT SANFORD. *The Authoritarian Personality*. New York: Harper, 1950.

AFRICA NEWS. "A Zaire Dossier." *Africa News* 11 (May 29, 1978): 5–9.

———. "Patching Over Old Differences." *Africa News* 11 (August 21, 1978): 5–8.

ALMANEY, ADNAN. "International and Foreign Affairs on Network Television News." *Journal of Broadcasting* 14 (1970): 499–509.

ALTHEIDE, DAVID L. *Creating Reality: How TV News Distorts Events*. Beverly Hills, California: Sage Publications, 1976.

ARGYRIS, CHRIS. *Behind the Front Page: Organizational Self-Renewal in a Metropolitan Newspaper*. San Francisco: Jossey-Bass, 1974.

ARLEN, MICHAEL, J. *Living-Room War*. New York: Viking Press, 1969.

ARTERTON, F. CHRISTOPHER. "The Impact of Watergate on Children's Attitudes toward Political Authority." *Political Science Quarterly* 89 (1974): 269–88.

———. "Campaign Organizations Face the Mass Media in the 1976 Presidential Nomination Process." Paper presented at the 1977 Annual Meeting of the American Political Science Association, Washington, D.C., September 1–4, 1977.

AULETTA, KEN. "Covering Carter is Like Playing Chess with Bobby Fischer." *More* 6 (1976): 12–22.

BAGDIKIAN, BEN H. *The Effete Conspiracy*. New York: Harper and Row, 1972.

———. "The Role of the Media Defended and Defined." Review of Lester Markel, *What You Don't Know Can Hurt You* (New York: Public Affairs

Press, 1972) and Hillier Krieghbaum, *Pressures on the Press* (New York: Thomas Y. Crowell Company, 1972), *New York Times Book Review* (June 11, 1972): 2ff.

———. "The Politics of American Newspapers." *Columbia Journalism Review* 10 (March/April, 1972): 8–13.

———. "The Fruits of Agnewism." *Columbia Journalism Review* 11 (January/February, 1973): 9–21, (1973a).

———. "The Myth of Newspaper Poverty." *Columbia Journalism Review* 11 (March/April, 1973): 19–25, (1973b).

———. "Fat Newspapers and Slim Coverage." *Columbia Journalism Review* 12 (September/October, 1973): 15–20 (1973c).

———. "Congress and the Media: Partners in Propaganda." *Columbia Journalism Review* 12 (January/February, 1974): 3–10.

———. "Watergate and the Press: Success and Failure." In Walter Lubars and John Wicklein, eds., *Investigative Reporting: The Lessons of Watergate.* Boston: Boston University School of Public Communication, 1975.

BAILEY, GEORGE. "Television War: Trends in Network Coverage of Vietnam, 1965–70." *Journal of Broadcasting* 20 (1976): 147–58 (1976a).

———. "Interpretive Reporting of the Vietnam War by Anchormen." *Journalism Quarterly* 53 (1976): 319–24 (1976b).

BALUTIS, ALAN P. "Congress, the President and the Press." *Journalism Quarterly* 53 (1976): 509–515.

BARBER, JAMES DAVID. *The Presidential Character.* Englewood Cliffs, New Jersey: Prentice-Hall, 1977, 2nd ed.

———. *The Pulse of Politics.* New York: Norton, 1980.

BARONE, MICHAEL. "Nonlessons of the Campaign." *New York Times Magazine* (November 28, 1976): 36–37, 101–104.

BARRETT, MARVIN, ed. *The Politics of Broadcasting, 1971–72.* New York: Thomas Y. Crowell, 1973.

———. *Moments of Truth?* New York: Thomas Y. Crowell, 1975.

BARTLETT, DOROTHY L., et al. "Selective Exposure to a Presidential Campaign Appeal." *Public Opinion Quarterly* 38 (1974): 264–70.

BATSCHA, ROBERT N. *Foreign Affairs News and the Broadcast Journalist.* New York: Praeger Special Studies, 1975.

BAUS, HERBERT M., AND WILLIAM B. ROSS. *Politics Battle Plan.* New York: Macmillan Company, 1968.

BECHER, JULES, AND DOUGLAS A. FUCHS. "How Two Major California Dailies Covered Reagan vs. Brown." *Journalism Quarterly* 45 (1968): 645-53.

BECHTOLT, WARREN, JR., JOSEPH HILYARD, AND CARL R. BYBEE. "Agenda Control in the 1976 Debates: A Content Analysis." *Journalism Quarterly* 54 (1977): 674–81, 689.

BECKER, LEE B., AND JOHN C. DOOLITTLE. "How Repetition Affects Evaluations of and Information Seeking about Candidates." *Journalism Quarterly* 52 (1975): 611–17.

BECKER, LEE B., MAXWELL E. McCOMBS, AND JACK M. McCLEOD. "The Development of Political Cognitions." In Steven H. Chaffee, ed., *Political Communication: Issues and Strategies for Research.* Beverly Hills, California: Sage Publications, 1975.

BELL, DAVID V. J. *Power, Influence, and Authority*. New York: Oxford University Press, 1975.

BELSON, WILLIAM. "Television and the Adolescent Boy." *Intermedia* 5 (December 1977): 20–24.

BENTLEY, ARTHUR F. *The Process of Government*. Cambridge, Massachusetts: Harvard University Press, 1967 (first published 1908).

BERELSON, BERNARD. "Democratic Theory and Public Opinion." *Public Opinion Quarterly* 16 (1952): 313–30.

BERELSON, BERNARD, PAUL F. LAZARSFELD, AND WILLIAM McPHEE. *Voting: A Study of Opinion Formation in a Presidential Campaign*. Chicago: University of Chicago Press, 1954.

BERELSON, BERNARD, AND PATRICIA J. SALTER. "Majority and Minority Americans: An Analysis of Magazine Fiction." In Bernard Rosenberg and David Manning White, eds., *Mass Culture, The Popular Arts*. New York: The Free Press, 1957.

BERG, MIE, PERTI HEMANUS, JAN EKECRANTZ, FRANDS MORTENSEN, AND PREBEN SEPSTRUP. *Current Theories in Scandinavian Mass Communication*. Grenna, Denmark: GMT, 1977.

BERGER, JOHN. *Ways of Seeing*. New York: Penguin Books, 1977.

BERK, LYNN M. "The Great Middle American Dream Machine." *Journal of Communication* 27 (Summer 1977): 27–31.

BERNSTEIN, BASIL B. *Class, Codes and Control*. New York: Schocken Books, 1975, 2nd rev. ed.

BERNSTEIN, CARL. "How America's Most Powerful News Media Worked Hand in Glove with the Central Intelligence Agency and Why the Church Committee Covered It Up." *Rolling Stone* (October 20, 1977): 55–67.

BLANCHARD, ROBERT O., ed. *Congress and the News Media*. New York: Hastings House, 1974.

BLUMLER, JAY G. "Audience Roles in Political Communication: Some Reflections on Their Structure Antecedents and Consequences." Paper presented at the Ninth World Congress of the International Political Science Association. Montreal, Canada, August 19–25, 1973.

BLUMLER, JAY G., AND DENIS McQUAIL. *Television in Politics: Its Uses and Influence*. Chicago: University of Chicago Press, 1969.

BOGART, LEO. "The Management of Mass Media." In W. Phillips Davison and Frederick T. C. Yu, eds., *Mass Communication Research*. New York: Praeger Publishers, 1974.

BOOTH, ALAN. "The Recall of News Items." *Public Opinion Quarterly* 34 (1970–71): 604–10.

BOWER, ROBERT T. *Television and the Public*. New York: Holt, Rinehart & Winston, 1973.

BOWERS, DAVID R. "A Report on Activity by Publishers in Directing Newsroom Decisions." *Journalism Quarterly* 44 (1967): 43–52.

BOWERS, THOMAS A. "Issues and Personality Information in Newspaper Political Advertising." *Journalism Quarterly* 49 (1972): 446–52.

BRAESTRUP, PETER. *The Big Story*. 2 vols. Boulder, Colorado: Westview Press, 1977.

BREED, WARREN. "Newspaper 'Opinion Leaders' and Processes of Standardization." *Journalism Quarterly* 32 (1955): 277–84, 328.

BROWN, LES. *Televi$ion: The Business behind the Box*. New York: Harcourt Brace Jovanovich, 1971.

BUNCE, RICHARD. *Television in the Corporate Interest*. New York: Praeger Publishers, 1976.

BUNGE, WALTER, ROBERT V. HUDSON, AND CHUNG WOO SUH. "Johnson's Information Strategy for Vietnam: An Evaluation." *Journalism Quarterly* 45 (1968): 419–25.

BUSBY, LINDA J. "Sex-Role Research on the Mass Media." *Journal of Communication* 25 (Autumn 1975): 107–31.

CALLOW, ALEXANDER B., JR. *The Tweed Ring*. New York: Oxford University Press, 1966.

CAMPBELL, ANGUS, PHILIP E. CONVERSE, WARREN E. MILLER, AND DONALD E. STOKES. *The American Voter*. New York: Wiley, 1960.

CAMPBELL, ANGUS, GERALD GURIN, AND WARREN E. MILLER. *The Voter Decides*. Evanston, Illinois: Row, Peterson, 1954.

CANTOR, MURIEL G. *The Hollywood TV Producer*. New York: Basic Books, 1971.

CAREY, JOHN. "How Media Shape Campaigns." *Journal of Communication* 26 (Spring 1976): 50–57.

CASPARY, WILLIAM R. "The 'Mood' Theory: A Study of Public Opinion and Foreign Policy." *American Political Science Review* 64 (1970): 536–47.

CATER, DOUGLASS. *The Fourth Branch of Government*. Boston: Houghton Mifflin Company, 1955.

CHAFFEE, STEVEN H. "The Interpersonal Context of Mass Communications." In F. Gerald Kline and Phillip J. Tichenor, eds., *Current Perspectives in Mass Communication Research*. Beverly Hills, California: Sage Publications, 1972.

———. "The Mass Media as Agents of Political Socialization." *International Journal of Political Education* 1 (1977–78): 127–42.

CHATTEN, ROBERT. "The Police and the Press: Criticism or Cooperation?" Paper submitted to Political Science 153, 154, *Politics and the Media*, Duke University, Durham, North Carolina, April 1978.

CHESEBRO, JAMES W., AND CAROLINE D. HAMSHER. "Communication, Values, and Popular Television Series." In Horace Newcomb, ed., *Television: The Critical View*. New York: Oxford University Press, 1976.

CHESTER, LEWIS, GODFREY HODGSON, AND BRUCE PAGE. *An American Melodrama*. New York: Viking Press, 1969.

CLAPP, CHARLES L. *The Congressman*. Garden City, New York: Doubleday Anchor, 1964.

CLARKE, PETER, ed. *New Models for Mass Communication Research*. Beverly Hills, California: Sage Publications, 1973.

CLYMER, ADAM. "More Conservatives Share Liberal View." *New York Times* (January 22, 1978): 1, 30.

———. "Poll Shows Sharp Rise Since 1977 in Opposition to Nuclear Plants." *New York Times* (April 10, 1979): 1, 16.

COHEN, BERNARD C. *The Press and Foreign Policy*. Princeton, New Jersey: Princeton University Press, 1963.

COHEN, STANLEY, AND JOCK YOUNG, eds. *The Manufacture of News*. Beverly Hills, California: Sage Publications, 1973.

COLE, BARRY, AND MAL OETTINGER. *Reluctant Regulators*. Reading, Massachusetts: Addison-Wesley Publishing Company, 1978.

COMSTOCK, GEORGE. "The Evidence So Far." *Journal of Communication* 25 (Autumn 1975): 25–34.

———. "Paradoxes in the Role of Mass Media." Paper prepared for the Workshop on Mass Media in Citizen Education, Marsh Center for the Study of Journalistic Performance, University of Michigan, Ann Arbor, Michigan, October 1977.

———. "The State of the Art of Television Research and the Young Adolescent." Paper presented at the Action for Children's Television Research Workshop on Televised Role Models and Young Adolescents, Harvard Graduate School of Education, Boston, Massachusetts, November 8, 1977.

CONNELL, R. W. *The Child's Construction of Politics*. Melbourne, Australia: Melbourne University Press, 1971.

CONVERSE, PHILIP E. "The Nature of Belief Systems among Mass Publics." In David E. Apter, ed., *Ideology and Discontent*. New York: The Free Press, 1964.

———. "Comment: The Status of Nonattitudes." *American Political Science Review* 68 (1974): 650–660.

———. "Public Opinion and Voting Behavior." In Fred I. Greenstein and Nelson W. Polsby, eds., *Handbook of Political Science*, vol. 4. Reading, Massachusetts: Addison-Wesley Publishing Company, 1975.

CONVERSE, PHILIP E., WARREN E. MILLER, JERROLD G. RUSK, AND ARTHUR C. WOLFE. "Continuity and Change in American Politics: Parties and Issues in the 1968 Election." *American Political Science Review* 63 (1969): 1083–1105.

CONVERSE, PHILIP E., AND GREGORY B. MARKUS. "Plus Ça Change . . . : The New C.P.S. Election Panel Study." *American Political Science Review* 73 (1979): 32–49.

COOPER, WENDY. "Zaire's Primrose Path to the Poorhouse." *The Nation* 229 (October 13, 1979): 333–37.

CORNWELL, ELMER E. *Presidential Leadership of Public Opinion*. Bloomington, Indiana: Indiana University Press, 1965.

COURTNEY, ALICE, AND THOMAS W. WHIPPLE. "Women in TV Commercials." *Journal of Communication* 24 (Autumn 1974): 110–18.

COX, HARVEY, AND DAVID MORGAN. *City Politics and the Press*. London: Cambridge University Press, 1973.

CRICK, BERNARD R. *The American Science of Politics: Its Origins and Conditions*. Berkeley, California: University of California Press, 1967.

CRONIN, THOMAS B. *The State of the Presidency*. Boston: Little, Brown and Company, 1975.

CROUSE, TIMOTHY. *The Boys on the Bus*. New York: Random House, 1973.

CULBERT, DAVID. "Historians and the Visual Analysis of Television News." In William Adams and Fay Schreibman, eds., *Television Network News: Issues in Content Research.* Washington, D.C.: George Washington University, 1978.

CULLEY, JAMES D., AND REX BENNETT. "Selling Women, Selling Blacks." *Journal of Communication* 26 (Autumn 1976): 160–79.

DAHLGREN, PETER. "TV News and the Suppression of Reflexivity." Paper, Department of Communication, Arts and Sciences, Queens College, City University of New York, New York, n.d.

DAVISON, W. PHILLIPS, JAMES BOYLAN, AND FREDERICK T. C. YU. *Mass Media: Systems and Effects.* New York: Praeger Publishers, 1976.

DAWSON, PAUL, AND JAMES ZINSER. "Broadcast Expenditures and Electoral Outcomes in the 1970 Congressional Elections." *Public Opinion Quarterly* 35 (1971): 398–402.

DAWSON, RICHARD E., KENNETH PREWITT, AND KAREN S. DAWSON. *Political Socialization.* Boston: Little, Brown and Company, 1977, 2nd ed.

DEAN, JOHN WESLEY. *Blind Ambition: The White House Years.* New York: Simon and Schuster, 1976.

DEFLEUR, MELVIN L., AND SANDRA BALL-ROKEACH. *Theories of Mass Communication,* New York: David McKay Company, 1975, 3rd ed.

DEVRIES, WALTER, AND V. LANCE TARRANCE. *The Ticket-Splitters: A New Force in American Politics.* Grand Rapids, Michigan, Erdmans, 1972.

DIAMOND, EDWIN. "Everybody into the Pool." *New York* 8 (March 10, 1975): 69.

DOLBEARE, KENNETH M., AND MURRAY J. EDELMAN. *American Politics: Policies, Power and Change.* Lexington, Massachusetts: D.C. Heath and Company, 1979.

DOMINICK, JOSEPH R. "Crime and Law Enforcement on Prime Time Television." *Public Opinion Quarterly* 37 (1973): 241–50.

――――. "Geographic Bias in National TV News." *Journal of Communication* 27 (Autumn 1977): 94–99.

DOMINICK, JOSEPH R., AND MILLARD C. PEARCE. "Trends in Network Prime-Time Programming, 1953–74." *Journal of Communication* 26 (Winter 1976): 70–80.

DONOHEW, LEWIS. "Newspaper Gatekeepers and Forces in the News Channel." *Public Opinion Quarterly* 31 (1967): 61–68.

DONOHEW, LEWIS, AND LEONARD TIPTON. "A Conceptual Model of Information Seeking, Avoiding, and Processing." In Peter Clarke, ed., *New Models for Communication Research.* Beverly Hills, California: Sage Publications, 1973.

DORFMAN, ARIEL, AND ARMAND MATTELART. *How to Read Donald Duck: Imperialist Ideology in the Disney Comic.* New York: International General Publishing Company, 1975.

DORMAN, WILLIAM A., AND EHSAN OMEED. "Reporting Iran the Shah's Way." *Columbia Journalism Review* 17 (January/February, 1979): 27–33.

DOWNS, ANTHONY. *An Economic Theory of Democracy.* New York: Harper and Row, 1957.

DREYER, EDWARD C. "Media Use and Electoral Choices: Some Political Consequences of Information Exposure." *Public Opinion Quarterly* 35 (1971–72): 544–53.

DRUMMOND, WILLIAM J. "Shackling the Free Press." *Public Information Center News* 2 (July/August, 1971): 6–8.

DRURY, ALLEN. *A Senate Journal, 1943–1945.* New York: McGraw-Hill, 1963.

DUNN, DELMER D. *Public Officials and the Press.* Reading, Massachusetts: Addison-Wesley Publishing Company, 1969.

EASTON, DAVID, AND JACK DENNIS. *Children in the Political System: Origins of Political Legitimacy.* New York: McGraw-Hill, 1969.

EDELMAN, MURRAY. *The Symbolic Uses of Politics.* Urbana. Illinois: University of Illinois Press, 1964.

———. "Language, Myths and Rhetoric." *Society* 12 (July/August, 1975): 14–21.

———. *Political Language: Words That Succeed and Policies That Fail.* New York: Academic Press, 1977.

EDWARDS, GEORGE C. "Presidential Influence in the House: Presidential Prestige as a Source of Presidential Power." *American Political Science Review* 70 (1976): 101–13.

EFRON, EDITH. *The News Twisters.* Los Angeles: Nash Publishers, 1971.

EHRENREICH, BARBARA. "Combat in the Media Zone." *Seven Days* (March 10, 1978): 13–14.

EINSIEDEL, E. F., AND M. JANE BIBBEE. "The News Magazines and Minority Candidates—Campaign '76." *Journalism Quarterly* 56 (1979): 102–105.

ENTMAN, ROBERT M. "The Influence of the Mass Media on Political Socialization and Attitude Change." In Thomas J. Volgy, ed., *Exploring Relationships between Mass Media and Political Culture.* Tucson, Arizona: University of Arizona Institute of Government Research, 1975.

———. "What the Neo-Conservatives Prescribe for Us." *The Nation* 222 (January 10, 1976): 21–23.

———. "The Mass Media and Power in American Politics." Paper presented at the 1978 Annual Meeting of the American Political Science Association, New York, August 31–September 3, 1978.

———. "The Imperial Media." In Arnold J. Meltsner, ed., *Politics and the Oval Office: Towards Presidential Governance.* San Francisco, California: Institute for Contemporary Studies, 1981.

ENTMAN, ROBERT M., AND BONNIE KOENIG. "Pack Journalism: The 'Conservative' Myth." *The Nation* 223 (July 17–24, 1976): 39–42.

ENTMAN, ROBERT M., AND DAVID L. PALETZ. "Making It: The Search for Academic Quality and the Striving after Success." *Liberal Education* 62 (1976): 576–84.

ENTMAN, ROBERT M., JAMES W. PROTHRO, AND EDWARD F. SHARP. "Watergate and Political Trust." *Working Paper.* Yale Institution for Social and Policy Studies. November, 1974.

ENTMAN, ROBERT M., AND FRANCIE SEYMOUR. "Close Encounters with the Third Reich." *Jump Cut* 18, (1978): 3–7.

EPSTEIN, EDWARD JAY. *News from Nowhere: Television and the News.* New York: Vintage, 1973.

———. *Between Fact and Fiction.* New York: Random House, 1975.

EPSTEIN, LAURILY KEIR. "Abortion and the Media: A Case Study in Agenda-Setting." Paper presented at the Annual Meeting of the Midwest Political Science Association, Chicago, Illinois, April, 1978.

ERBRING, LUTZ, EDIE GOLDENBERG, AND ARTHUR H. MILLER. "Front Page News and Real World Cues: Another Look at Agenda-Setting by the Media." Center for Political Studies, Institute for Social Research, University of Michigan, July, 1978.

ERICSON, DAVID. "Newspaper Coverage of the Supreme Court: A Case Study." *Journalism Quarterly* 54 (1977): 605–607.

ERSKINE, HAZEL. "The Polls: Opinion of the News Media." *Public Opinion Quarterly* 34 (1970–71): 630–43.

EWEN, STUART. *Captains of Consciousness: Advertising and the Social Roots of the Consumer Culture*. New York: McGraw-Hill, 1976.

FAIRLIE, HENRY. "The Unreal World of Television News." In David Manning White and Richard Averson, eds., *Sight, Sound and Society*. Boston: Beacon Press, 1968.

FAULK, JOHN HENRY. *Fear on Trial*. New York: Simon and Schuster, 1964.

FASS, PAULA S. "Television as Cultural Document: Promises and Problems." In Richard Adler and Douglass Cater, eds., *Television as a Cultural Force*. New York: Praeger Publishers, 1976.

FEARING, FRANKLIN. "Influence of the Movies on Attitudes and Behavior." In Denis McQuail, ed., *Sociology of Mass Communications*. Baltimore, Maryland: Penguin Books, 1972.

FEDLER, FRED, AND PHYLLIS TAYLOR. "Broadcasting's Impact on Selection of News Stories by Readers." *Journalism Quarterly* 55 (1978): 301–305, 333.

FENNO, RICHARD F., JR. "If, as Ralph Nader Says, Congress Is 'the Broken Branch,' How Come We Love Our Congressmen So Much?" In Norman J. Ornstein, ed., *Congress in Change: Evolution and Reform*. New York: Praeger Publishers, 1975.

———. "U.S. House Members in Their Constituencies: An Exploration." *American Political Science Review* 71 (1977): 883–917.

FIELD, MERVIN. "Sending a Message: Californians Strike Back." *Public Opinion* 1 (July/August, 1978): 3–7.

FIORINA, MORRIS I. *Congress: Keystone of the Washington Establishment*. New Haven, Connecticut: Yale University Press, 1977.

FISHEL, JEFF. "Agenda-Building in Presidential Campaigns: The Case of Jimmy Carter." Paper presented at the 1977 Annual Meeting of the American Political Science Association. Washington, D.C., September 1–4, 1977.

———, ed. *Parties and Elections in an Anti-Party Age*. Bloomington, Indiana: Indiana University Press, 1978.

FLEISHMAN, JOEL L., AND CAROL S. GREENWALD. "Public Interest Litigation and Political Finance Reform." *Annals of the American Academy of Political and Social Science* 425 (May, 1976): 114–23.

FOGELSON, ROBERT M. *Violence as Protest: A Study of Riots and Ghettos*. Garden City, New York: Doubleday, 1971.

FOSS, PHILLIP O. *Politics and Grass: The Administration of Grazing on the Public Domain*. New York: Greenwood Press, 1969.

FRADY, MARSHALL. "The Transformation of Bobby Kennedy." *New York Review* 25 (October 12, 1978): 42–51.

FRANCIS, MICHAEL J. "The U.S. Press and Castro: A Study in Declining Relationships." *Journalism Quarterly* 44 (1967): 257–66.

FRANK, ROBERT S. *Message Dimensions of Television News.* Lexington, Massachusetts: Lexington Books, D.C. Heath, 1973.

———. "The IAS Case against CBS." *Journal of Communication* 25 (Autumn 1975): 186–89.

FRANKEL, MAX. "Letter." *Commentary* 52 (July, 1971): 6ff.

FRANZWA, HELEN H. "Working Women in Fact and Fiction." *Journal of Communication* 24 (Spring 1974): 104–109.

FREEDMAN, STANLEY R. "The Salience of Party and Candidate in Congressional Elections: A Comparison of 1958 and 1970." In Norman R. Luttbeg, ed., *Public Opinion and Public Policy.* Homewood, Illinois: Dorsey Press, 1974, 2nd ed.

FREEMAN, J. LEIPER. *The Political Process: Executive Bureau-Legislative Committee Relations.* Garden City, New York: Doubleday, 1955.

FRIENDLY, FRED W. *Due to Circumstances beyond Our Control.* New York: Random House, 1967.

FRITSCHLER, A. LEE. *Smoking and Politics: Policymaking and the Federal Bureaucracy.* New York: Appleton-Century-Crofts, Educational Division, 1969.

FROHLICH, NORMAN, JOE A. OPPENHEIMER, JEFFREY SMITH, AND ORAN R. YOUNG. "A Test of Downsian Voter Rationality: 1964 Presidential Voting." *American Political Science Review* 72 (1978): 178–97.

FROMAN, LEWIS A., JR. "On a Realistic Approach to Campaign Strategies and Tactics." In M. Kent Jennings and L. Harmon Zeigler, eds., *The Electoral Process.* Englewood Cliffs, New Jersey: Prentice-Hall, 1966.

FRYKLUND, RICHARD. "Covering the Defense Establishment." In Ray E. Hiebert, ed., *The Press in Washington.* New York: Dodd, Mead and Company, 1966.

GALLUP, GEORGE H. *The Gallup Poll: Public Opinion 1972–1977,* vol. I. Wilmington, Delaware: Scholarly Resources, 1978.

GALTUNG, JOHAN, AND MARI RUGE. "The Structure of Foreign News." *Journal of Peace Research* 2 (1965): 64–91.

GANS, HERBERT J. *Deciding What's News: A Study of CBS Evening News, NBC Nightly News, Newsweek and Time.* New York: Pantheon Books, 1979.

GARDNER, JOHN W. "America: Toward New Priorities." *Current* 123 (November, 1970): 3–8.

GARROW, DAVID J. *Protest at Selma: Martin Luther King and the Voting Rights Act of 1965.* New Haven, Connecticut: Yale University Press, 1978.

GERBNER, GEORGE, AND LARRY GROSS. "Living with Television: The Violence Profile." *Journal of Communication* 26 (Spring 1976): 172–99.

GERBNER, GEORGE, et al. "TV Violence Profile No. 8: The Highlights." *Journal of Communication* 27 (Spring 1977): 171–80.

GERBNER, GEORGE, AND GEORGE MARVANYI. "The Many Worlds of the World's Press." *Journal of Communication* 27 (Winter 1977): 52–66.

GERGEN, DAVID. "A Report from the Editors on the 'Crisis of Confidence.'" *Public Opinion* 2 (August/September, 1979): 2–4, 54.

GITLIN, TODD. "Sixteen Notes on Television and the Movement." In George White and Charles Newman, eds., *Literature in Revolution.* New York: Holt, Rinehart & Winston, 1972.

————. "Media Sociology: The Dominant Paradigm." *Theory and Society* 6 (1978): 205–53.

————. *The Whole World Is Watching*. Berkeley, California: University of California Press, 1980.

GLASS, ANDREW J. "Common Cause." In J. G. Smith, ed., *Political Brokers: Money, Organizations, Power and People*. New York: Liveright, 1972.

GLASER, WILLIAM A. "Television and Voting Turnout." *Public Opinion Quarterly* 29 (1965): 71–86.

GOLDENBERG, EDIE N. *Making the Papers*. Lexington, Massachusetts: Lexington Books, D.C. Heath and Company, 1975.

GOLDSEN, ROSE K. "Television's Modes of Address." *Journal of Communication* 25 (Spring 1975): 44–49.

GOLDSTEIN, JEFFREY H., AND BRENDA J. BREDEMEIR. "Socialization: Some Basic Issues." *Journal of Communication* 27 (1977): 154–59.

GORMLEY, WILLIAM T., JR. "How Cross Ownership Affects Newsgathering." *Columbia Journalism Review* 16 (May/June 1977): 38–44.

GRABER, DORIS A. "The Press as Opinion Resource during the 1968 Presidential Campaign." *Public Opinion Quarterly* 35 (1971): 168–82.

————. "Press and Television as Opinion Resources in Presidential Campaigns." *Public Opinion Quarterly* 40 (1976): 285–303.

————. *Mass Media and American Politics*. Washington, D.C.: Congressional Quarterly Press, 1980.

GRABER, DORIS, AND YOUNG Y. KIM. "Media Coverage and Voter Learning during the Presidential Primary Season." Paper presented at the Annual Meeting of the Midwest Political Science Association, Chicago, Illinois, April 21–23, 1977.

GREENBERG, BRADLEY S., AND BRENDA DERVIN. "Mass Communications among the Urban Poor." *Public Opinion Quarterly* 34 (1970): 224–35.

GREENFIELD, JEFF. "Down to the Last Detail." *Columbia Journalism Review* 14 (March/April, 1976): 16–17.

GREENSTEIN, FRED I. "What the President Means to Americans . . ." In James David Barber, ed., *Choosing the President*. Englewood Cliffs, New Jersey: Prentice-Hall, 1974.

————. "The Benevolent Leader Revisited: Children's Images of Political Leaders in Three Democracies." *American Political Science Review* 69 (1975): 1371–98.

GREENWALD, CAROL S. *Group Power: Lobbying and Public Policy*. New York: Praeger Publishers, 1977.

GREY, DAVID L. *The Supreme Court and the News Media*. Evanston, Illinois: Northwestern University Press, 1968.

GROSS, LARRY, AND SUZANNE JEFFRIES-FOX. "What Do You Want to Be When You Grow Up, Little Girl? Approaches to the Study of Media Effects." In Gaye Tuchman et al., eds., *Hearth and Home: Images of Women in the Mass Media*. New York: Oxford University Press, 1978.

GROSSMAN, MICHAEL BARUCH, AND MARTHA JOYNT KUMAR. "White House Press Operations and the News Media: The Phases of a Continuing Relationship." Paper presented at the Annual Meeting of the American Political Science Association, Washington, D.C., September 1–4, 1977.

GROSSMAN, MICHAEL BARUCH, AND FRANCIS E. ROURKE. "The Media and the Presidency: An Exchange Analysis." *Political Science Quarterly* 91 (1976): 455–70.

GUTMAN, JONATHAN. "Self-Concepts and Television Viewing among Women." *Public Opinion Quarterly* 37 (1973): 388–97.

HACKER, ANDREW. "Safety Last." *New York Review* 24 (September 15, 1977): 3–8.

HAIN, PAUL L. "How an Endorsement Affected a Non-Partisan Mayoral Vote." *Journalism Quarterly* 52 (1975): 337–40.

HALBERSTAM, DAVID. "CBS: The Power and the Profits." *The Atlantic Monthly* 237 (February, 1976): 52–91.

———. *The Powers That Be.* New York: Knopf, 1979.

HALE, F. DENNIS. "A Comparison of Coverage of Speech and Press Verdicts of Supreme Court." *Journalism Quarterly* 56 (1979): 43–47.

HALL, STUART. "External Influences on Broadcasting." In F. S. Bradley, ed., *Fourth Symposium on Broadcasting Policy.* University of Manchester, Dept. of ExtraMural Studics, n.d.: 91–105.

———. "Deviancy, Politics and the Media." Paper presented at the British Sociological Conference, 1971.

———. "External Influences on Broadcasting." Stencilled Occasional Papers, University of Birmingham Centre for Contemporary Cultural Studies, February, 1972.

———. "Encoding and Decoding in the Television Discourse." Stencilled Occasional Papers, University of Birmingham Centre for Contemporary Cultural Studies, 1973 (1973a).

———. "The 'Structured Communication' of Events." Stencilled Occasional Papers, University of Birmingham Centre for Contemporary Cultural Studies, October, 1973 (1973b).

———. "Television as a Medium and Its Relation to Culture." Stencilled Occasional Papers, University of Birmingham Centre for Contemporary Cultural Studies, 1975.

HALLIN, DANIEL. "The War in Vietnam and the Crisis in American Politics." Ph.D. dissertation, University of California, Berkeley, 1980.

HALPERIN, MORTON H. *Bureaucratic Politics and Foreign Policy.* Washington, D.C.: The Brookings Institution, 1974.

HALPERN, PAUL. *Consumer Politics and Corporate Behavior: The Case of Automobile Safety.* Ph.D. dissertation, Harvard University, 1972.

HARRIS, RICHARD. *The Real Voice.* New York: Macmillan Company, 1964.

HARRIS, WILLIAM F. "Government without Newspapers?" Paper presented at the World Congress of Sociology, Uppsala University, Uppsala, Sweden, August 14–19, 1978 (1978a).

———. "The News Story and Political Theory: Binding Mind and Polity." Paper presented at the Annual Meeting of the American Political Science Association, New York, August 31–September 3, 1978 (1978b).

HERSH, SEYMOUR M. "The Story Everyone Ignored." *Columbia Journalism Review* 8 (Winter 1969–70): 55–58.

HESTER, AL. "Five Years of Foreign News on U.S. Television Evening News-casts." *Gazette* 24 (1978): 86–95.

HICKEY, NEIL. "Hassle in Duluth." *TV Guide* 19 (November 13, 1971): 8–14.

HOBBES, THOMAS. *The Leviathan*. New York: E. P. Dutton, 1907.

HOFFMANN, STANLEY. "The Case of Dr. Kissinger." *New York Review* 26 (December 6, 1979): 14–29.

HOFSTETTER, C. RICHARD, et al. *Bias in the News: Network Television Coverage of the 1972 Election Campaign*. Columbus: Ohio State University Press, 1976.

HOFSTETTER, C. RICHARD, AND TERRY F. BUSS. "Politics and Last-Minute Political Television." Paper presented at the 1978 Annual Meeting of the Midwest Political Science Association, Chicago, Illinois, April 20–22, 1978.

HOFSTETTER, C. RICHARD, AND CLIFF ZUKIN. "Television Network News and Advertising in the Nixon and McGovern Campaigns." *Journalism Quarterly* 56 (1979): 106–15, 152.

HOLSTI, OLE R. "Cognitive Process Approaches to Decision Making: Foreign Policy Actors Viewed Psychologically." *American Behavioral Scientist* 20 (1976): 11–32.

HOUGH, JERRY F. "The Mass Media and the Policy-Making Process in the Soviet Union and the United States: Implications for Comparative Studies." Paper presented at the 1967 Annual Meeting of the American Political Science Association, Chicago, September 5–9, 1967.

HOWKINS, JOHN. "Television May Never Be the Same Again." *Sight and Sound* 48 (1979): 148–50.

HUBBARD, J. T. W. "Business News in Post-Watergate Era." *Journalism Quarterly* 53 (1976): 488–93.

HUGHES, EMMETT JOHN. *The Ordeal of Power*. New York: Atheneum, 1963.

———. *The Living Presidency*. New York: Coward, McCann and Geoghegan, 1973.

HUNTINGTON, SAMUEL P. "The Democratic Distemper." *Public Interest* 41 (1975): 9–38.

HURWITZ, LEON, BARBARA GREEN, AND HANS SEGAL. "International Press Reactions to the Resignation and Pardon of Richard M. Nixon." *Comparative Politics* 9 (1976): 107–23.

HYMAN, HERBERT H. "Mass Communication and Socialization." In W. Phillips Davison and Frederick T. C. Yu, eds., *Mass Communication Research*. New York: Praeger Publishers, 1974.

JACOBSON, GARY C. "The Effects of Campaign Spending in Congressional Campaigns." *American Political Science Review* 72 (1978): 469–91.

JANIS, IRVING. *Victims of Groupthink*. Boston: Houghton Mifflin, 1972.

JERVIS, ROBERT. *Perception and Misperception in International Politics*. Princeton, New Jersey: Princeton University Press, 1976.

JOHNSON, RICHARD M. *The Dynamics of Compliance: Supreme Court Decision-Making from a New Perspective*. Evanston, Illinois: Northwestern University Press, 1967.

JOHNSTONE, JOHN W. C., EDWARD J. SLANSKI, AND WILLIAM W. BOWMAN.

The News People: A Sociological Profile of American Journalists and Their Work. Urbana, Illinois: University of Illinois Press, 1976.

JOSLYN, RICHARD A. "The Impact of Political Television on Nonpartisan Voting Behavior." Paper presented at the Annual Meeting of the American Political Science Association, Washington, D.C., September 1–4, 1977.

KAID, LYNDA LEE. "Newspaper Treatment of a Candidate's News Release." *Journalism Quarterly* 53 (1976): 135–37.

KAMPELMAN, MAX M. "The Power of the Press: A Problem for Our Democracy." *Policy Review* 6 (1978): 7–40.

KATZ, ELIHU, AND PAUL F. LAZARSFELD. *Personal Influence.* New York: The Free Press, 1955.

KATZ, ELIHU, JAY G. BLUMLER, AND MICHAEL GUREVITCH. "Uses of Mass Communication by the Individual." In W. Phillips Davison and Frederick T. C. Yu, eds., *Mass Communication Research.* New York: Praeger Publishers, 1974.

KATZ, ELIHU, HANNA ADONI, AND PRINA PARNESS. "Remembering the News: What the Picture Adds to Recall." *Journalism Quarterly* 54 (1977): 231–39.

KATZMAN, N. "Television Soap Operas: What's Been Going On Anyway?" *Public Opinion Quarterly* 36 (1972): 200–212.

KEISLER, CHARLES, BARRY COLLINS, AND NEAL MILLER. *Attitude Change.* New York: Wiley, 1970.

KELLNER, HELLA. "Television as a Socialization Factor." *European Broadcasting Union Review* 29 (March, 1978): 13–16.

KELLY, CLIFFORD W., AND F. FLOYD SHOEMAKER. "United States Foreign Policy: An In-Depth Study of Attitudes and Values." Paper presented at the Annual Conference of the American Association for Public Opinion Research, Asheville, North Carolina, May 13–16, 1976.

KEMPTON, MURRAY. "The Right People and the Wrong Times." *The New York Review* 16 (April 18, 1971): 31–35.

KEY, V. O., JR. *Public Opinion and American Democracy.* New York: Alfred A. Knopf, 1961.

KEY, WILSON BRYAN. *Subliminal Seduction.* New York: Signet Books, 1973.

KINGDON, JOHN W. *Candidates for Office: Beliefs and Strategies.* New York: Random House, 1966.

———. *Congressmen's Voting Decisions.* New York: Harper and Row, 1973.

KLAPPER, JOSEPH T. *The Effects of Mass Communication.* New York: Free Press, 1960.

KLEIN, JEFFREY. "Semi-Tough: The Politics behind 60 Minutes." *Mother Jones* 4 (September/October, 1979): 26–31, 40.

KLEIN, WOODY. *Lindsay's Promise: The Dream That Failed.* New York: Macmillan Publishing Company, 1970.

KNIGHTLEY, PHILLIP. *The First Casualty from the Crimea to Vietnam: The War Correspondent as Hero, Propagandist, and Myth Maker.* New York: Harcourt Brace Jovanovich, 1975.

KNOPF, TERRY ANN. "Plugola: What the Talk Shows Don't Talk About." *Columbia Journalism Review* 15 (January/February, 1977): 44–46.

KNUDSON, JERRY W. "U. S. Coverage Since 1952 of Bolivia: The Unknown Soldier of the Cold War." *Gazette* 22 (1977): 185–97.

KOPKIND, ANDREW. "Times Square." *New York Review* 8 (May 4, 1967): 12–15.

KRASNOW, ERWIN G., AND LAWRENCE D. LONGLEY. *The Politics of Broadcast Regulation.* New York: St. Martin's Press, 1978, 2nd ed.

KRAUS, SIDNEY, ed. *The Great Debates.* Bloomington, Indiana: Indiana University Press, 1962.

———. *The Great Debates: Carter vs. Ford, 1976.* Bloomington, Indiana: Indiana University Press, 1977.

KRAUS, SIDNEY, AND DENNIS DAVIS. *The Effects of Mass Communication on Political Behavior.* University Park, Pennsylvania: Pennsylvania State University Press, 1976.

KRIENEMAN, RODNEY M., AND JOSEPH E. WRIGHT. "News Policies of Broadcast Stations for Civil Disturbances and Disasters." *Journalism Quarterly* 52 (1975): 670–77.

KRUGER, HAROLD. "Hoover's FBI: The Media and the Myth." *Feed/Back* 4 (1978): 7–15.

KRUGMAN, HERBERT E., AND EUGENE L. HARTLEY. "Passive Learning from Television." *Public Opinion Quarterly* 34 (1970): 184–90.

KRULL, ROBERT, JAMES H. WATT, JR., AND LAWRENCE W. LICHTY. "Entropy and Structure: Two Measures of Complexity in Television Programs." *Communication Research* 4 (1977): 61–86.

KUMAR, MARTHA JOYNT, AND MICHAEL BARUCH GROSSMAN. "The Manager of the Message: The Press Secretary to the President of the United States." Paper presented at the Annual Meeting of the Southern Political Science Association, New Orleans, Louisiana, November 2–7, 1977.

KUTTNER, BOB. "The TV Cameraman in Washington." *The Washington Post/ Potomac* (December 3, 1972): 16ff.

LADD, EVERETT C., JR. "The Polls: The Question of Confidence." *Public Opinion Quarterly* 40 (1976–77): 544–52.

———. "Is America Going Right? An Editorial View." *Public Opinion* 1 (September/October, 1978): 33.

———. "What the Polls Tell Us." *Wilson Quarterly* 3 (1979): 73–83.

LADD, EVERETT C., JR., WITH CHARLES D. HADLEY. *Transformations of the American Party System.* New York: Norton, 1975.

LADD, EVERETT C., JR., WITH MARILYN POTTER, LINDA BASILICK, SALLY DANIELS, AND DANA SUSZKIW. "The Polls: Taxing and Spending." *Public Opinion Quarterly* 43 (1979): 126–35.

LAING, ROBERT B., AND ROBERT L. STEVENSON. "Public Opinion Trends in the Last Days of the Nixon Administration." *Journalism Quarterly* 53 (1976): 294–302.

LANE, ROBERT E. *Political Ideology.* New York: Free Press, 1962.

———. "Patterns of Political Belief." In Jeanne Knutson, ed., *Handbook of Political Psychology.* San Francisco: Jossey-Bass, 1973.

LANG, GLADYS ENGEL, AND KURT LANG. "Immediate and Delayed Responses to the Carter–Ford Debate: Assessing Public Opinion." *Public Opinion Quarterly* 42 (1978): 322–41.

LANG, KURT, AND GLADYS ENGEL LANG. *Politics and Television*. Chicago: Quadrangle Books, 1968.

LARSON, CHARLES U. "A Content Analysis of Media Reporting of the Watergate Hearings." *Communication Research* 1 (1974): 440–48.

LARSON, JAMES, AND ANDY HARDY. "International Affairs Coverage on Network Television News: A Study of News Flow." *Gazette* 23 (1977): 241–56.

LASSWELL, HAROLD D. *Psychopathology and Politics*. Chicago: The University of Chicago Press, 1930.

LAZARSFELD, PAUL F., BERNARD BERELSON, AND HAZEL GAUDET. *The People's Choice: How the Voter Makes Up His Mind in a Presidential Campaign*. New York: Duell, Sloan and Pearce, 1944.

LAZARSFELD, PAUL F., AND ROBERT K. MERTON. "Mass Communication, Popular Taste, and Organized Social Action." In Bernard Rosenberg and David Manning White, eds., *Mass Culture*. New York: Free Press, 1957.

LAZIN, FRED A. "How the Police View the Press." Paper presented at the Annual Meeting of the American Political Science Association, New York, August 31–September 3, 1978.

LEARY, MARY ELLEN. "California 1974: The Browning of Campaign Coverage." *Columbia Journalism Review* 15 (July/August, 1976): 18–21.

LEFCOURT, HERBERT M. *Locus of Control: Current Trends in Theory and Research*. Hillsdale, New Jersey: Lawrence Erlbaum Associates, 1976.

LEFEVER, ERNEST W. *TV and National Defense*. Boston, Virginia: Institute for American Strategy Press, 1974.

LEMERT, JAMES B. "Content Duplication by the Networks in Competing Evening Newscasts." *Journalism Quarterly* 51 (1974): 238–44.

LEMERT, JAMES B., BARRY N. MITZMAN, MICHAEL A. SEITHER, ROXANA H. COOK, AND REGINA HACKETT. "Journalists and Mobilizing Information." *Journalism Quarterly* 54 (1977): 721–26.

LENIN, V. I. *What Is to Be Done?* New York: International Publishers, 1969 (first published, 1902).

LESLIE, DAVID W. "The Supreme Court in the Media: A Content Analysis." Paper presented at the Annual Meeting of the International Communication Association, Portland, Oregon, April 15, 1976.

LEUTHOLD, DAVID A. *Electioneering in a Democracy*. New York: Wiley, 1968.

LEVIN, JACK, AND ALLAN J. KIMMEL. "Gossip Columns: Media Small Talk." *Journal of Communication* 27 (Winter 1977): 169–75.

LEVITIN, TERESA E., AND WARREN E. MILLER. "Ideological Interpretations of National Elections: Problems in the Analysis of Change." Paper presented at the Annual Meeting of the American Political Science Association, New York, August 31–September 3, 1978.

LIEBLING, A. J. *The Press*. New York: Ballantine Books, 1961.

LINDBLOM, CHARLES E. *Politics and Markets*. New York: Basic Books, 1978.

LINNÉ, OLGA. "Violence in Television Programmes." *European Broadcasting Union Review* 29 (March, 1978): 30–36.

LIPPMANN, WALTER. *Public Opinion*. New York: Free Press, 1965 (first published, 1922).

LIPSET, SEYMOUR MARTIN, AND WILLIAM SCHNEIDER. "How's Business? What the Public Thinks." *Public Opinion* 1 (July/August, 1978): 41–47.

———. "The Public View of Regulation." *Public Opinion* 2 (January/February, 1979): 6–13.

LIPSKY, MICHAEL. *Protest in City Politics.* Chicago: Rand McNally, 1970.

LITTLEWOOD, THOMAS B. "What's Wrong with Statehouse Coverage." *Columbia Journalism Review* 10 (March/April, 1972): 39–45.

LOWI, THEODORE J. *The End of Liberalism.* New York: Norton, 1969.

LOORY, STUART H. "The CIA's Use of the Press: A 'Mighty Wurlitzer.' " *Columbia Journalism Review* 13 (September/October, 1974): 9–18.

LUKAS, J. ANTHONY. "The White House Press 'Club.' " *New York Times Magazine* (May 15, 1977): 22ff.

LUMBY, MALCOLM E. "Ann Landers' Advice Column: 1958 and 1971." *Journalism Quarterly* 53 (1976): 129–32.

LUTZKER, PAUL. *The Politics of Public Interest Groups: Common Cause in Action.* Ph.D. dissertation, The Johns Hopkins University, 1973.

MACDOUGALL, MALCOLM D. "How Madison Avenue Didn't Put a Ford in Your Future." *New York* 10 (February 21, 1977): 46–54.

McCLENGHAN, JACK SEAN. "Effect of Endorsements in Texas Local Elections." *Journalism Quarterly* 50 (1973): 363–66.

McCOMBS, MAXWELL E. "Mass Communication in Political Campaigns: Information, Gratification and Persuasion." In F. Gerald Kline and Phillip J. Tichenor, eds., *Current Perspectives in Mass Communication Research.* Beverly Hills, California: Sage Publications, 1972.

———. "Setting the Stage for Public Attention: The Agenda-Setting Influence of the Press." Paper prepared for National Conference on Measuring the Effectiveness of Public Relations, sponsored by the University of Maryland, October 4–5, 1977.

McCOMBS, MAXWELL E., AND DONALD L. SHAW. "The Agenda-Setting Function of Mass Media." *Public Opinion Quarterly* 36 (1972): 176–87.

McCONNELL, GRANT. *Private Power and American Democracy.* New York: Knopf, 1966.

McFARLAND, ANDREW S. "The Complexity of Democratic Practices within Common Cause." Paper presented at the Annual Meeting of the American Political Science Association, Chicago, Illinois, September 2–5, 1976.

McGINNISS, JOE. *The Selling of the President.* New York: Trident Press, 1969.

McGUIRE, WILLIAM J. "Persuasion, Resistance and Attitude Change." In Ithiel de Sola Pool et al., eds., *Handbook of Communication.* Chicago: Rand McNally, 1973.

McLAUGHLIN, JAMES. "The Doctor Shows." *Journal of Communication* 25 (Summer 1975): 182–84.

McLEOD, JACK M., JANE D. BROWN, LEE B. BECKER, AND DEAN A. ZIEMKE. "Decline and Fall at the White House." *Communication Research* 4 (1977): 3–22, 35–39.

MACNEIL, ROBERT. *The People Machine.* New York: Harper and Row, 1968.

McQUAIL, DENIS, ed. *Sociology of Mass Communication.* New York: Penguin Books, 1972.

MANDER, JERRY. *Four Arguments for the Elimination of Television*. New York: Morrow, 1978.

MANHEIM, JAROL B. "Can Democracy Survive Television?" *Journal of Communication* 26 (Spring 1976): 84–90.

MANLEY, JOHN F. "White House Lobbying and the Problem of Presidential Power." Paper presented at the Annual Meeting of the American Political Science Association, Washington, D.C., September 1–4, 1977.

MANNING, ROBERT A., AND STEPHEN TALBOT. "Swallowing Carter's Zaire Line." *Inquiry* (July 24, 1978): 8–11.

MARETH, PAUL. "America's Public Broadcasting Service: Public Visions, Private Voices." *Sight and Sound* 46 (1976–1977): 14–17.

MATTHEWS, DONALD R. *U. S. Senators and Their World*. Chapel Hill, North Carolina: University of North Carolina Press, 1960.

MAY, ERNEST R., AND JANET FRASER, eds. *Campaign '72: The Managers Speak*. Cambridge, Massachusetts: Harvard University Press, 1973.

MAYER, MARTIN. *About Television*. New York: Harper and Row, 1972.

MAYHEW, DAVID R. *Congress: The Electoral Connection*. New Haven, Connecticut: Yale University Press, 1974.

MAZLISH, BRUCE. *In Search of Nixon: A Psychological Inquiry*. New York: Basic Books, 1972.

MEERLOO, JOOST A. M. *The Two Faces of Man*. New York: International Universities Press, 1954.

MENDELSOHN, HAROLD. "The Neglected Majority: Mass Communications and the Working Person." In Ithiel de Sola Pool, ed., *Talking Back: Citizen Feedback and Cable Technology*. Cambridge, Massachusetts: M.I.T. Press, 1975: 24–53.

MERELMAN, RICHARD M. "Power and Community in Television." *Journal of Popular Culture* 2 (1968): 63–80.

MILBRATH, LESTER W. *Political Participation*. Chicago: Rand McNally and Company, 1977, 2nd ed.

MILIBAND, RALPH. *The State in Capitalist Society: An Analysis of the Western System of Power*. New York: Basic Books, 1969.

MILLER, ARTHUR H. "Political Issues and Trust in Government, 1967–70." *American Political Science Review* 68 (1974): 951–72.

———. "The Institutional Focus of Political Distrust." Paper presented at the 1979 Annual Meeting of the American Political Science Association, Washington, D.C., August 30–September 2, 1979.

MILLER, ARTHUR H., AND WARREN E. MILLER. "Issues, Candidates and Partisan Divisions in the 1972 American Presidential Election." *British Journal of Political Science* 5 (1975): 393–434.

———. "Partisanship and Performance: 'Rational' Choice in the 1976 Presidential Election." Paper presented at the Annual Meeting of the American Political Science Association, Washington, D.C., September 1–4, 1977.

MILLER, ARTHUR H., WARREN E. MILLER, ALDEN S. RAINE, AND THAD A. BROWN. "Majority Party in Disarray: Policy Polarization in the 1972 Election." *American Political Science Review* 70 (1976): 753–78.

MILLER, ARTHUR H., EDIE N. GOLDENBERG, AND LUTZ ERBRING. "Type-Set Politics: Impact of Newspapers on Public Confidence." *American Political Science Review* 73 (1979): 67–84.

MILLER, SUSAN H. "News Coverage of Congress: The Search for the Ultimate Spokesman." *Journalism Quarterly* 54 (1977): 459–65.

———. "Congressional Committee Hearings and the Media: Rules of the Game." *Journalism Quarterly* 55 (1978): 657–63.

MILLER, WARREN E. "Misreading the Public Pulse." *Public Opinion* 2 (October/November 1979): 9–15, 60.

MILLER, WARREN E., AND TERESA E. LEVITIN. *Leadership and Change: The New Politics and the American Electorate.* Cambridge, Massachusetts: Winthrop, 1976.

MINOW, NEWTON M., JOHN BARTLOW MARTIN, AND LEE M. MITCHELL. *Presidential Television.* New York: Basic Books, 1973.

MOLOTCH, HARVEY, AND MARILYN LESTER. "News as Purposive Behavior: On the Strategic Use of Routine Events, Accidents and Scandals." *American Sociological Review* 39 (1974): 101–12.

———. "Accidental News: The Great Oil Spill as Local Occurrence and National Event." *American Journal of Sociology* 81 (1975): 235–60.

MORGAN, DAVID. "Polls, Presidents and Reporters: The Case of Jimmy Carter." Paper presented at the American Politics Group Conference of the Political Studies Association, University of Bristol, January 3–5, 1979.

MORISON, SAMUEL E., AND HENRY STEELE COMMAGER. *The Growth of the American Republic.* New York: Oxford University Press, 1962.

MORLEY, DAVID. "Industrial Conflict and the Mass Media." Occasional paper, University of Birmingham Centre for Contemporary Studies, n.d.

MORRIS, ROGER. "Henry Kissinger and the Media: A Separate Peace." *Columbia Journalism Review* 13 (May/June, 1974): 14–25 (1974a).

———. "Through the Looking Glass in Chile: Coverage of Allende's Regime." *Columbia Journalism Review* 13 (November/December 1974): 15–26 (1974b).

———. "Kissinger and the Press—Revisited." *Columbia Journalism Review* 14 (September/October, 1975): 49–52.

———. "Carter's Cabinet: The Who's Who Treatment." *Columbia Journalism Review* 15 (March/April 1977): 34–35.

———. "Reporting the Race War in Rhodesia." *Columbia Journalism Review* 17 (March/April, 1979): 32–34.

MOYNIHAN, DANIEL P. "The Presidency and the Press." *Commentary* 51 (March 1971): 41–52.

MUELLER, CLAUS. *The Politics of Communication.* New York: Oxford University Press, 1973.

MUELLER, JOHN E. "Choosing among 133 Candidates." *Public Opinion Quarterly* 34 (1970): 395–404.

MURDOCK, GRAHAM. "Political Deviance: The Press Presentation of a Militant Mass Demonstration." In Stanley Cohen and Jock Young, eds., *The Manufacture of News: Social Problems, Deviance and the Mass Media.* London: Constable, 1973.

NATIONAL CENTER FOR STATE COURTS. *The Public Image of the Courts.* Williamsburg, Virginia, March 19–22, 1978.

NAVASKY, VICTOR S. Review of *FBI* by Sanford J. Ungar and *Cointelpro,* Cathy

Perkus, ed. *The New York Times Book Review* (March 14, 1976): 2–3, 16, 18, 20.

NEUMAN, W. RUSSELL. "Patterns of Recall among Television News Viewers." *Public Opinion Quarterly* 40 (1976): 115–23.

NEUSTADT, RICHARD E. *Presidential Power.* New York: Wiley, 1960.

NEUSTADT, RICHARD, AND RICHARD PAISNER. "How to Run on TV." *The New York Times Magazine* (December 15, 1974): 20ff.

NEWCOMB, HORACE, ed. *Television: The Critical View.* New York: Oxford University Press, 1976.

NIE, NORMAN H., SIDNEY VERBA, AND JOHN PETROCIK. *The Changing American Voter.* Cambridge, Massachusetts: Harvard University Press, 1976.

NIMMO, DAN D. *Newsgathering in Washington.* New York: Atherton Press, 1964.

———. *The Political Persuaders.* Englewood Cliffs, New Jersey: Prentice-Hall, 1970.

———. *Political Communication and Public Opinion in America.* Santa Monica, California: Goodyear Publishing Company, 1978.

NIXON, RICHARD M. "National Association of Broadcasters: The President's Remarks in a Question–Answer Session at the Association's Annual Convention in Houston, Texas." *Presidential Documents* 10, No. 12, (March 19, 1974): 335–45.

NOBLE, GRANT. *Children in Front of the Small Screen.* Beverly Hills, California: Sage Publications, 1975.

NOELLE-NEUMANN, ELISABETH. "The Spiral of Silence: A Theory of Public Opinion." *Journal of Communication* 24 (Spring 1974): 43–51.

———. "Turbulence in the Climate of Opinion: Methodological Applications of the Spiral of Silence Theory." *Public Opinion Quarterly* 41 (1977): 143–58.

NOLL, ROGER G., MERTON J. PECK, AND JOHN J. McGOWAN. *Economic Aspects of Television Regulation.* Washington, D.C.: The Brookings Institution, 1973.

NORTHCOTT, HERBERT C., JOHN F. SEGGAR, AND JAMES L. HINTON. "Trends in Television Portrayal of Blacks and Women." *Journalism Quarterly* 52 (1975): 741–44.

O'DONNELL, WILLIAM J., AND KAREN J. O'DONNELL. "Update: Sex Role Messages in Television Commercials." *Journal of Communication* 28 (Winter 1978): 156–58.

O'KEEFE, GARRETT J. "Political Campaigns and Mass Communication Research." In Steven H. Chaffee, ed., *Political Communication.* Beverly Hills, California: Sage Publications, 1975.

OLSON, MANCUR. *The Logic of Collective Action.* Cambridge, Massachusetts: Harvard University Press, 1965.

OWEN, BRUCE M., JACK H. BEEBE, AND WILLARD G. MANNING, JR. *Television Economics.* Lexington, Massachusetts: D. C. Heath and Company, 1974.

PALETZ, DAVID L. "Perspectives on the Presidency." *Law and Contemporary Problems* 35 (1970): 429–44.

————. "The Neglected Context of Congressional Campaigns." *Polity* 4 (1971): 195–217.

————. "Some Delegates' Views of Television Coverage of the 1968 Democratic Convention." *Journal of Broadcasting* 16 (1972): 441–52.

————. "Television Drama: The Appeals of the Senate Watergate Hearings." *The Midwest Quarterly* 18 (1976): 103–109.

————. "Underground." *Film Quarterly* 30 (1977): 34–37.

————. "Influence of the Media on the 1976 Presidential Election." In Jeff Fishel, ed., *Parties and Elections in an Anti-Party Age*. Bloomington, Indiana: Indiana University Press, 1978.

PALETZ, DAVID L., AND LYNN C. BAUMBLATT. "A Little Star Is Born." Unpublished manuscript, 1978.

PALETZ, DAVID L., AND ROBERT DUNN. "Press Coverage of Civil Disorders: A Case Study and Analysis of Winston-Salem, 1967." *Public Opinion Quarterly* 33 (1969): 328–45.

PALETZ, DAVID L., AND MARTHA ELSON. "Television Coverage of Presidential Nominating Conventions: Now You See It, Now You Don't." *Political Science Quarterly* 91 (1976): 103–32.

PALETZ, DAVID L., AND WILLIAM H. HARRIS. "Four-Letter Threats to Authority." *Journal of Politics* 37 (1975): 955–79.

————. "Getting the Word Out: The News on 'Four-Letter Threats to Authority.'" *South Atlantic Quarterly* 76 (1977): 263–72.

PALETZ, DAVID L., AND DENNIS R. LAFIURA. "The Press and Authority: Portrayals of a Coach and a Mayor." *Journalism Monographs* 50 (August 1977): 33pp.

PALETZ, DAVID L., AND ROBERTA E. PEARSON. "The Way You Look Tonight: A Critique of Television News Criticism." In William Adams and Fay Schreibman, eds., *Television Network News: Issues in Content Research*. Washington, D.C.: George Washington University, 1978.

PALETZ, DAVID L., AND RICHARD J. VINEGAR. "Presidents on Television: The Effects of Instant Analysis." *Public Opinion Quarterly* 41 (1977–78): 488–97.

PALETZ, DAVID L., KATHY R. CHANDLER-HENRY, AND PAGE GARDNER. "Interest Groups and the Media: A Study of Common Cause." Paper presented at the Annual Meeting of the Southern Political Science Association, New Orleans, Louisiana, November 3–5, 1977.

PALETZ, DAVID L., ROBERTA E. PEARSON, AND DONALD L. WILLIS. *Politics in Public Service Advertising*. New York: Praeger Publishers, 1977.

PALETZ, DAVID L., PEGGY REICHERT, AND BARBARA MCINTYRE. "How the Media Support Local Government Authority." *Public Opinion Quarterly* 35 (1971): 80–92.

PALETZ, DAVID L., JUDITH KOON, ELIZABETH WHITEHEAD, AND RICHARD B. HAGENS. "Selective Exposure: The Potential Boomerang Effect." *Journal of Communication* 22 (March 1972): 48–53.

PARKIN, FRANK. *Class Inequality and Political Order*. New York: Praeger, 1971.

PARRY, GERAINT, AND PETER MORRISS. "When Is a Decision Not a Decision?" In Ivor Crewe, ed., *Elites in Western Democracy*. Vol. I of the British Political Sociology Yearbook. London: Croom Helm, 1974.

PATTERSON, THOMAS E. "The Media Muffed the Message." *The Washington Post* (December 5, 1976): B1 ff.

———. "Press Coverage and Candidate Success in Presidential Primaries: The 1976 Democratic Race." Paper presented at the Annual Meeting of the American Political Science Association, Washington, D.C., September 1–4, 1977.

PATTERSON, THOMAS E., AND ROBERT D. MCCLURE. *The Unseeing Eye: The Myth of Television Power in National Politics.* New York: G. P. Putnam's Sons, 1976.

PAULU, BURTON. "The American Scene." *European Broadcasting Union Review* 29 (March, 1978): 39–43.

PEARSON, ROBERTA E. "Interest Group Interactions with the Media: A Case Study of the White House Conference on Food, Nutrition and Health." Paper presented at the Annual Meeting of the Southern Association for Public Opinion Research, Chapel Hill, North Carolina, March 12–14, 1978.

PEEK, CHARLES W., JON P. ALSTON, AND GEORGE D. LOWE. "Comparative Evaluation of the Local Police." *Public Opinion Quarterly* 42 (1978): 370–79.

PERETZ, PAUL. "There Was No Tax Revolt!" Paper presented at the 1980 Annual Meeting of the American Political Science Association, Washington, D.C., August 28–31, 1980.

PETERS, CHARLES. "Why the White House Press Didn't Get the Watergate Story." *The Washington Monthly* 4 (July/August 1973): 5–9.

PHILLIPS, E. BARBARA. "Novelty without Change." *Journal of Communication* 26 (Autumn 1976): 87–92.

POLLOCK, JOHN C., AND CHRISTOPHER L. GUIDETTE. "Mass Media, Crisis and Political Change: A Comparative Approach." Paper presented at the meeting of the American Political Science Association, Washington, D. C., September 1–4, 1977.

POLLOCK, JOHN C., JAMES LEE ROBINSON, JR., AND MARY CARMEL MURRAY. "Media Agendas and Human Rights: The Supreme Court Decision on Abortion." *Journalism Quarterly* 55 (1978): 544–48, 561.

POMPER, GERALD. *Voter's Choice: Varieties of American Electoral Behavior.* New York: Dodd, Mead and Company, 1975.

———. "The Decline of the Party in American Elections." *Political Science Quarterly* 92 (1977): 21–41.

POPKIN, SAMUEL, JOHN W. GORMAN, CHARLES PHILLIPS, AND JEFFREY A. SMITH. "Comment: What Have You Done for Me Lately? Toward an Investment Theory of Voting." *American Political Science Review* 70 (1976): 779–805.

PORTER, WILLIAM E. *Assault on the Media: The Nixon Years.* Ann Arbor, Michigan: University of Michigan Press, 1976.

PREWITT, KENNETH. "Political Socialization Research in the United States: Can We Get Where We Should Be Going from Where We Have Been?" *International Journal of Political Education* 1 (1977–78): 111–26.

PRIDE, RICHARD A., AND BARBARA RICHARDS. "Denigration of Authority? Television News Coverage of the Student Movement." *Journal of Politics* 36 (1974): 637–60.

———. "The Denigration of Political Authority in Television News: The Ecology Issue." *Western Political Quarterly* 28 (1975): 635–45.

PUTNAM, ROBERT D. *The Comparative Study of Elites*. Englewood Cliffs, New Jersey: Prentice-Hall, 1976.

RAINVILLE, RAYMOND, AND EDWARD MCCORMICK. "Extent of Covert Racial Prejudice in Pro Football Announcers' Speech." *Journalism Quarterly* 54 (1977): 20–26.

REAL, MICHAEL R. *Mass-Mediated Culture*. Englewood Cliffs, New Jersey: Prentice-Hall, 1977.

REEVES, RICHARD. "The Prime-Time President." *New York Times Magazine* (May 15, 1977): 17–18.

RESTON, JAMES. *Artillery of the Press*. New York: Harper and Row, 1967.

RINTELS, DAVID W. "How Much Truth Does 'The FBI' Tell about the FBI?" *New York Times*, March 5, 1972, Section 2, pp. 1, 17.

RITCHIE, MICHAEL. "How the CBS Censor Wiped the 'Smile' from My Face." *New West* 2 (January 17, 1977): 55–57.

RIVERS, WILLIAM L. *The Opinion Makers*. Boston: Beacon Press, 1965.

ROBINSON, GERTRUDE JOCH, AND VERNONE M. SPARKES. "International News in the Canadian and American Press: A Comparative News Flow Study." *Gazette* 22 (1976): 203–18.

ROBINSON, JOHN P. "TV Violence Research Resuscitated." *Public Opinion Quarterly* 36 (1972): 440–41.

———. "Toward a Post-Industrious Society." *Public Opinion* 2 (August/September 1979): 41–46.

ROBINSON, JOHN P., ROBERT PISKALN, AND PAUL HIRSCH. "Protest Rock and Drugs." *Journal of Communication* 26 (1976): 125–36.

ROBINSON, MICHAEL J. "A Twentieth-Century Medium in a Nineteenth-Century Legislature: The Effects of Television on the American Congress." In Norman J. Ornstein, ed., *Congress in Change: Evolution and Reform*. New York: Praeger Publishers, 1975.

———. "Public Affairs Television and the Growth of Political Malaise: The Case of 'The Selling of the Pentagon.' " *American Political Science Review* 70 (1976): 409–32.

———. "Television and American Politics: 1956–1976." *The Public Interest* 48 (1977): 3–39.

———. "Prime Time Chic: Between Newsbreaks and Commercials the Values are L.A. Liberal." *Public Opinion* 2 (March/May, 1979): 42–48.

ROBINSON, MICHAEL J., AND CLIFFORD ZUKIN. "Television and the Wallace Vote." *Journal of Communication* 26 (Spring 1976): 79–83.

ROBINSON, MICHAEL J., AND KAREN A. MCPHERSON. "Television News Coverage before the 1976 New Hampshire Primary: The Focus of Network Journalism." *Journal of Broadcasting* 21 (1977): 177–86.

ROPER ORGANIZATION REPORT. *Public Perceptions of Television and Other Mass Media: A Twenty-Year Review, 1959–1978*. New York: Television Information Office, 1979.

ROSENSTEIN, JAY. "What Became of That 'Heavy Vote'?" *Columbia Journalism Review* 15 (January/February, 1977): 37–39.

ROSHCO, BERNARD. *Newsmaking*. Chicago: University of Chicago Press, 1975.

ROTHCHILD, JOHN. "Views of the Press: The Stories Reporters Don't Write." *The Washington Monthly* 3 (June 1971): 20–27.

ROURKE, FRANCIS E. "The United States." In Itzhak Galnoor, ed., *Government Secrecy in Democracies*. New York: Harper Colophon Books, 1977.

ROUSSEAU, JEAN-JACQUES. *Politics and the Arts: Letter to M. D'Alembert on the Theater*. Ithaca, New York: Cornell University Press, 1960.

RUBIN, ALAN M. "Telelvision in Children's Political Socialization." *Journal of Broadcasting* 20 (1976): 51–60.

RUTKUS, DENNIS S. *A Report on Simultaneous Television Network Coverage of Presidential Addresses to the Nation*. Washington, D. C.: Congressional Research Service (January 12, 1976).

RYTER, MARK. "COINTELPRO: Corrupting American Institutions." *First Principles* 3 (Center for National Security Studies) (May 1978): 1–5.

SAFIRE, WILLIAM. "The Press Is the Enemy: Nixon and the Media." *New York* 8 (January 27, 1975): 41–50 (1975a).

———. *Before the Fall*. New York: Doubleday and Company, 1975 (1975b).

SALZMAN, EDWARD. "The Pitiful Plight of the Democratic Liberals." *California Journal* 10 (April, 1979): 131–32.

SANFORD, BRUCE W. "No Quarter from This Court." *Columbia Journalism Review* 18 (September/October 1979): 59–63.

SAYER, CHRISTOPHER. "Patriot Sleeps through Elections." *Harrisburg Independent Press* (June 17–24, 1977): 1.

SCHAMBRA, WILLIAM. "More Buck for the Bang; New Public Attitudes toward Foreign Policy." *Public Opinion* 2 (January/February 1979): 47–48.

SCHANBERG, SYDNEY H. "The Saigon Follies, or, Trying to Head Them Off at Credibility Gap." *New York Times Magazine* (November 12, 1972): 38ff.

SCHATTSCHNEIDER, E. E. *The Semi-Sovereign People*. New York: Holt, Rinehart & Winston, 1960.

SCHILLER, HERBERT I. *The Mind Managers*. Boston: Beacon Press, 1973.

SCHMIDT, BENNO C., JR. *Freedom of the Press vs. Public Access*. New York: Praeger Special Studies, 1976.

SCHORR, DANIEL. *Clearing the Air*. Boston: Houghton Mifflin, 1977.

SCHRAMM, MARTIN. *Running for President*. New York: Stein and Day, 1977.

SCHRAMM, WILBUR, AND RICHARD F. CARTER. "Effectiveness of a Political Telethon." *Public Opinion Quarterly* 23 (1959): 121–26.

SCHREIBER, E. M. "Anti-War Demonstrations and American Public Opinion on the War in Vietnam." *British Journal of Sociology* 27 (1976): 225–36.

SCHUBERT, GLENDON A. *The Judicial Mind Revisited: Psychometric Analysis of Supreme Court Ideology*, New York: Oxford University Press, 1974.

SCHULMAN, MARK A. "The Impact of Three Mile Island." *Public Opinion* 2 (1979): 7–9.

SCHWARTZ, BERNARD. *The Professor and the Commissions*. New York: Knopf, 1959.

SCHWARTZ, TONY. *The Responsive Chord*. Garden City, New York: Anchor Press/Doubleday, 1973.

Sears, David O. "The Debates in Light of Research: An Overview of the Effects." Paper presented at the Annual Meeting of the American Political Science Association, Washington, D.C., September 1–4, 1977.

Sears, David O., and John B. McConahay. *The Politics of Violence: The New Urban Blacks and the Watts Riot.* Boston: Houghton Mifflin, 1973.

Sears, David O., and Richard E. Whitney. *Political Persuasion.* Morristown, New Jersey: General Learning Press, 1973.

Sennett, Richard, and Jonathan Cobb. *The Hidden Injuries of Class.* New York: Vintage Books, 1973.

Seymour-Ure, Colin. "Presidential Power and Communication: The Eisenhower and Nixon Perspectives." Paper presented at the American Politics Group Conference of the Political Studies Association, University of Bristol, January 3–5, 1979.

Sherrod, Drury. "Selective Perception of Political Candidates." *Public Opinion Quarterly* 35 (1971–72): 554–62.

Sickels, Robert J. *Presidential Transactions.* Englewood Cliffs, New Jersey: Prentice-Hall, 1974.

Siegel, Roberta S. "Image of the American Presidency: Part 11 of an Exploration into Popular Views of Presidential Power." *Midwest Journal of Political Science* 10 (1966): 123–37.

Sigal, Leon V. *Reporters and Officials.* Lexington, Massachusetts: D.C. Heath and Company, 1973.

Simon, Herbert J., and Frederick Stern. "The Effect of Television upon Voting Behavior in Iowa in the 1952 Presidential Election." *American Political Science Review* 49 (1955): 470–77.

Smith, Anthony. *The Shadow in the Cave.* Urbana, Illinois: University of Illinois Press, 1973.

Smith, Don D. "Mass Media Effectiveness and the Public's Right to Know." Paper presented at the Annual Meeting of the Southern Association for Public Opinion Research, Chapel Hill, North Carolina, March 12–14, 1978.

Smith, M. Brewster. "Political Attitudes." In Jeanne N. Knutson, ed. *Handbook of Political Psychology.* San Francisco: Jossey-Bass, 1973.

Sniderman, Paul M., et al. "Stability of Support for the Political System: The Initial Impact of Watergate." *American Politics Quarterly* 3 (1975): 437–57.

Sobel, Judith, and Edwin Emery. "U.S. Dailies' Competition in Relation to Circulation Size: A Newspaper Data Update." *Journalism Quarterly* 55 (1978): 145–49.

Spragens, William C. *The Presidency and the Mass Media in the Age of Television.* Washington, D.C.: University Press of America, 1978.

Stanworth, Philip H. "Property Class and the Corporate Elite." In Ivor Crewe, ed., *Elites in Western Democracy.* Vol. 1 of the British Political Sociology Yearbook. London: Croom Helm, 1974.

Steinbruner, John D. *The Cybernetic Theory of Decision.* Princeton, New Jersey: Princeton University Press, 1974.

Stone, Walter. "A Panel Analysis of Representation in Congress: A Preliminary Report." Paper presented at the Annual Meeting of the American Political Science Association, Washington, D.C., September 1–4, 1977.

TALBOT, STEPHEN. "About Those Cubans." *International Bulletin* 5 (July 31, 1978): 1–2.

TALESE, GAY. *The Kingdom and the Power*. New York: World Publishing Company, 1969.

TANNENBAUM, PERCY H. "The Effects of Headlines on the Interpretation of News Stories." *Journalism Quarterly* 30 (1953): 189–97.

TATE, EUGENE D., AND STUART H. SURLIN. "Agreement with Opinionated TV Characters across Cultures." *Journalism Quarterly* 53 (1976): 199–204, 210.

TEDESCO, NANCY S. "Patterns of Prime Time." *Journal of Communication* 24 (Spring 1974): 119–24.

THOMPSON, HUNTER S. *Fear and Loathing: On the Campaign Trail '72*. San Francisco, California: Straight Arrow Books, 1973.

THOMSON, JAMES C., JR. "Government and Press." *New York Times Magazine* (November 25, 1973): 33ff.

TICHENOR, PHILLIP J., G. A. DONOHUE, AND C. N. OLIEN. "Mass Communication Research: Evolution of a Structural Model." *Journalism Quarterly* 50 (1973): 419–25.

TILLINGHAST, DIANA. "Inside the *Los Angeles Times:* Organizational Constraints on News about the 1976 Presidential Election Campaign." Paper presented at the Annual Meeting of the Western Political Science Association, San Francisco, California, March 1980.

TOPOLSKY, MARY. "Common Cause." *Worldview* 17 (April 1974): 35–39.

TOWNLEY, RICHARD. "Through the Tube Darkly." *TV Guide* (May 29, 1971): 39–46.

TRACEY, MICHAEL. *The Production of Political Television*. London: Routledge and Kegan Paul, 1978.

TRUMAN, DAVID B. *The Governmental Process*. New York: Knopf, 1951.

TUCHMAN, GAYE. *Making News*. New York: Free Press, 1978.

———, ed. *The Television Establishment: Programming for Power and Profit*. Englewood Cliffs, New Jersey: Prentice-Hall, 1974.

TUCHMAN, GAYE, ARLENE K. DANIELS, AND JAMES BENET, eds. *Hearth and Home: Images of Women in the Mass Media*. New York: Oxford University Press, 1978.

TUNSTALL, JEREMY. *The Westminster Lobby Correspondents*. London: Routledge and Kegan Paul, 1970.

TUROW, JOSEPH. "Advising and Ordering: Daytime, Prime Time." *Journal of Communication* 24 (Spring 1974): 138–41.

UNITED STATES, CONGRESS, HOUSE OF REPRESENTATIVES, COMMITTEE ON THE JUDICIARY, SUBCOMMITTEE ON CIVIL AND CONSTITUTIONAL RIGHTS. *Hearings, FBI Oversight*. Ninety-Fourth Congress, First and Second Sessions, October 21, December 11, 12, 1975; February 11, May 13, 20, 27, June 10, July 29, September 16, 29, 1976; Serial No. 2, Part 3.

UNITED STATES, CONGRESS, HOUSE OF REPRESENTATIVES, SELECT COMMITTEE ON ASSASSINATIONS. *Executive Session*, March 17, 1977.

VERBA, SIDNEY, AND NORMAN H. NIE. *Political Participation*. New York: Harper and Row, 1972.

VIDMAR, NEIL, AND MILTON ROKEACH. "Archie Bunker's Bigotry: A Study in Selective Perception and Exposure." *Journal of Communication* 24 (Winter 1974): 36–47.

WACKMAN, DANIEL B., DONALD M. GILLMOR, CECILIE GAZIANO, AND EVER-ETTE E. DENNIS. "Chain Newspaper Autonomy as Reflected in Presidential Campaign Endorsements." *Journalism Quarterly* 52 (1975): 411–20.

WALL, ROBERT. "Special Agent for the FBI." *New York Review* 17:12 and 18:1 (January 27, 1972): 12–18.

WALTERS, ROBERT. "The Howard Baker Boom." *Columbia Journalism Review* 12 (November/December, 1973): 33–38.

WALZER, MICHAEL. Review of Lindblom, Charles E. *Politics and Markets.* New York: Basic Books, 1978. In *New York Review* 25 (July 20, 1978): 40–42.

WARDELL, NANCY NEEDHAM. "The Corporation." *Daedalus* 107 (1978): 97–110.

WARNER, MALCOLM. "Television Coverage of International Affairs." *Television Quarterly* 7 (1968): 60–75.

WARREN, DENISE. "Commercial Liberation." *Journal of Communication* 28 (Winter 1978): 169–73.

WAWANASH, SHEILA. "Television's 'Medical Center' Sells Self-Determination." *Jump Cut* 16 (November, 1977): 29–33.

WEAVER, PAUL T. "Is Television News Biased?" *The Public Interest* 26 (1972): 57–74.

WEINBERG, LOUISE. "A New Judicial Federalism?" *Daedalus* 107 (1978): 129–41.

WEISS, WALTER. "Effects of the Mass Media of Communication." In Gardner Lindzey and Elliot Aronson, eds., *Handbook of Social Psychology,* vol. 5., 2nd ed. Reading, Massachusetts: Addison-Wesley Publishing Company, 1969.

WEISSMAN, STEPHEN R. "CIA Covert Action in Zaire and Angola: Patterns and Consequences." *Political Science Quarterly* 94 (1979): 263-86.

WEST AFRICA. "What Happened in Zaire?" *West Africa* (May 29, 1978): 1008–1009.

WESTIN, AV. Untitled paper presented at the Duke Fellows in Communication, Duke University, 1975.

WHEELER, MICHAEL. *Lies, Damn Lies, and Statistics.* New York: Liveright, 1976.

WHITE, THEODORE H. *The Making of the President, 1960.* New York: Atheneum, 1961.

———. *The Making of the President, 1968.* New York: Atheneum, 1969.

WHITEHEAD, ALFRED NORTH. *Adventures of Ideas.* New York: Macmillan, 1933.

WICKER, TOM. *A Time to Die.* New York: Quadrangle, 1975.

WIEBE, G. D. "Responses to the Televised Kefauver Hearings: Some Social Psychological Implications." *Public Opinion Quarterly* 16 (1952); 179–200.

———. "Two Psychological Factors in Media Audience Behavior." *Public Opinion Quarterly* 33 (1969–70): 523–36.

WILENSKY, HAROLD L. "Class, Class Consciousness, and American Workers." In Maurice Zeitlin, ed., *American Society, Inc.* Chicago: Markham, 1970.

WILHOIT, G. CLEVELAND. "Political Symbol Shifts in Crisis News." *Midwest Journal of Political Science* 13 (1969): 313–19.

WILLIAMS, BRIEN R. "The Structure of Televised Football." *Journal of Communication* 27 (Summer 1977): 133–39.

WILLIAMS, CAROL TRAYNOR. "It's Not So Much 'You've Come a Long Way, Baby' as 'You're Gonna Make It after All.'" In Horace Newcomb, ed., *Television: The Critical View.* New York: Oxford University Press, 1976.

WILLIAMS, RAYMOND. *Television, Technology and Cultural Form.* New York: Schocken Books, 1974.

WILLIAMS, WENMOUTH, JR., AND WILLIAM D. SEMLAK. "Structural Effects of TV Coverage on Political Agendas." *Journal of Communication* 28 (Autumn 1978): 114–19.

WILLS, GARY. "Carter on His Own." *New York Review* 23 (November 25, 1976): 30–34.

WILSON, JAMES Q. *Political Organizations.* New York: Basic Books, 1973.

WINDHAUSER, JOHN W. "How the Metropolitan Press Covered the 1970 General Election Campaign in Ohio." *Journalism Quarterly* 53 (1976): 264–70.

WINN, MARIE. *The Plug-In Drug.* New York: Bantam Books, 1977.

WISE, DAVID. *The Politics of Lying.* New York: Random House, 1973.

WOLFSON, LEWIS W. "The Press Covers Government: The Nixon Years from 1969 to Watergate." *Department of Communication,* The American University, Washington, D.C., 1973.

————. "A Report on the State of the Presidential Press Conference." *The National News Council,* New York November 1975.

WOLIN, SHELDON S. "The State of the Union." *New York Review* 25 (May 18, 1978): 28–31.

WOODWARD, BOB, AND CARL BERNSTEIN. *All the President's Men.* New York: Simon and Schuster, 1974.

WOODWARD, BOB, AND SCOTT ARMSTRONG. *The Brethren: Inside the Supreme Court.* New York: Simon and Schuster, 1979.

WRIGHT, JAMES D. "Life, Time and the Fortunes of War." *Trans-Action* 9 (January, 1972): 42–52.

WYCKOFF, GENE. *The Image Candidates.* New York: Macmillan, 1968.

Index

ABC (American Broadcasting Company),
7, 12, 17, 62, 75, 119, 127, 185
coverage of Watergate by, 159
network, 168
percentage of foreign news coverage by,
9
Adamany, David, 146
Adorno, Theodor, 169
Advertisements, 170
on television, 178–180
see also Messages
Afghanistan, 190
Africa, 200, 216, 229, 230
Agnew, Spiro, 65, 160
Alger, Horatio, 174
Allende, Salvador, and the media, 213–214
"All in the Family," 177–178
America, 136
diplomatic and economic goals of, 18
mood of, 196, 198, 199
political culture of, 206
political, economic, and social system in,
6, 146
political power in, 4
see also United States
American Bar Association, 245
American Can Company, 246
American Medical Association, 135
American Stock Exchange, 12
Anchorpersons, 81, 182
as legitimators, 24
Anderson, John, 44
Angola, 224, 227, 229
AP (Associated Press), 80, 217
stories on the Supreme Court, 104
stories on Zaire, 227–228
Arterton, F. Christopher, 43, 51
Asia, 200
Astrology Today, 13
Astrology: Your Daily Horoscope, 13
Atlanta, Georgia, 46
Atlantic, 185
Auden, W. H., 29
Authority
and the FBI, 117–121, 122
holders of, 5, 99, 124, 154
legitimacy of, 5, 18
and police, 111, 122–123
of presidents, 64, 74

and ritual, 74
of the Supreme Court, 107
transformation from power into, 4

Bagdikian, Ben, 11, 22, 159
Baker, Howard, 31, 43
Barnaby Jones, 168
Barron's, 185
Bay of Pigs, Cuba, 213
Bayh, Birch, 35, 38
Begin, Menachem, 232
Belgium, 222, 227
Bentley, Arthur, 4
Benton, M. C., 115
Bernstein, Carl, 56, 159, 217
Bigart, Homer, 15
Bill of Rights, 12, 108
Binder, Al, 9
Black Panthers, 127
"Bonanza," 182
Boston, Massachusetts, 42
television station in, 11
Boston Globe, 37, 126
Bradley, Ed, 71
Broder, David, 196
Brooke, Edward, 83
Brown, Edmund G. (Jerry), Jr., 37
media and, 41–42
1974 campaign of, 238
Buckley, James, 66–67
Bunker, Archie, 177–178
Burch, Dean, 62
Burke, Kenneth, 22
Burger, Warren, 164
Bush, George, 36
1980 campaign strategy of, 43
Business and mass media, 131–137

Caddell, Pat, 71
California, 33, 41, 42, 206, 238
Calley, William, 15
Calorie Control Council, 135
Cambridge, Massachusetts, 201
Camp David, Maryland, 73
Candidates
and advertisements, 45–47
and the "conservative mood," 204
and the media, 32–37, 42–44
tasks of, 31, 32